WALK THE BARRIO

Cultural Frames, Framing Culture

ROBERT NEWMAN, EDITOR
JUSTIN NEUMAN, ASSOCIATE EDITOR

WALK THE BARRIO

The Streets of Twenty-First-Century Transnational Latinx Literature

Cristina Rodriguez

University of Virginia Press • *Charlottesville and London*

University of Virginia Press

© 2022 by the Rector and Visitors of the University of Virginia

All rights reserved

Printed in the United States of America on acid-free paper

First published 2022

ISBN 978-0-8139-4805-8 (hardcover)
ISBN 978-0-8139-4806-5 (paper)
ISBN 978-0-8139-4807-2 (ebook)

9 8 7 6 5 4 3 2 1

Library of Congress Cataloging-in-Publication Data

Names: Rodriguez, Cristina, author.

Title: Walk the barrio : the streets of twenty-first-century transnational Latinx literature / Cristina Rodriguez.

Description: Charlottesville : University of Virginia Press, 2022. | Series: Cultural frames, framing culture | Includes bibliographical references and index.

Identifiers: LCCN 2022008348 (print) | LCCN 2022008349 (ebook) | ISBN 9780813948058 (hardcover ; acid-free paper) | ISBN 9780813948065 (paperback) acid-free paper) | ISBN 9780813948072 (ebook)

Subjects: LCSH: American literature—Hispanic American authors—History and criticism. | American literature—21st century—History and criticism. | Literature and transnationalism—United States. | Hispanic American neighborhoods in literature. | Place (Philosophy) in literature. | Immigrants in literature. | LCGFT: Literary criticism.

Classification: LCC PS153.H56 R626 2022 (print) | LCC PS153.H56 (ebook) | DDC 810.9/868073—dc23/eng/20220420

LC record available at https://lccn.loc.gov/2022008348

LC ebook record available at https://lccn.loc.gov/2022008349

Publication of this volume has been supported by *New Literary History*.

All photographs by the author unless otherwise noted.

Cover photo: Simons bricks. (Photo by the author)

For my mom

And for all the immigrants, who, like her, were brave enough to make a home for themselves in the unknown

You gotta walk outside your life
To where the neighborhood changes . . .

—Ani DiFranco, "Willing to Fight"

CONTENTS

WALK THE BARRIO

INTRODUCTION

My Hometown, Silver Spring, and the Method of *Walk the Barrio*

IN THE neighborhood I grew up in, everybody seemed to be from somewhere else. In the 1980s and 1990s, our corner of metropolitan Silver Spring, Maryland (zip code 20901), was increasingly Salvadoran, as well as Ethiopian, Haitian, and Jamaican. The local dollar theater turned into a Spanish Pentecostal church when I was a kid, and the main drag of my neighborhood, Flower Avenue, increasingly boasted predominantly Latin American stores and restaurants. El Gavilán, up the street by the Giant supermarket, was the neighborhood Salvadoran hot spot: I remember being accosted by the boisterous music and circulating sizzling skillets of fajitas as a preteen, and then proudly bringing friends back to this "authentic" hole-in-the-wall dining experience as an adult. Around the corner, you could get *pupusas* from the food truck outside the Giant's parking lot, or fresh cuts of meat (and jewelry!) from the Pan American Market in the mini strip mall; a little further down toward the Silver Spring Metro stop African fashion shops, Ethiopian restaurants, and the varied commerce of Sixteenth Street and Georgia Avenue rubbed shoulders with the quirky down-and-out legacies of a bygone era (the Tastee Diner, the old Silver Spring Theater, The Woodside Deli, "Old Blair" High School, the take-out seafood joints). The neighborhood at that time was somewhat divided: our section of Flower Avenue was mostly single-family homes, with a lot of neighbors whose parents were from Indiana, or Virginia, who I'm sure could trace their time in this country at least a few generations back. Yet just "up the hill," Silver Spring turned into what my mom liked to call *Cowboylandia,* a full-blown *colonia* of Salvadoran life. I see echoes of my hometown in every barrio I visit.

My best friends in grade school had parents from the Philippines, Ethiopia, Nigeria, Ghana, and Ireland. Nonimmigrant families felt like the minority. So I never had to explain my mother's accent, or the (harrowing, scarring) experience of Saturday Argentine School,[1] or my occasional strangely pronounced word. I would go to my friends' houses and hear their parents and relatives speaking in Tagalog or look over what

1

goods a family friend had brought them from Ethiopia, and the awkwardness my friends felt walking through the scene, dodging questions in that other language, matched my own when I was a host.

As I grew up, the schools and neighborhoods I was part of became more and more monochromatic. By high school my white friends teased me about the idiosyncratic expressions and norms of my household ("so much hugging and kissing!" was the consensus). My sister befriended Latinas (a *dominicana* and *colombiana* from our neighborhood), but I was intimidated by the Latin American set. Applying to college, the idea that I, the middle-class daughter of an international civil servant who was once told by a disgruntled immigration officer at JFK Airport, "Lady, you speak English better than *I* do," would be considered a "diversity" student seemed absurd. Yet at Reed College I was the only one of my friends from an immigrant family. After college, to my friends in Boston I was the token "ethnic friend," if only in name and in jest.

I largely embraced my own personal *blanqueamiento,* since I never really felt Latina enough to claim it as an identity anyway. Only my mom was a Latin American immigrant. While my dad's surname and his father are both Puerto Rican, my father is more from Long Island than anywhere else (New Hyde Park and its surroundings are truly a world of their own). Speaking Spanish in public was a hardship of bruised pride. I looked white. I *was* white. Better to not self-identify. Somebody might call me out. Say I didn't speak Spanish well enough. Or worse, that my Spanish was learned, not innate. Or that I didn't look Latina enough. Or that I wasn't really "ethnic" enough. I'm not sure who I thought was policing the border of identity claims, but I feared them for exposing me as a fraud.

It was only much, much later that I realized that my particular experience of identity anxiety might be shared. I had never read any Latinx literature before graduate school. Harboring the unexamined belief that literature about social identity was inferior to "great" "universal" works of fiction (I cringe as I type), I went to the University of California, Irvine to study Thomas Pynchon and Don DeLillo and the other canonical (all male, largely white) writers of the twentieth century. When I was placed with Professor Rodrigo Lazo as my advisor, I thought, "Typical. They are trying to pigeonhole me, to push me into Latinx studies."[2] Yet as I plodded my way through coursework and talked out ideas with my mentors, the issue of identity kept cropping up for me; it crystallized during my master's exam. I had written about how Gayl Jones experiments with form in her novel *Mosquito* to create for the reader the lived experience of a black female narrator who can only find belonging in the Southwest borderlands. As I defended my thesis, the chair, either assuming from my surname or deducing from my analysis, asked me: how does your research relate to your own experiences of identity? It literally had not occurred to me prior to that moment that there was any connection between what I wanted to study and who I was. Yet as I answered the panel, stumbling over my interest in narratives of unbelonging, I realized that I was drawn to stories like my own, stories that wonder: what does it mean to feel between identities? How does it happen? What does it look like?

Indeed, I knew from childhood that there were whole neighborhoods of kids like me, who weren't quite of the place their parents were from and weren't quite fully of here either. I saw in my UC Irvine students too, whose parents were from Mexico, Vietnam, the Philippines, Japan, that these questions of where and how to belong were relevant. Investigating my family tree further, I found that each of my parents had undergone a similar self-fashioning: my mother, Veronica Hanglin, a third- and fourth-generation Anglo Argentine, recounts how as a child she and her siblings would avoid the kitchen and its potential for stilted conversation during visits from her English-speaking relatives in Argentina before she learned the language from her Scotch Argentine grandmother. My father, on frequent trips to Puerto Rico with his father, would bluff and blunder his way through a family and land and language largely foreign to him. I had in fact inherited identity awkwardness. Surely, I thought, in this era of globalization and widespread immigration I was not alone in feeling this way. Surely writers were talking about this, and as the world was only getting smaller and more interconnected, surely we all needed to be talking about this. I started to believe that *this* experience of identity was underrepresented in academic scholarship. I wanted to study, and promote, the literature that spoke to this way of being in the world.

In that body of work, what I found was that, in the face of uncertainty over who they were, authors tightened their grip on *where* they were. They claimed their neighborhoods all the more fiercely because of the ambivalence with which they claimed other aspects of themselves, like their dominant language, ethnicity, nationality, and class. An anxiety over being "authentic" enough, meaning Latinx *enough,* working-class *enough* (or for some, middle-class enough), Spanish-speaking *enough,* expressed itself in the form of the writing. As someone whose sense of self still gains strength from where I grew up, who still references that locally shared immigrant identity I felt as a kid to try to cobble a sense of genuine *latinidad* for myself,[3] to keep the identity "border patrol" at bay, this discovery rang true.

How writers describe that process, and what it can tell us about new forms of identity construction in the late twentieth and early twenty-first centuries, is the focus of this book. This project taught me that my own experience growing up in the US, in a Silver Spring barrio forged by one diaspora among many other diasporas, in a community I was and was not a part of, was far from unique; that, to put it mawkishly, I am not alone.

Introductory Claims

Walk the Barrio starts from an almost obvious premise: immigrants, and their communities, have a particular and intensified relationship to place. Authors from transnational social fields evince in their work a sharpened perception of and connection to their local spaces, which we can see in their writing from, of, and about their neighborhoods. When I tell nonacademics this, most nod their heads vigorously, asserting "of course that's true." Scholars agree; we are not only aware of the link but also know which questions to ask as a consequence: if immigrants have a distinct connection to place, how does that manifest? What forms does that connection take? How does it impact the way immigrants construct their own identities and their own physical communities? And how does it emerge in art and literature? How might we trace the network of linkages between self, place, and nation(s)?

Although most of us accept the initial point about immigrants and place identity, and some of us ask the right questions, very few have followed where those questions should lead. That's because, as academics, we tend to look down at the page for answers, rather than looking around. *To write about place, you have to experience place.* This is the second, not-so-obvious premise of the book. By "experience" here I don't mean just plumbing the local archives or reading about the town's history: I mean walking the streets, talking to people (often the authors themselves), and placing oneself physically in the spaces that one is attempting to understand. You cannot experience place remotely. There are a lot of theorists who masterfully expound upon this idea—Henri Lefebvre, David Harvey, Gloria Anzaldúa, Bruce Novoa, Gaston Bachelard, Michel de Certeau—but I hardly need them to defend the underlying postulate, since this is another concept that makes sense to most people as soon as you say it. We *know* that spaces are unique and must be felt in the body, and yet rarely do we as scholars employ that knowledge, or behave in accordance with that knowledge, when we are writing about place identity and authorship.

The effect of these two premises is quite simple: in a book about immigrants, writing, and places, I talk to immigrants, interview authors, and go to places. I visit the immigrant community being written about, follow in the steps of the author or protagonists, and tease out the connections between the character of the place and the form of the literary work. However, I am not a sociologist, and this is not a purely journalistic exercise. What draws me to each neighborhood is the work of literature that was fueled and inspired by that neighborhood, and literary interpretation is at the core of each chapter. The goal is to see how the specific culture of each local community informs the writing of the text. How did the author innovate upon, trouble, or generally break the rules of his or her genre in order to capture in words an embodied experience of the barrio? A number of literary techniques surface, elements characteristic of each author based on his or her barrio, and his or her position in regard to class, gender, race, sexual orientation, or nationality. However, a common thread also emerges: an authorial anxiety over being the representative for a given Latinx community, combined with a pronounced demonstration of barrio knowledge. Place settings in these works cement the authors in their social identities. *Walk the Barrio* thus surveys a developing body of literature: twenty-first-century transnational Latinx[4] writing on place.

For a book about immigrants, writing, and place, it will be helpful to frame each of these three aspects. You'll notice how even in trying to talk about one of these elements I end up talking about the others: in reality the three facets of the project bleed into each other. With that caveat in mind, let's start with immigrants.

1. IMMIGRANTS

One might argue that immigrants have always had an intensified relationship to place, but one of the theses of this book is that contemporary globalization and its attendant transnational flows have transformed in fundamental ways how immigrants conceptualize their identities. Immigration is no longer the linear, one-way process of resettlement and generational assimilation it had generally been historically. In the late twentieth and twenty-first centuries, immigrants continue to move between their home and host countries, maintaining social, economic, and political ties in two or more places: as a result, transnational subjects in the US can often experience even more difficulty establishing cultural belonging—in either culture—than in earlier forms of immigration. As a consequence of this more profound destabilization of identity, many subjects hew all the more strongly to place as a way to claim and assert a fixed sense of self.

Thus, the anxiety over authenticity evinced by the authors in this study reflects fairly recent migration shifts.

TRANSMIGRANCY AND TRANSNATIONALISM

I follow contemporary sociologists in utilizing the term "transmigrant" to refer to "immigrants who develop and maintain multiple relationships— familial, economic, social, organizational, religious, and political—that span borders" (Basch et al. 7). In the past thirty years, transnationalism has come to prominence as a promising theoretical mode for grappling with the social, cultural, and political effects of contemporary globalization, with its concomitant increase in the movement of persons, goods, and capital between countries. In their book *Nations Unbound,* the trio of sociology/anthropology scholars largely responsible for the development of transnationalism as a field of study, Linda G. Basch, Nina Glick Schiller, and Cristina Szanton Blanc, offer a theory of transnationalism based on case studies involving the immigrations of St. Vincentians, Grenadians, Haitians, and Filipinos to the New York City area. While *Nations Unbound* does not include Latin America, based on the "common trends" for transnational immigration, which include being from a postcolonial state that has been intensively penetrated by global capital, "the domination" of the country by the United States, "a resultant deterioration of the standard of living for all but the dominant classes," and "a vast emigration, from all classes, including broad sections of the middle strata" (228–29), we can safely relate the findings of Basch et al. to immigration from Mexico, Cuba, Puerto Rico, the Dominican Republic, Guatemala, and El Salvador.

The simplest definition of transnationalism is living across geographic boundaries. Basch et al. describe transnationalism as "the processes by which immigrants forge and sustain multi-stranded social relations that link together their societies of origin and settlement" (7). The chief premises of transnational theory are both economic and social. Transnational migration is inextricably linked to global capitalism and must be understood within the context of global relations between capital and labor. Yet these migrations also entail cultural shifts as transmigrants, through their political and social relationships, build social fields that cross-national boundaries.

Transnationalism is the result of the worldwide economic crises of the past twenty-five years, the deindustrialization of the US in an era of post-Fordism, changes to US immigration laws, and global restructurings of capital that have disrupted local economies throughout the third world (25). These economic dislocations in both "core" and "periphery" countries have increased immigration to capitalist core nations, yet as the economies of *those* have declined, it has become more difficult for immigrants to build secure economic bases in their new host countries: "global economic dislocations, long-term economic retrenchment and recession, and the restructuring of production processes throughout the world have either reduced or unexpectedly altered demands for labor" (26). Genuine transnational migration is thus largely limited to the late twentieth and twenty-first centuries.

Common transnational strategies include building extended kinship networks and splitting up labor, childcare, and nuclear families across two or more countries in order to extend the family's economic base; using remittances from the host country to accumulate property or wealth in the country of origin; maintaining two residences and/or political standing in two communities to translate economic gains abroad to cultural status "back home"; sending a family member to live with a distant relative abroad to secure employment and begin the visa process to help other family members immigrate later. While these practices result in the downside of extended separation, transnational networks allow their practitioners "to resist specific state policies aimed at controlling and exploiting their labor and also to challenge the terms of their subordinated insertion into structures of global capital" (82). Such strategies entail complicity with the instability of present socioeconomic conditions and perpetuate the need for ongoing migration, yet they largely result in financial and status gains in one or both countries and allow immigrants to evade becoming assimilated into the often oppressive racial and xenophobic ordering of the United States. The endemic racism at work in the US, combined with increasingly meager opportunities for economic advancement, deters transmigrants from fully severing ties to their nation of origin.

Walk the Barrio pursues the *literary* implications of these momentous contemporary social and political shifts in migrancy, which remain undertheorized. *Nations Unbound* asserts that while social scientists may use the term "transnationalism," "it is only in contemporary fiction . . . that this state of 'in-betweeness' has been fully voiced" (8). *Walk the Barrio* showcases authors who are articulating versions of this heretofore largely unarticulated "transnational identity." First-, second-, and even third-generation transmigrants become inscribed in transnational social fields, subject to the forces of colonization and globalization, oppressive social paradigms, and economic incentive to split families and divide homelands that fuel contemporary transmigrancy.

The authors in *Walk the Barrio* are first-generation, second-generation, and in-between (generation 1.5). These authors live in the midst of what sociologist Luis Eduardo Guarnizo calls "binational social fields,"[5] and their lived experience of transmigrancy leaves aesthetic marks upon their artistic production. They hail from the largest Latinx immigration groups of the last twenty years: the Hispanic Caribbean, Mexico, and Central America. They also come from neighborhoods in the top three US cities for contemporary Latinx immigration: Los Angeles, New York, and Miami. Since Puerto Ricans technically don't immigrate internationally, I have left them out, despite the similarities between Puerto Rican and other Hispanic Caribbean migration patterns, and Puerto Ricans' hefty literary contributions, particularly in the canon of writing about barrios (it was a tough decision and may my Puerto Rican ancestors forgive me).[6] Each country of origin has its own unique history, which informs its culture as well as its diaspora: to prevent flattening out the Latinx immigration experience, the introduction of each part of the book includes the relevant history of the home nation of the author(s) in relation to the US, providing an outline of Mexican, Dominican, Cuban, Salvadoran, and Guatemalan immigrations.

2. WRITING

Another thesis of this book is that, in the twenty-first-century wake of sweeping globalization, a new form of transnational Latinx literature has arisen, one marked by a particularly intimate relationship to locality. I argue that many contemporary Latinx authors, enmeshed in transnational social fields, are deploying actual barrio spaces to write fictionalized, often highly experimental, accounts of identity and dislocation. These authors have vastly different voices and span the spectrum of distinct Latinx immigrant groups, and yet every writer in this study, in composing a literary account of his/her hometown, even an extremely surreal or abstract account, refrains from fictionalizing the literal, physical aspects of his or her barrio when reconstructing it as setting. In other words, these authors describe their barrios as they are, with minimal fabrication: writing about the actual dwellings, bus lines, street names, businesses, and geographic features of their neighborhoods.[7] In fact, the settings reflect the physical places so accurately that I can find the streets, houses, landmarks, of each work in my own visit to the place. Such devotion to capturing the neighborhood *as it is,* even while utilizing narrative innovations to get at a particular form of subjective experience, is powerful evidence of just how important the claiming of place identity can be for contemporary transnational authors.

This minute attention to real-life place detail gestures to another shared attribute among the writers in this book, which I argue reflects the keenness of identity uncertainty at work in binational social fields. There is an anxiety about identity operating, at various levels, in each of these texts. At times the fear is that a beloved neighborhood is under threat of erasure from the forces of urban planning or gentrification: in the novels of Helena María Viramontes and Angie Cruz, for instance, we see a narrative impulse to "save" the barrio and get it down on paper, before the city of Los Angeles or Manhattan's hordes of white yuppies and hipsters (are those groups even different anymore?) come to change its character indelibly. Elsewhere, as in Junot Díaz or Héctor Tobar, there's an implicit desire to be seen as Latinx enough, closer to the diaspora and its working class: demonstrating intimate—and again, true to life—knowledge of neighborhoods that were once less upwardly mobile as a way to declare the authenticity of past experience. If the goal is to show how well you know the Latinx barrio you were raised in, getting it "right" is paramount.

Please note that my claim that these authors reveal an anxiety over identity belonging is not a critique or a judgment: as Díaz says in *Oscar Wao*, "*like, after all, recognizes like*" (97). After several failed attempts at gentrification (an international school, a mall), downtown Silver Spring began to transform with the arrival of the Discovery building in 1998. After I left for college, the changes to the neighborhood intensified, all flowing from the commerce and foot traffic brought in by Discovery Communications. Years later, when I was home for a visit, my mom took me out to dinner "downtown" and my jaw dropped: apartment buildings had been razed and replaced with a pleasantly designed arcade, complete with a mosaic fountain, full of high-end restaurants and shops. The town I liked to jokingly call a "poor man's Bethesda" (the fancy urban enclave one town over) was now basically just . . . Bethesda.

Painfully aware of this shift in Silver Spring's reputation, I find myself explaining to people that this is not the same neighborhood I grew up in. I cite shootings at "Old Blair" or the Tastee Diner in the 1990s. I reference the tiny, off-the-beaten-path Malaysian and Ethiopian restaurants I used to frequent. I take friends to El Gavilán or to the *pupusa* truck. I tell them how ugly and dirty the Metro used to look, how my sister's car got stolen out of our driveway once, how I used to drive to Prince George's County to buy alcohol at Tick Tock as an underage teen, how my high school friends would join University of Maryland crews to break-dance nearby at College Park on Monday nights. "Dave Chapelle is from Silver Spring!" I tell anyone who will listen. My town's street cred is my own, and my town's gentrification threatens to gentrify my own already precarious identities, as Latina, daughter of immigrants, and of an acceptable level (read: not too rich) of middle class.

I'll venture that this anxiety over one's hometown affects many of us. How many of us have claimed knowledge of some wayward piece of our childhood neighborhood, to perform our ownership of the space? How many of us from the middle class have tried, perversely, to describe how much less middle-class our neighborhood used to be?[8] Yet the role of place in claiming a fixed identity gains particular prominence for these authors, some of whom are not fully accepted by their home of origin or the home of their parents, all of whom are offered a very qualified and complicated belonging in the United States. We will see how several of these authors perform barrio expertise in their texts, both for those of their readers in the know and for themselves, to write their way to a more anchored sense of self. The archive of author interviews, published and unpublished, in this book serves to contextualize the authors' own connections to place and identity.

3. PLACE

Merriam-Webster Dictionary defines "barrio" as "a Spanish-speaking quarter or neighborhood in a city or town in the U.S." and tells us the word first enters the English lexicon in 1833. In Spanish, "barrio" means something closer to district and does not have the ethnic connotation; when speaking of US Latinx neighborhoods, a more common term (or at least one better recognized by the Real Academia de la Lengua Española, the bible of Peninsular Spanish[9]) is "colonia." "Colonia" has the advantage of bringing with it the idea of colonization and of a group of people displaced within a broader cultural hegemony. However, "barrio," as English-language dictionaries define it, refers specifically to Latinx communities in the US context, making it more appropriate for this project. A barrio, then, is a Spanish-language dominant section of a larger city or town in the United States. Each of the neighborhoods studied here fits these criteria.

LATINX LITERARY THEORIES OF SPACE

Walk the Barrio focuses on Latin American immigration because Latinx literature in particular has a rich tradition of vivid neighborhood depiction. Everyone knows Sandra Cisneros's *The House on Mango Street,* with its quirky vignettes about a working-class Mexican and Puerto Rican barrio in Chicago. Then there's El Barrio, the New York City neighborhood that has been home to the Puerto Rican diaspora, captured by the Young Lord poets of the 1970s and Piri Thomas's memoir *Down These Mean Streets*. Head south to the edge of the Eastern Seaboard, and the Cuban exiles (Cristina Garcia, Ana Menendez, Achy Obejas) will tell you about their Miami's Little Havana. Fly west to the Texas borderlands that inspire Gloria Anzaldúa's *mestiza* consciousness in *Borderlands/La Frontera* and then to New Mexico to find the Albuquerque barrio that makes Jimmy Santiago Baca a poet. At the coast you have the Sacramento of Richard Rodriguez's memoirs and the aspiring Mexican families of Ernesto Galarza's *Barrio Boy*. The literary barrios in this study join an already storied canon.

Latinx letters, and Chicanx literary criticism in particular, has also been at the forefront of conceptualizing the role of space in narrative and analyzing the relationship between transnationalism and place identity in literature.[10] Juan Bruce-Novoa, a Chicanx theorist writing during the Chicano Movement of the 1970s, asserts that Chicano/as occupy "the intercultural possibilities" of a space neither fully Mexican nor fully American; he argues that Chicanx art and literature "opens a space for itself" to combat the chaos of discontinuity and rupture in everyday life (98–99). Gloria Anzaldúa's groundbreaking *Borderlands/La Frontera*, itself an experimental hybrid of memoir, poetry, and theory, levied this salvo, which opened up a new field of inquiry for Latinx literature: "the Borderlands are physically present wherever two or more cultures edge each other, where people of different races occupy the same territory, where under, lower, middle and upper classes touch, where the space between two individuals shrinks with intimacy" (1). As an area of study, "borderlands" refers to both the geographic region incorporating the southwestern US-Mexico border and the particular cultural productions—generally characterized by experimental forms—that result from the sociopolitical interactions endemic to such contested terrain. The concept of the borderlands not just as a physical, geographic space but as an abstract space was taken up and pursued by critics interested in exploring its manifestations in literature. In the 1990s and into the 2000s, Chicanx literary critics like Ramón Saldívar, Mary Pat Brady, and Raúl Homero Villa have interpreted literature in terms of its spatial reasoning and its production of a literary borderlands.

My methodology shares similarities with the work of both Mary Pat Brady and Raúl Homero Villa, who also personally visit the spaces— towns, regions, cities—whose literary production they are examining in order to interrogate the relationship between actual place identity and fictional representation. Brady, in particular, in her *Extinct Lands, Temporal Geographies*, expertly teases out the relations between the form of the narrative in question and the locale to which it refers. Yet Brady, Saldívar, Anzaldúa, and others working in borderlands theory focus on regional literatures of the Southwest. Villa turns to the city, and his knowledge of the cultural practices and place memory of Chicano/as in Los Angeles in *Barrio-Logos* illuminates his interpretation of the spaces of poetry and fiction created by Latino/as in urban spaces. *Walk the Barrio*, however, narrows the scope, by applying theories of space in narrative at the level of the individual barrio. This specificity matches the specificity of the texts I study, which detail houses and streets of a particular neighborhood, and thus allows me to focus on making direct connections between each narrative choice and its potential analog in the real-life setting it evokes.

A GENEALOGY OF SPACE THEORY

While Raúl Homero Villa and Mary Pat Brady are this project's nearest theoretical predecessors, I lean on space theory lineage more broadly. From Henri Lefebvre I have adopted the operating premise of *The Production of Space* that "(social) space is a (social) product" (26) and tailored his terminology regarding the tripartite division of space.[11] Lefebvre famously postulates that a form of economic production will secrete its own unique mode of spatial organization. Within a given society, Lefebvre offers a hermeneutic for how the same social space will change, based on whether one is perceiving the space (space as society's macrostructure), conceiving of the space (space as an abstraction of maps, plans, routes, and data), or living in the space (space as the experience of a user or inhabitant). Lived space is highly symbolic, often nonverbal, and absolutely embodied.

Like a good, cynical Marxist, Lefebvre doesn't offer much hope for the possibility of rival productions of space operating within a late-capitalist superstructure; he does, however, hint at the potential for subversive modes of producing space: "In this same space there are, however, other forces on the boil. . . . The violence of power is answered by the violence of subversion. . . . These seething forces are still capable of rattling the lid of the cauldron of the state and its space, for differences can never be totally quieted" (23). I would argue that these subversive modes of spatial production—what Lefebvre will call "differential space" (73)—hail from space as lived, embodied experience, that is, from the space produced on the ground by users and inhabitants.

While Lefebvre himself does not (to my knowledge) discuss transnationalism, the consequences of his theory are apparent for transnational spaces. If we each are both a product of and a producer of a society's iteration of space, surely we do not immediately cease to operate in that mode once we are placed in a new social space. We carry with us our embodied experiences of past spaces. The distinct spatial organization of many immigrant communities in the US points to how a space's users and inhabitants are not only shaped by their spaces but shape those spaces, often according to logics adhering in other, prior spaces they have lived in. The differential space created by this clash of spatial productions can "rattle the lid of the cauldron" of the reigning mode of spatial organization by secreting a novel perception of space that results in a quite literally new (social) space.

While we're talking about Marxism, Mike Davis (*City of Quartz, Magical Urbanism*) and Dolores Hayden (*The Power of Place*) are also central to my thinking about how various spaces are battlegrounds for the territorial struggles of people of color, women, LGBTQ+, and the working class. While David Harvey (*Social Justice and the City*, and of course, *The Conditions of Postmodernity*, which no self-respecting UC Irvine critical theory student was ever without) and Fredric Jameson (in *Postmodernism*, obviously) have both informed my approach to space—particularly when dealing with Los Angeles—and concepts like Harvey's time-space compression or Jameson's spatialization of time are useful for understanding the impact of globalization upon twenty-first-century neighborhoods, they are the foregrounding rather than the model for my own work.[12]

My praxis has two parents: human geography and narrative journalism. Human geography is "the branch of geography dealing with how human activity affects or is influenced by the earth's surface" (*OED*): human geographers combine demographics, knowledge of the natural and built environment, and analysis of spatial organization and social processes of people in a place, to create a picture of the interplay between a group of people and their surroundings. Human geography is already interdisciplinary, pulling from anthropology, sociology, economics, and political science, but there is also a subbranch that applies these tools to literature: human geographers like Edward Soja (in *Thirdspace*, but also in *Postmodern Geographies*), Douglas Pocock (*Humanistic Geography and Literature: Essays on the Experience of Place*), and David Ley and James Duncan (*Place/Culture/Representation*) demonstrate how effective this approach to space is as a lens for literary analysis.

Jane Jacobs's fantastic *The Death and Life of Great American Cities* best illustrates my methodology's other inheritance. Jacobs begins her narrative with a neighborhood sidewalk, and her personal experiences in Boston's

North End, ultimately presenting a compelling, *embodied* analysis of the failures of urban planning and myopic urban renewal projects, incorporating history, statistics, and, most important, reportage. Jacobs is not a sociologist or ethnographer but a journalist. Jacobs adheres to the essential rules of journalism: an obligation to the "truth," a loyalty to the public interest, consistent verification, objectivity/distance from the subject, and purposeful storytelling.[13] As a discipline, journalism allows a writer to synthesize first-person reporting, personal interviews, historical and statistical research, analysis, and argumentation into a holistic account.

My own training, before graduate school, from 2005 to 2009, was in local news journalism. As a "news stringer" for WATD in Massachusetts ("The South Shore's radio station," as they call themselves), I learned that you always had to interview the key players, always had to include and vet your sources, and always needed to research the history of the issue you were presenting. For news radio, I effaced myself as speaker, stuck to the facts, and kept the sentences short and punchy. However, in forays into narrative journalism,[14] I learned how to include my perspective and to speak from an explicitly first-person interpretation of events. The tools of narrative journalism allow me to link elements of human geography and the underpinnings of literary theory to an embodied account of neighborhood space.

"Barriography": Putting Together Immigrants, Writing, and Place

Every immigrant neighborhood has a particular history, and a specific set of cultural norms that I ultimately excavate in each of the texts. I offer what I call a "barriography" for each of the barrios included in *Walk the Barrio*: this entails first-person reportage of the barrio,[15] interviews with the author, museum curators, and/or locals, archival research, demographic and historical data, and a literary analysis of the work focused on how stylistic elements relate to the influence of place identity upon the author and his/her formal choices. I never know exactly what I will find when I go to the place: but it always unlocks some aspect of the text that would remain hidden otherwise. With this methodology, I explore El Monte with Salvador Plascencia; East Los Angeles with Helena María Viramontes; Van Nuys and Lincoln Heights with William Archila; Downtown L.A. and Little Armenia with Héctor Tobar; Washington Heights with Angie Cruz; Parlin and New Brunswick, New Jersey, with Junot Díaz; and Little Havana with Richard Blanco.

Latinx literary criticism, which historically homed in on the role of place in narrative, has widened rather than narrowed its geographic scope, adopting a transnationalist lens focused on international movements and changing immigration patterns. While the transnational turn is necessary, we risk losing sight of the neighborhood at just the moment when it is regaining centrality to Latinx literature. The field needs a model for interpreting the stylistic uses of local geography, for mapping the effects of contemporary transnationalism upon literary form. I humbly offer "barriography" as such a model. Walk the Barrio demonstrates that the need for both a more localized analysis and the crucial intervention of transnationalist theory do not have to be antithetical: examining the unique cultural and historical norms of a neighborhood illuminates the greater transnational movements of its Latinx community. By grounding the effects of transmigrancy in concrete locations, the barriographies of Walk the Barrio present a comprehensive vision of the contemporary US Latinx immigrant experience, without generalizing from its myriad versions and numerous sites.

Where Are the Puerto Ricans? And Other Absences

I know. The absence of Puerto Rican New York City in Walk the Barrio is glaring.[16] Puerto Rican migration was markedly transnational before transnationalism, strictly speaking, existed: the Puerto Rican presence in metropolitan New York is over a century old, and Puerto Ricans' status as US citizens has allowed for continued connections between the island and the mainland. El Barrio, or Spanish Harlem, in New York City is the premier, quintessential Latinx barrio. The South Bronx—the birthplace of hip hop, itself a cultural production stemming from the confluence of Puerto Rican, African American, and Jamaican traditions—is another storied neighborhood with a rich Latinx literary history. My own grandfather came from the island to New York City, believing, as Lin-Manuel Miranda (himself a storied New York Rican from Inwood) famously put it in Hamilton, "in New York you can be a new man" (a postulate, incidentally, that this book disproves). My grandparents met on a Central Park tennis court (he pretended to lose the first set, then turned up the heat, and most likely the charm). My father self-identifies as a nuyorican. I know from experience that, despite citizenship, despite the status of many Puerto Ricans (including my grandfather and great-grandfather) as US Army war veterans, despite a hundred years of settlement on the mainland, Puerto Ricans are still immigrants in the eyes of the mainstream and adopt many of the transnational strategies of other Latinx groups. The honest truth is I ran out of space, and out of time. COVID-19 prevented me from completing research on a nuyorican chapter, and, facing a manuscript that was already far too long, I decided to excise Puerto Ricans on the technicality of US citizenship. I sketch the bare contours of this would-be chapter in the conclusion.

"Claim Hialeah fiercely since it's all people ask you about anyway" (160), Jennine Capó Crucet's protagonist asserts in the eponymous story from *How to Leave Hialeah*. Crucet's book, which—funny story—is actually on display behind the bar at La Cocina, the sleek new Hialeah night spot I went to for research on Cuban Americans in South Florida (research trips are tough), forms part of a cohort of contemporary writing about Hialeah, Miami's less famous and more working-class Cuban American barrio. Today's Little Havana, described in chapter 7, has consistently defined itself in opposition to Little Mariano (Hialeah's nickname) as the two locales pit two very different waves of the Cuban diaspora against each other: while Little Havana was built by the 1960s "Golden Exiles," thus named because of their levels of wealth, education, and whiteness, Hialeah was largely settled by later waves of Cuban immigration more representative of the Cuban population in terms of their socioeconomic and racial makeup. I gesture to this barrio's unique history in the introduction to Cuban Floridians, but Crucet's book, and the city of Hialeah, deserves a chapter it does not get.

Another thing *Walk the Barrio* does *not* provide is a barrio "greatest hits." Many of these barrios are not obvious choices for a barriography: that is because I was guided in my selection not by the reputation or fame of the barrio but by the form and quality of the writing. The book's aim is to be a model for interpreting an emergent form of Latinx literature that evinces a new transnational mode of experiencing place identity: that specific goal required setting multiple limits on the field of study. In addition to its simple chronological boundary (the book largely focuses on works from the last twenty years), this book's criteria for inclusion was fourfold: authors either needed to be immigrants themselves or part of a transnational community; the authors needed to be writing about their own US neighborhoods; the neighborhood setting had to form an integral part of the work; and the text had to utilize form in some unexpected way. This narrow scope allowed me to find fascinating resonances between stylistic choices and neighborhood aesthetics, as discovered through close reading and first-person experience. It also allows me to present to you what I hope are compelling accounts of the three metropolitan centers for Latinx immigration in the US, showing you the character of a handful of twenty-first-century Latinx neighborhoods and the Mexican, Chicanx, Dominican, Cuban, and Central American populations that give them life.

Where to Now?

The book is divided into three parts, based on the top cities for Latinx immigration. Part 1 begins in Greater L.A., a fitting start as some Chicanx families in the Southwest never immigrated to the United States, having been here since it was Spanish and then Mexican territory. Chapters 1 and 2 present barriographies of El Monte and East L.A., two long-standing Mexican and Chicanx barrios whose histories are irrevocably tangled up in the making of the urban monster that is Los Angeles, through two novels: Salvador Plascencia's *The People of Paper* and Helena María Viramontes's *Their Dogs Came with Them*. Part 2 considers the more recent immigration waves from the Northern Triangle (Honduras, Guatemala, and El Salvador) to L.A.'s downtown. In Héctor Tobar's novel *The Tattooed Soldier* (chapter 3) and William Archila's poetry collection *The Art of Exile* (chapter 4), we see how the effects of civil war and trauma in one's country of origin inform and even transform space in Los Angeles for its transplanted residents. Part 3 moves to Greater New York, exploring how gender roles disrupted in the Dominican diaspora play out for Dominican Americans, both those who identify as male and those who identify as female. By traveling to Junot Díaz's New Brunswick and London Terrace housing projects in Parlin, New Jersey, in *This Is How You Lose Her* (chapter 5), and Angie Cruz's Washington Heights neighborhood in *Soledad* (chapter 6), we discover how the particularly pronounced instability of Dominican transnationalism results in a toxic masculinity that haunts both male and female second-generation protagonists. Both neighborhoods share a panoptic atmosphere—of female elders policing and the male gaze menacing—that our protagonists must grapple with and ultimately heal from in order to build healthy relationships. Part 4 treats greater Miami by comparing two works by Richard Blanco, his early poetry collection (*City of a Hundred Fires*) and his most recent memoir (*The Prince of Los Cocuyos*). To capture his experience growing up as a gay Cuban American man in Little Havana's surrealistically self-aware barrio, Blanco queers the genre of the bildungsroman, building a multifaceted coming-of-age narrative for his intersectional identities: the burgeoning poet must find himself in the midst of a Cuban Golden

Exile community that yearns to be elsewhere, when where they are is the only home he has ever known. The conclusion opens with a snapshot of Mexico City in Sandra Cisneros' *Caramelo* to briefly sketch the potential for other barriographies; I go on to explore the model's use for other neighborhoods (such as the South Bronx and El Barrio) and for earlier texts, closing with a very short guide to teaching students how to close read their own neighborhoods.

PART I

WEST

Mexican American East Los Angeles

CALIFORNIOS TO CALIFORNIANS: A BRIEF HISTORY OF MEXICAN AMERICAN LOS ANGELES

To UNDERSTAND the character of the Mexican American[1] Eastside it is necessary to trace its history, which is woven into the history of L.A. Founded in 1781 as a Spanish pueblo, part of New Spain, the city we now call Los Angeles has gone from Spanish control, to Mexican, to US, and in the case of East L.A., back to Latinx again. In the late eighteenth and early nineteenth centuries, most pueblo residents were self-identified "*californios,*" citizens of *Nueva Espana* who were born in California. Wealthy Mexicans owned ranches in the basin and maintained second residences in town, where whites formed a minority: "numbering less than fifty families in Los Angeles in 1848, Anglo Americans and Europeans lived alongside the Mexican residents" (Romo 4).

Two nearly simultaneous events, the gold rush in 1849 and California statehood in 1850, following Mexico's war defeat and the subsequent treaty granting the US much of Texas and the southwest, radically changed the composition of Los Angeles. US citizens, and others, began to settle in Los Angeles in increasing numbers (22): "A migration of Anglos, Chinese, Jews, Germans, and Blacks to California followed . . . In a short time most Anglo settlers had established residences and businesses beyond the old plaza community. They clustered together and attempted to restrict Mexican voting rights and to prohibit cultural practices native to the Mexican community. The Mexican population did not grow at the same rate as the Anglo population and remained near the center of town" (5). The plaza offered a Catholic church, bilingual schools, and Spanish-speaking, Mexican-owned shops: Mexicans continued to live and work there, even as Los Angeles's main business district shifted to southwest Los Angeles (5). Anglos and other European settlers moved away from the original core, which began to be called "Sonoratown" or "Little Mexico" (5). However, trade continued to draw Mexicans to the region, especially Sonorans, and the pueblo remained predominantly Mexican into the 1850s (24).

The city changed again following the arrival of the railroads in the early 1880s. The Southern Pacific and Santa Fe Railroad companies branded Los Angeles as a halcyon suburban paradise and outdid one another offering inexpensive one-way fares—once as low as a dollar—from Midwestern points to the city (Hutchinson 22). The population of the town doubled within a decade, and continued to grow, from a town of 100,000 people in 1900 to a metropolis of over a million by 1930 (Romo 5). For Mexican residents this meant the loss of numerical supremacy, and a loss of political power. As the Santa Fe Railroad and the interurban railway expanded, depots were built on the plaza, bringing new industry to the area and forcing Mexican migrants to spread out, mainly eastward. A majority Mexican town up until the 1880s, by 1910 the Mexicans become a minority in their former pueblo. George Sánchez writes that, "by the turn of the century, the native-born element in the population had been reduced to a relatively insignificant constituency in the life of the metropolis" (71).

Extraordinary, sustained growth, "at a rate never matched by any other American metropolis," characterized Los Angeles in the early twentieth century, which quadrupled in population from 1910 to 1930 (Sánchez 71). This rapid industrialization of Los Angeles depended, however, on Mexican labor. In the 1920s, amidst the city's radical economic growth, industries in need of both skilled and unskilled workers turned to Mexico.[2] Thus, despite being moved from the plaza, Mexican residents continued to form a crucial part of the city's economy, and by the 1930s Los Angeles's industries had grown dependent on the "reliable and cheap" local Mexican labor force (Romo 6, 7).

Railroads and interurban railway companies like Pacific Electric recruited Mexicans and provided them with company housing, usually along the track lines in labor camps, which were often shack towns, on the outskirts of any existing part of town (Romo 69); these camps would transform into barrios in many cases, dotting the east of L.A.: "small oases of Mexican residents became surrounded by suburban residents of a different class and nationality. In the middle of suburbia these small Mexican communities evolved into isolated urban satellite barrios outside of the political and cultural mainstream" (69). The El Monte barrio began as "Hicks Camp," a shanty town established in the early 1900s to house *braceros* working on the Los Angeles Interurban Electric Railway. The railways that Mexicans helped build furthered their own isolation, however, as improved urban transportation "hastened the decentralization of the city" (6), and the extended interurban railway line to Boyle Heights helped spark "the massive exodus of Mexicans from the Plaza to the east side" (68). The history of East Los Angeles is thus profoundly intertwined with the history of Los Angeles transportation in the nineteenth and twentieth centuries.

By 1930 the East Los Angeles barrio was the largest Mexican city in the US, rivaling in size many major US cities (Romo vii). During this period, rapid suburbanization and industrial growth pushed Mexican Americans eastward (61). The barrio formed out of a combination of factors: the rapid increases in migration from Mexico between 1910 and 1920 (during Mexico's revolutionary war and World War I), the booming industry and commerce in the old Mexican plaza that eliminated inner-city residential areas, the decentralizing effects of interurban transportation; and a rise in racial tension and subsequent efforts to segregate Mexican residents, which prevented immigrants from moving into the north or west sections of the city, all contributed to the making of East Los Angeles (61–62).

Ricardo Romo writes that the move to the Eastside gave the Mexican "*colonia*" more cohesiveness, and insulation, than it had experienced downtown:

> In the Plaza area, Mexicanos mingled with Europeans and sections of the neighborhood crossed into Chinatown and the Black community. On the east side, by contrast, the barrio had more clearly defined boundaries that gave the community an insulated character. Sociologists of that era considered the segregated features of the Mexican *colonia* an inevitable consequence of racism . . . but they also moved in great numbers to the east side for the opportunity to maintain social relationships that made their transitions to American life easier. In the *colonias* they found Spanish spoken in the stores and churches, and there they could expect to receive credit and meet with others from their village or homeland. (148–49)

The colonia's self-sufficiency as a community also diminished Mexican residents' need to interact with the Anglo residents of the city, reinforcing its cultural insulation. The transformation of Los Angeles's public transportation system and urban planning schema in the mid-1920s will solidify the neighborhood cohesion, making it not just unnecessary but excessively difficult for Eastside residents to move outside the Eastside.

In her book *Imagining Transit: Race, Gender, and Transportation in Los Angeles,* Sikivu Hutchinson argues that the changing transportation systems of the city have determined the aggressively segregated and sprawling landscape of Los Angeles. Hutchinson claims that the streetcar companies of the 1910s and 1920s "profoundly influenced the racialization of space in the city," as "the Pacific Electric's path neatly presaged the suburban shift to eastern counties propelled by highway development" (118). These streetcar lines allowed the movement of Mexicans and Mexican Americans to the Eastside; however, as railways made way for freeways, the Eastside became cut up and cordoned off by new interstates and state highways running through the barrio. Part of a Depression-era "sea change" in American city planning, L.A.'s urban planners embraced decentralization, turning away "from their promotion of 'core-city oriented systems'" in the wake of downtown traffic congestion, dwindling support for public transportation initiatives, and integration of the auto into city landscapes (121). In 1924 the city planners, led by Gordon Whitehall, announced their vision for a "horizontal city of the future," which would break with the conventions of eastern cities and seize upon the automobile as the key to the city's long-standing, paradoxical desire for antiurban urban development (122). Los Angeles planners decided to avoid costly and time-consuming "core-city problems" by focusing their resources on suburban expansion outside the city center, essentially abandoning the inner city in favor of developing freeway access to spaces further afield.

The "horizontal city of the future" plan led to two key changes in urban planning that have resulted in the segregation of L.A.'s contemporary landscape: the creation of the planning commission and the institution-alization of zoning laws (122). The planning commission was composed of land developers, real estate agents, and bankers who had no ties to the communities that would be under development and who pushed for street and regional highway development, facilitating "the massive segregation of land use and concomitant preservation of private space during the superhighway era" (123). Zoning laws segregated residential space from retail and manufacturing spaces, increasing the need for the automobile and undermining the mixed-use spaces of the central city. Together, these initiatives "helped solidify the model of the decentered, auto-dependent, racially segregated antiurban city" (122).

The implementation of this new model inordinately affected the El Monte and East L.A. barrios, as freeways and public structures began being built upon their community. During the 1950s, when parts of *The People of Paper* are set and just before *Their Dogs Came with Them* takes place, East L.A. barrio residents faced dual challenges, subject to hous-ing and employment discrimination and thus unable to move, and subject to "urban renewal" projects that disrupted their neighborhood, as "giant earth movers began carving up East Los Angeles" (Sánchez 169). In the late 1950s and into the 1960s, massive construction of freeways connecting

Anglo suburban communities with the city center included the building of high overpasses and six-lane freeways, which crisscrossed the east side (170). Thousands of residents were relocated. Freeway construction eliminated trolley lines and disrupted public transit, further isolating the neighborhoods of East Los Angeles from other areas of town. The highway system would thus radically change the physical landscape of greater Los Angeles while conversely radically stabilizing the character of barrios like the Eastside and El Monte as Mexican American and Chicanx colonias.

"Cautious of Paper": Mexican East L.A. in Salvador Plascencia's *The People of Paper* and Helena María Viramontes's *Their Dogs Came with Them*

In the midst of *The People of Paper*'s metafictional battle for the right to tell the story of a neighborhood, the fictional novelist's fictional financial backers Ralph and Elise Landis (humorous stand-ins for Plascencia's own Paul and Daisy Soros Foundation grant for the book) step in and take a side: "if we had learned anything from this story it was to be cautious of paper—to be mindful of its fragile construction and sharp edges, but mostly to be cautious of what is written on it" (Plascencia 219). In Helena María Viramontes's *Their Dogs Came with Them*, East L.A. resident Ermila, facing a barrio quarantine, representative of the very real campaign to simultaneously police and pathologize Eastside residents, voices a similar fear: "The city officials demanded paper so thin and weightless, it resisted the possibility of upholding legal import to people like herself . . . No one on the eastside believed in paper" (63). Paper in these twenty-first-century texts misrepresents; it erases histories and entire communities from the East Los Angeles landscape; it labels, categorizes, and criminalizes Chicano/as and Mexicans, at the same time that it literally papers over their long-standing presence and their many contributions to the region.

Plascencia and Viramontes are thus faced with the same dilemma: how to use the very material that curbs their community in order to represent that community? How to put a real place down on the page without falling into the trap of paper, which purports to record indelibly the single, objective history of an individual, or a community, or a city? The two novels treat two different East L.A. barrios, with distinct histories and unique cultures, and the resulting stylistic choices differ as well: where Plascencia embraces metafiction to call attention to the construction of his story, to essentially point out that paper *is* paper, Viramontes deploys the techniques of literary realism. Yet both novelists conscientiously shape narrative form to correct the inherent dangers of paper, to criticize the way it has pigeonholed and corralled their communities, and even implicate their own authorship, to capture their barrios without commodifying them. While the methods are quite dissimilar, part 1 will show how Viramontes and Plascencia each precisely craft their aesthetic to match the particularities of their community.

East L.A. and El Monte have different histories and distinct cultural aesthetics. East L.A. arose out of the development and gentrification of downtown L.A., serving as a catchall immigrant neighborhood, first housing them, then serving their dead in the dozen cemeteries that sprouted up beginning in the 1800s. East L.A. becomes ground for a massive freeway interchange for an increasingly sprawling metropolis, subject to the irony of being hyperconnected and yet increasingly disconnected, pressures that ethnically homogenized the population and physically isolated the neighborhood. El Monte's Chicanx community was segregated from the start, growing out of a camp of Mexican laborers first brought across the border to build the interurban railway and then to tend the flowers. Unlike East L.A., there have always been (at least) two El Montes.

Both communities are consistently infused with ongoing transnational migrations from Mexico, and both share a history of fierce solidarity and cultural unity in the face of exclusion from the outside. Yet while Plascencia's El Monte battles the abstract erasure of the official Anglo El Monte narrative, Viramontes's Eastside battles the very concrete erasure (literally!) of its neighborhood by the forces of urban expansion and "renewal." These two authors must thread the needle between defending, preserving, and paying homage to their neighborhoods and offering up those places to a broader community of uninitiated readers: they run the risk of literary gentrification, allowing outsiders to move in. The gamble is worth it to capture the inimitable character of the barrios that made them who they are.

1

"A World Built on Cement"

THE EL MONTE AESTHETIC IN SALVADOR PLASCENCIA'S
THE PEOPLE OF PAPER

> Saturn arrived in El Monte, the El Monte where he had first touched her
> waist and tasted her split ends and dandruff, this El Monte, not the El
> Monte of warfare and lead houses.
>
> —Salvador Plascencia, *The People of Paper*

THE REAL El Monte is a city of 115,000 inhabitants some twelve miles
east of downtown Los Angeles. With a 61 percent Mexican population,
according to the 2010 census, it is an outpost of Mexican culture more
than a hundred miles from the southern border of the United States. Its
long-standing barrio, with a history of Mexican American braceros and
flower-picking labor, is home to El Monte Flores (EMF), one of the oldest
Chicanx gangs in the region. Salvador Plascencia's debut novel *The People
of Paper* contains several versions of El Monte, each claiming various levels
of recourse to the real. The novel's "nonfictional" El Monte is the barrio in
its gritty present, where Saturn—the name the self-aware characters know
Salvador Plascencia by in his text—grows up, falls in love, and has his heart
broken prior to writing the book we hold in our hands. The "El Monte of
warfare and lead houses" is populated by Saturn's characters and set in the
1950s, when Mexican immigrants and Chicano/as labored together in the
Bodger Seed Company flower fields. This fictionalized El Monte takes up
most of the story but finally defers to the "real" El Monte of the present,
the one of "split ends and dandruff," of "pachuco gangs," "drug turf and
street names" (49) that propels the novel. Plascencia reveals himself to be
not only the author but a character and a tyrant as well, weaving stories of
heartache for his fictional characters and looking back to an earlier, more
idyllic El Monte from the vantage of its less glamorous present.

The most striking feature of the novel is its formal experimentation.
The page layout alternates between chapters with multiple columns of
independently labeled characters whose thoughts are narrated in third
person, chapters with one narrative or three narratives told from a

SATURN

Federico de la Fe did not win a single game of lotería. He thought that perhaps an evil omen was at work. The only pictures he ever placed a bean over were those of the devil and the grim reaper.

Little Merced did not win a game either, but none of her cards pointed to any signs of evil or premature death—only benign images of watermelons and banjos.

Just before midnight they left the cobblestone bingo park and headed to the red-brick bus depot.

They boarded Bus Number 8 on its north route to the border city of Tijuana. Federico de la Fe led Little Merced by the hand into the last two seats at the back of the bus, next to the toilet stall. Little Merced shoved her pillowcases beneath her seat and fell asleep across the burgundy cushions that smelled of sugarcane.

Ten minutes after the bus pulled out of the brick bus depot, four miles into the trip, Federico de la Fe looked out the window and then down at his daughter. He felt a slight inkling of the old sadness and feared that if he fell asleep he would soak his seat.

Out of this fear, Federico de la Fe went into the toilet stall and pulled out his sickle and heated it with a bit of phosphorus until it burned red. He lifted his wool Sunday shirt and pressed the glowing red sickle into his stomach until the sadness receded.

22

LITTLE MERCED

I bought three limes from an old salt Indian who sold fruits and blocks of sodium. I hid the limes in my pillowcases and pushed them underneath my bus seat.

I fell asleep and did not wake until four hours later as the bus meandered around the curves of the Chapoltenec canyon. My father, who could sleep through almost anything, snored, but I could hear a woman talking in a baby voice. I looked over the seat and saw a woman wearing a wool Indian poncho with twigs tangled into the thread. On her lap was a slobbering baby who moved only his lower lip.

"He's meditating. He was born in a meditative state," the woman said. "At first I thought that he was brain dead; the doctors said that he was as dumb as a turnip." She explained that she had nearly killed him. But, as she was buying rat poison for her baby turnip, the curandero behind the counter looked into the baby's eyes. The curandero told her that the baby was actually a very powerful soothsayer who was meditating. "One day he will break his trance and add to the parchment texts of Nostradamus."

"I know it seems like he is dead inside but just yesterday I looked in his eyes and I saw the history of the world on the inside of his retina. I saw us as jellyfish and apes, and then the ships of Columbus.

"And it's not just this world. Sometimes I see Saturn and stars and planets that telescopes have never been pointed at. The universe whirls around in his head, and one day he will be able to tell us about it."

I wanted a glimpse of the future; I thought that in the contained vastness of the baby's head, maybe I could spot my mother's black hair. I wiped the baby's slobber with my sleeve and stared into his eyes.

23

BABY NOSTRADAMUS

FIGURE 1. The unorthodox layout of Salvador Plascencia's *The People of Paper*

particular character's point of view, and a few chapters with as many as six voices per page crowded into columns. The text itself undergoes stress and interruption: Names are scratched out; text is blacked out, crossed out; and the occasional graffito or diagram or image is placed throughout the novel (see fig. 1). The narrative is equally self-conscious: Salvador Plascencia enters the story as an author being fought by his characters, who desire freedom from the incursion of omniscient narration into their private lives. Such narrative experimentation clearly implores the reader to think about the formal and stylistic choices of the author. Yet in its public reception, *The People of Paper*'s literary strangeness has often been glossed over. Critics either assume that Plascencia, as a Latinx writer, is operating in a Latin American tradition, and quickly relegate the novel to the category of magical realism, or they assume that Plascencia, as a Latinx writer, is engaged in a literary project of Chicanx social justice and highlight the novel's more straightforward depiction of Mexican and Chicanx flower pickers.

These dual tendencies are evidenced by reviews of the debut novel, in the *Los Angeles Times, Publishers Weekly,* and *The Guardian,* among others, which overwhelmingly referred to *The People of Paper* as magical realist; those that didn't claim the text as magical realist emphasized its Chicanx side: for instance *New York Times* reviewer Nathaniel Rich connected *The People of Paper* to *Music of the Mill,* the debut novel by former L.A. gang member and Chicanx activist poet Luis J. Rodriguez, calling them both "Cal-Mex." The early literary criticism of the novel largely followed suit. In his chapter on *The People of Paper* and Karen Tei Yamashita's *Tropic of Orange,* Kevin Cooney interprets the experimental formatting of Plascencia's text as an inheritor of the Latin American magical realist tradition, viewing the novel as an act of "postcolonial resistance" engaged in "mapping the city from its racial and geographic margins" (207). In this reading, the novel's unusual formatting functions to create the textual geography of a public space such as the Los Angeles Plaza and to move these voices to the center of a Los Angeles that had pushed communities like El Monte to the periphery. (In reality, El Monte was never part of the city of Los Angeles, peripheral or otherwise, as the El Monte Township was formed in 1866, and the city of El Monte was incorporated in 1912.) Cooney rightly argues that these formal elements "raise profound questions about the relationship between literature and place." However, his claim that this "metafictional mapping" is specifically connected to postcolonial modes of resistance miscategorizes Plascencia's project as part of a Latin American tradition.

Ramón Saldívar catches the link Cooney and others overlook between Plascencia and what Mark McGurl has called "the Program Era" of American literature fueled by an institutionalized MFA style and avers that Plascencia's text "share[s] more with the form and aesthetics" of contemporary postmodernist writers such as Michael Chabon and Mark Z. Danielewski than with those of the Latin American magical realist tradition ("Historical Fantasy" 576). Saldívar expands on what he calls a "postrace, neo-fantasy, transnational turn in American ethnic fiction" in a monograph in *Narrative,* where he argues that the twenty-first century has introduced among US ethnic writers "a hybrid amalgam of realism, magical realism, metafiction, and genre fictions, including science fiction, graphic narrative, and fantasy proper" ("Second Elevation" 13). While I agree that there has been a shift in contemporary modes of narration in African American, Latinx, and Asian American fiction, I disagree that these writers all necessarily share an investment in "reconfiguring the thematics of race," which Saldívar sees as a chief element of the new style (5). Placing them in this category of "postrace aesthetic" also gains

us little in terms of analyzing the particular function or aim of experimental form in the case of each work.

As for the subject matter of *The People of Paper*, Saldívar reads Plascencia's project as a protest for social justice for an underserved Chicanx
community, ultimately claiming that both Plascencia and Junot Díaz are
"sharing the goal of ethnic writers to imagine a state of achieved social
justice," while telling their "protest stories" ("Historical Fantasy" 593).
Saldívar engages explicitly with the form of the novel, and he refreshingly
avoids placing Plascencia's work in a magical realist tradition out of hand.
However, once the experimentation of the novel is explained with this
new label of "postrace aesthetics," Saldívar emerges with a reading that,
while perceptive and nuanced, ultimately situates *The People of Paper* in
the same category of "Chicanx social protest" that critics and reviewers
who *didn't* grapple with the novel's form utilized.

My reading resists categorizing the novel as part of preexisting traditions
like Latin American magical realism or Chicanx protest literature; instead,
I take my cue from the vivid presentation of the town of El Monte and seek
specific neighborhood sources for Plascencia's innovative narrative strategies. *The People of Paper* expresses a unique formal relationship between the
author and his neighborhood of El Monte: the text thus insists on a localized analysis, which connects Plascencia's stylistic choices to the novel's setting and deals with those experimental innovations in the terms dictated
by the work itself. My barriography will provide a more precise hermeneutic for interpreting *The People of Paper*. I argue that the actual El Monte's
cultural practices of *con safos* and *rasquachismo* inform the text's unusual
author/character relationship and the unorthodox physical layout of the
novel. Interpreting these narrative choices locally elucidates the transnational identity of the author, himself an immigrant from Guadalajara to El
Monte, inscribed in the novel, a valence lost when the text is read as part of
a generic literary tradition, such as metafiction or magical realism.

A barriography of El Monte reveals a barrio that is closed off, ideologically and culturally at odds with the city that surrounds it. The city of El
Monte disavows its Mexican past as well as its Mexican present, while its
barrio community persists in producing its own endemic aesthetic practices, informed by both native Chicanx and Mexican immigrant culture.
Considering the explicit references to turf wars and graffiti tags in the text,
I propose that the role of writing in the novel is governed by the practice of
con safos, a Southwestern Chicanx mode of understanding public writing
as sacred and vulnerable. Viewed in this light, the novel becomes a graffiti
tag and reveals Plascencia's anxiety toward his own textual production by

evoking the graffiti tagger's authorial power in proclaiming his or her name publicly, as well as the fear of potential defamation of one's own name that might result. The unorthodox page formatting, when interpreted in terms of the neighborhood, can be understood as operating according to the principles of Chicanx *rasquachismo*, an aesthetic sensibility characterized by "a witty, irreverent, and impertinent posture that recodes and moves outside established boundaries" (Ybarra-Frausto 155), which pervades the contemporary decor of the El Monte barrio. The novel enacts the aesthetic practices of El Monte through its *rasquache* production, creating juxtapositions and hybridizations that can stylistically approximate the barrio. This method allows Plascencia to reappropriate in order to avoid appropriating the character of the place that has inspired his story.

The Official El Monte

The danger of paper is palpable in the official history of the nonfictional El Monte. In Plascencia's novel, El Monte appears to be a Mexican American world unto itself, a town wholly devoted to flower picking and solely occupied by Mexican and Chicanx laborers. Yet a visit to the El Monte Historical Museum reveals that a very different history is being cultivated and curated. The uncomfortable juxtaposition of these two versions of El Monte's history demonstrates the stakes of *The People of Paper's* wariness of paper and Plascencia's strategies for reappropriating the materials of narrative construction.

The official history of El Monte, as purveyed by the El Monte Historical Museum in South El Monte, California, is already revisionist.[1] Apparently fed up with assumptions that their town was a mere latecomer outer L.A. suburb, the museum insists that El Monte was one of the earliest (Anglo) settlements in Southern California. Donna Crippen, the museum's curator, tells me that El Monte was "the first all-American settlement in Los Angeles County" (Crippen). The phrase "all-American," aside from its frisson-producing implications of who is and is not an American according to this categorization, is meant not only to distinguish the town from the earlier Native American, Spanish, and Mexican settlements in California but also ostensibly to indicate that the whole of this "first" settlement was Anglo in its composition. The first wagon train left from Independence, Missouri, in 1849, spurred on by the California gold rush. The self-avowed main attractions of the town's history are Gay's Lion Farm, former home to the MGM lion; its walnut and flower industries; and one of the first public schools in the state of California, founded in 1852.

The claim of first Anglo settlement in California is belied by the name, "El Monte," which is of course Spanish in origin. "Monte" in contemporary Spanish means hill or mountain, yet as Plascencia notes, the town of El Monte has neither: "The town was called El Monte, after the hills it did not have. But everything else was named after flowers" (Plascencia 33). In the pamphlet, "A Brief History of El Monte," free with your free entrance to the museum, Jack Barton explains the discrepancy:

> Most non-Hispanic persons with some knowledge of Spanish assume that the name El Monte must pertain to a hill or a mountain of some sort. If this were true, it would belie the physical realities of El Monte as a place, for there are no hills or mountains in any evidence. . . . Rather, one must search for a meaning to the name "El Monte" in the obscure and somewhat archaic definitions which were current in Spanish-usage in the late 18th century. For it was in the 1770s that a group of Spanish soldiers and missionaries first explored this part of Southern California. . . . And, one among their number, first used the term in Spanish which, at that time (1770s) would best describe this beautiful "wooded spot." (1–2)

The Spanish appreciated El Monte's "precious soil, abundant wood (for fuel), and deep, rich alluvial topsoil" (1), and named the town, yet they are not considered the town's founders or its original inhabitants. It does seem strange, however, that mere passersby would be so appreciative of the soil quality. Barton calls the Spaniards "journeyers," referring to a series of decades, including the era of the missions of the 1770s to 1830s and the "land grant" ranchos of the 1830s, where El Monte functioned merely as "a natural resting place for whatever weary journeyer came its way" (2). Barton notes that, even before its naming, El Monte was "frequented" by small bands of "nomadic" Indians, which is evidenced by Indian burial sites and "kitchen middens" (2). Familiarity with the topsoil, the establishment of missions, and the inherent land use natural to the economic mode of ranch production all imply some form of residency, as do the earlier burial and kitchen sites. However, the museum avers that it was only the great gold rush of the 1840s and 1850s "that brought the first permanent residents to El Monte" (2).

The strategic qualification of an unavoidable Spanish past here echoes what Raúl Homero Villa calls the "Spanish Romance" version of the history of greater Los Angeles. As a tactic for "the neutralization or erasure of present, lived forms of expression, historical consciousness, and material iconography reflecting the city's actual Mexican legacy," a "Spanish

Romance" or "fantasy heritage" was manufactured and promoted for the region, which acknowledges and emphasizes the much earlier Spanish presence in order to downplay the more recent and, more important, still ongoing Mexican presence in Los Angeles and its environs (55). This history of the area, told through heavily publicized tourist events such as "days of the don" and "mission days" or the promotion of "authentic" Spanish marketplaces such as the Olvera Street market in downtown L.A., is a ploy for increasing regional tourism that also tries to recast California's Mexican culture as a quaint, disappearing inheritance of *Los Angeles* culture, now "accessible only in the reified object-form of a pseudo-historical cultural landscape and iconography" (55). El Monte cannot escape its Spanish past, despite a battle in the 1860s to change the town name to "Lexington," and so its history acknowledges the influence, while mitigating this past by refusing to cede actual prior settlement rights to the Spaniards, or the Native Americans who in turn preceded them.

The "Spanish Romance" telling of El Monte's history is placed in relief by the artifacts exhibited in the museum itself. Early Spanish artifacts are displayed side by side with older Native American ones, tucked in the back corner of the museum. The only reference to Mexicans or Mexican Americans is a small subsection of images, labeled "Mexican-Americans," showing a dozen black and white photographs from the 1940s and 1950s of community dances at Medina Court, ostensibly the Chicanx neighborhood in old El Monte, though it is not explained in the exhibit. Considering that El Monte's current population, according to 2018 census data, is 61 percent Mexican (50 percent of whom were born in Mexico), with 70 percent of the town Hispanic/Latinx (South El Monte, where the museum is located, is a whopping 84 percent), the elision of the Mexican history of El Monte is startling. Despite these erasures, however, this history still manages to resurface.

Looking over an El Monte photo album with the curator, Donna Crippen, a lifelong native of El Monte, we come across a photo of "Hicks Camp," and she notes that it was taken before the renovation of the area, which had become a slum. When pressed further, she tells me Hicks Camp was initially established in the 1910s for braceros (my word, not hers), migrant laborers solicited from Mexico to work first in the fields and later on the trolley network and housed in what began as temporary housing. The braceros and their families stayed, and eventually housing was renovated to reflect permanent rather than temporary—or perhaps "journeyers"?—settlement. Crippen added that "they were not segregated," although "they" lived in a different part of town. She explains that

El Monte's second public school was *not* built as a segregated school; it was merely a grammar school where Spanish-speaking children could learn English. Crippen relates that it was considered an incentive for Mexican and Mexican American students, who could attend the unsegregated high school if they attained the requisite level of English at their own elementary school.

In reality, Hicks Camp was envisioned by its owner and founder, Robert Hicks, as a source of pliable migrant Mexican labor to be contracted out to surrounding farms during the growing season. Hicks, a labor contractor, began recruiting Mexicans to the site with promotional flyers in the 1910s. El Monte's restrictive housing covenants kept even upwardly mobile Mexicans and Mexican Americans from living outside of the camp, which for decades consisted of dirt roads, boxcar houses, and a marked absence of city services such as police, fire, and trash pickup; the camp had to rely on Los Angeles County emergency response (Rasmussen). The city of El Monte's local parks were off-limits to Mexicans, and its school system was segregated (separate schools for whites, Mexicans, and Japanese) until the 1950s (Morales).

The Mexican American presence is felt but left unnamed as Jack Barton goes on to describe the twentieth-century history of El Monte. The Bodgers Seed Company arrived in El Monte in the 1910s, when agriculture formed the town's main economy, and remained in business until 2010. The seed company's vast flower fields were famous in the area through the first half of the twentieth century: "During blooming season, these fields of blossoms—precisely laid out in geometric patterns—were visited by people from all over the San Gabriel valley. The farm workers employed to tend these magnificent floral gardens affectionately named the area Las Flores—a name which persists today in designating that part of the 'island' of El Monte" (6). Much like the "journeyer" versus "permanent settler" rhetoric of the early history of El Monte, the language here refuses inclusion of Mexican residents. The Spanish speakers who named the land are insistently tied to their work rather than the place, with almost absurd redundancy: As "workers" "employed" "to tend," their role is strictly economic, as laborers who in this telling appear to be passing through, though the permanence of the town's name implies they were residents and citizens of the town in addition to its employed labor. The adjective "affectionately" also rings false, as the name "Las Flores" is a noun with no descriptive power in Spanish, signifying, simply, "the flowers." The modern-day legacy of these workers, and their naming, is the El Monte Flores street gang.

Funded by the Works Progress Administration, El Monte's museum and its literature chiefly represent archiving and research done only up through the 1930s. While the museum has collected artifacts for the second half of the twentieth century, the bulk of materials are from El Monte's early history until World War II. This may account for the seeming dearth of information about El Monte's ethnic communities, not only the Latinx population but also the Japanese American and newer Chinese and Vietnamese communities in the city. Yet even with this caveat, the museum's insistence on a pioneer narrative, reflected in the majority of its exhibits as well as its literature, systematically elides or subsumes the Spanish and then Mexican presence that has been in the town since before its founding (see fig. 2).

With this persistent elision of the Mexican American presence in El Monte in mind, Plascencia's version of the town's history takes on new valence, as an attempt to revise the "official" narration. Plascencia frames El Monte with a different origin myth from that of the Anglo pioneers and consistently reiterates the ties between the city and Mexico through a series of cultural practices native to the city but inherited from or inspired by Mexico.

FIGURE 2. The interior of the El Monte Historical Museum, 2013. (Photo by the author; by permission of the City of El Monte)

The *Other* El Monte

In its first pages, *The People of Paper* distinguishes itself as a New World story. It opens with a surreal prologue recounting the Vatican decree to forbid the making of people "from the ground or from the marrow of bones," which up until the declaration had been a wildly successful enterprise, perfected by Catholic monks. The decree leaves only the method of creation "from the propulsions and mounts performed underneath bedsheets" (at which the monks were markedly less successful): we track a unit of saddened monks who are forced to close their people factory and march until they forget its coordinates (Plascencia 11). Plascencia locates his origin myth of fabricated people in the Americas: the monks "walked south to the Argentine land of fire and back north to the glacial cliffs of Alaska" (11), and when one monk, the rebellious #53, refuses to march any further, he absconds in "the desert basin," presumably the area containing parts of California and Chihuahua, Mexico. Eager to create his first entire person of paper, the Guadalajaran origami surgeon Antonio finds monk #53 by way of the church gossip mill, learns the factory coordinates, and journeys there in a poncho with a wheelbarrow full of construction paper. Our narrative begins, then, in an otherworldy Mexico, where the ability to create life (of mud, or ribs, or paper) is limited only by papal decree and the scope of human endeavor.

Plascencia thus very consciously claims origin myths for the Americas, and Mexico specifically. The Garden of Eden is located not in some Mesopotamian valley but in Oaxaca, also home to a breed of songbirds that can cure loneliness:

> Pío-Pío descended from one of the flocks that had willingly left the Garden in pursuit of Eve. Pío-Pío's ancestors were faithful to the first couple until they bore Cain. Attending to the duties of a new father, Adam neglected the fields, and when the crops wilted he began to caress the plump meat of the songbirds' wings and bellies. The first bird migration began on the brink of man's discovery of white meat. The flocks were not seen again until the years of Cortez. At that time the mestizos, who had learned from their colonizers, began to cage the Oaxacan songbirds. (79)

This version of the first man and woman transforms Adam and Eve into native Mexicans and marks change by the chronology of the Conquest: The birds abandon the Garden, but though they fear being eaten, this indignity pales in comparison to the treatment of birds that come with "the years of Cortez," when the songbirds are caged for their performance. Prehistory in this text, then, is anchored firmly in Mexico.

The fluidity of these transmigrations, from the monks' early exploration of the Americas to the terrified songbirds of paradise fleeing Mexican Adam and Eve, offers a version of history that recognizes the arbitrariness of national lines as well as the absurdity of claiming swaths of the Southwest for Anglo pioneers as their first settlement. *The People of Paper*'s fictional account of the prehistory of the hemisphere gestures towards the very real history of the original inhabitants of North and South America, who are reluctantly acknowledged by the official history of a town like El Monte but denied the role of protagonist or first settler. Yet Plascencia's alternate history counters the history forwarded by the El Monte Historical Museum without explicitly condemning it or attempting to supplant it; the author abstains from building just another "official" account, with all its attendant elisions or inevitably biased perspectives. His playful historical account points to the created nature of *all* accounts.

After the prologue, *The People of Paper*'s narrative speeds forward to the 1950s, arriving in Frederico de la Fe's small town of Las Tortugas, Mexico. Plagued by heartbreak and sadness, de la Fe and his daughter Little Merced ultimately settle in El Monte. As Mexican immigrants the pair stand out, even in a town with El Monte's history of imported braceros. Frederico de la Fe's coworkers are largely Chicano/as, and they note that his Spanish is unbroken by English, unlike their own (69). However, in El Monte both father and daughter find a culture seemingly transplanted from their Mexican homeland: "El Monte was one thousand four hundred forty-eight miles north of Las Tortugas and an even fifteen hundred miles from the city of Guadalajara, and while there were no cockfights or wrestling arenas, the curanderos' botanica shops, the menudo stands, and the bell towers of the Catholic churches had also pushed north, settling among the flowers and sprinkler systems" (34). The phrase "had also pushed north" is ambiguous, but the "also" seems to refer to Little Merced and Frederico de la Fe, implying that it was not only immigrants that had "pushed north" from Mexico. Yoking concrete objects—the *botánica* shops, the menudo stands, the Catholic church towers—to the migration of individuals, complete with these objects' "settling" in town, reflects the ongoing cultural assimilation of El Monte to its Mexican and Mexican American citizens. The elements of a Mexican town have pushed north in their entirety, appearing to take over all of the town aside from its flower beds, which of course represent the labor that drew Mexican migrants in the first place. This description indicates the impossibility of immigration occurring on a massive scale without carrying with it a migration of culture as well.

Little Merced's version of El Monte history, in fact, speaks of the exodus rather than the migration of the pioneer settlers, scared off by the cultural assault from Mexico that has come with the flower pickers: "The original settlers of El Monte, people who had come from the east using the path of Santa Fe and the paved route of 66, gradually moved from El Monte to the foothills of Arcadia and Pasadena, towns that did not have the foot traffic of flower pickers or the smell of oregano and lard bubbling from the boiling pots of menudo stands. The only time the pioneers of El Monte returned was in December, when they bought flowers to decorate the motorized carts that floated down the avenues of their newly adopted towns" (34). Little Merced has already been educated in the official history of El Monte, which is obvious by her conflation of the town's past to its present, believing the original settlers arrived by highway. Yet she views the pioneers as inhabiting El Monte's past, as *her* El Monte is settled only by flower pickers; in this recasting of the "Spanish Romance" as the "Anglo Romance," Little Merced acknowledges the town's pioneer past but sees little evidence of it in the town's present. Her swift dismissal of Pasadena's annual Rose Bowl parade, defamiliarized here as flowers and carts used to decorate "newly adopted towns," highlights the slight but ostentatious presence of these pioneers. This version of El Monte leaves the Mexican and Chicanx laborers as the permanent inhabitants and ironically turns the "original settlers" into *migrants,* who live elsewhere and yet return annually based on the growing season. It is to these permanent inhabitants that we now turn.

Plascencia's Literary *Con Safos*

At the center of *The People of Paper* is a battle over the power to create and name and the question of how to shoulder the responsibility that comes with that power. This conflict is staged through the novel's adherence to graffiti logic, particularly the deployment of *con safos*. A concept unique to Chicanx cultures of the Southwest and practiced by the gangs of El Monte and greater Los Angeles, *con safos* operates according to a set of regulations, which Plascencia applies to his own writing in the novel.

In the fictional 1950s El Monte, Frederico de la Fe joins his fellow flower-pickers in their burgeoning gang, El Monte Flores (EMF); but Plascencia did not invent EMF. The real modern-day city of El Monte is *still* home to El Monte Flores or EMF, which was begun by Bodger Seed Company laborers in the 1950s, a group united by their work in El Monte's flower-picking industry (Baeder). As of 2009, EMF had about 400 members. In a section of the novel that takes place in the present, EMF leader and El Monte native Froggy notes the changes to the neighborhood that he sees as an old man: "instead of flowers, gasoline pumps and lampposts rose from El Monte, all marked by the EMF tags" (Plascencia 46). While the old EMF also tagged their barrio, Froggy laments a loss of precision in the application of the tags that he sees in present-day El Monte: "even the old gang tag had lost some of its formality, now posted haphazardly and sloppily etched" (49). The new tags betray a lack of pride in the act of claiming territory, merely applied to mark ownership of a street for drug dealing. Froggy's preoccupation, not with the acts of tagging themselves but with their loss of aesthetic precision, indicates the cultural importance of graffiti tags and gestures toward a specific relationship between the tagger and his or her tag.

Unlike the ubiquitous "curanderos' botanica shops, the menudo stands, and the bell towers of Catholic churches" (34) of El Monte, graffiti is not a cultural inheritance from Mexico. The first tags that EMF posts across its city, and the later ones "haphazardly etched," function as urban territorial markers—something Frederico de la Fe or his rural Mexican compatriots did not need, something born from "a world that was built on cement and not mud" (19) as Little Merced says. Yet while the contemporary resurgence of graffiti is a widespread urban phenomenon, Froggy's reverence for proper graffiti form hints at the idea of *con safos*.

The term *con safos* defies English translation, but in usage it is "primarily associated with names" (Grider 133). The Los Angeles-based bilingual magazine *Con Safos* explains the term as "protective symbolism used by Chicano graffiti artists appearing usually by a person's name or the name of his *barrio*, meaning the same to you; ditto, likewise" (Flores 65). Whatever criticism or defacement has been written over the tag then applies to the new tagger. In her essay "Con Safos: Mexican-Americans, Names and Graffiti," Sylvia Ann Grider argues that "*con safos* is a surrogate for a physical bodyguard which can protect a written name" (134). The danger of placing one's name in a public location is mitigated by the application of a *con safos*, which allows taggers to proclaim themselves without suffering the humiliation of possible public defacement.

Grider affirms that the phrase *con safos* is unique to Chicanx communities and expressive of "Chicano attitudes and values," chief among these the "penchant for naming" and the importance or sacredness of naming (133). Tagging of course is often about naming, and projecting that name to the public. Yet the addition of the written *con safos*, "C/S," or equivalent protection so common in Chicanx tagging implies a different, more intimate relationship between the tagger and his or her tag: "The problem that such public presentation of names creates for the individual who writes them is the necessity of protecting these inscriptions from defacement and further insult because the graphic depiction of *the name is regarded as a tangible extension of the person himself*" (Grider 133; emphasis added). The insistence that the name be protected and the power of a *con safos* to do so suggest that in Chicanx tagging culture, in defiance of Ferdinand de Saussure, the name *is* the person, and the signifier is tied to the signified in a meaningful way (see fig. 3).

Users of the *con safos* presume a community that will respect that connection between name and self. For a *con safos* to be effective, it must be used where those who see it understand its implications: "the youth write their names for people who know and recognize them, not for hostile strangers" (Grider 137). Graffiti serves several functions, as an artistic outlet, social statement, territorial marker, or self-aggrandizement. However, Grider insists that Chicanx graffiti protected by a *con safos* is distinct from graffiti motivated by defacing "public property as a sign of their contempt for society" (137): "it is instead one aspect of a *communication code* which places extremely high value on personal names" (139; emphasis added). The application of a *con safos* to a tag thus simultaneously describes the tagger/artist and indicates his or her audience.

Picking up on this community aspect of *con safos,* in his work on Chicanx culture and urban spaces, Raúl Homero Villa extends the tradition beyond individual identity preservation. Describing "the ubiquitous emblem" "C/S" signed on to Chicanx territorial graffiti throughout the city of Los Angeles, Villa writes: "Of uncertain origin and without an exact translation, 'C/S' is generally posted as a challenge or warning by the writer-artist to those who would disrespect the neighborhood by disfiguring the public imprint of *place identity*" (153; emphasis added). He adds that these tags are "weaving together town shreds of barrio social space" (153). For example, Villa reads the large number of "plaqueasos" (scripted declarations of territory) in the 1960s near the San Gabriel freeway (I-605) that split the Jim Town Hoyo barrio as uniting symbolically what was once a geographically united neighborhood (154). In contemporary El Monte graffiti the "C/S" has become stylized, represented by small exes on either side of the tag, which Plascencia mimics in his own graffiti in the text (such as fig. 4). We can thus read EMF's tags in *The People of Paper* as announcing the name, and marking off the place, of the El Monte barrio.

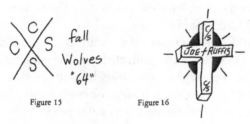

FIGURE 3. Examples of graffiti utilizing *"con safos."* (From Sylvia Ann Grider, "Con Safos: Mexican-Americans, Names and Graffiti"; by permission of the author)

The fictional denizens of El Monte operate under the assumption of semiotic ipseity indicated by *con safos,* believing that name and extension are of the same entity. These characters objected to being written about, especially considering the heartbreaking storylines their heartbroken storyteller was forcing them to act out for his own catharsis, because their representation on paper was as real to them as their flesh-and-blood world. We see this in the habitual substitution of ink for blood in the text; for instance, when Smiley's orders are to slit Saturn's throat and "let his ink drip," "because if that is what he wants, to write, let him write his own blood letter" (Plascencia 105). The characters, aware that they are fictional, recognize their own blood is ink; and when Saturn enters the story as a character, his blood too becomes textualized.

When read in relation to the rules of *con safos,* especially the intimacy between name and named, Saturn's relationship to his novel becomes far more nuanced. After Salvador Plascencia's characters successfully revolt against their author the first time, Saturn returns to present-day El Monte, which is in ruins: "El Monte was ravaged, the telephone poles splintered in half, the roads eroded, the crows dispersed, cart pushers on strike, and the tags of EMF etched everywhere—on trees, on windows, and on bakery walls. Only the church of Guadalupe was spared. And every time Saturn came across one of the tags he crossed it out" (111; see fig. 4). Saturn's act of crossing out is a declaration of war on EMF. It is an insult not just to the tag itself but to the gang represented by the tag, and a challenge to their claim of ownership of the neighborhood. Grider writes that in Chicanx gang culture one way to precipitate a fight with an opposing gang is to write the barrio name *without* the *con safos* bodyguard, wait until the other gang defaces the name, and then use that act as an excuse for retaliation (136). The idea of defiling a tag that *has* a *con safos* is not even mentioned, because it is so profane. Thus, when Saturn exes out every "EMF" tag he sees, even those with the exes protecting them, he is attempting to erase the actual EMF from El Monte.

Yet based on the logic of *con safos*—with its dictum, "the same now goes for you," if you defile the protected tag—when Saturn crosses out every EMF tag he sees, he is also negating himself. Present-day El Monte figures very little in the novel; it is largely overshadowed by the 1950s El Monte of the author's imagination. The author is in both El Montes: in one he is chiefly known as Saturn, the omniscient narrator and creator, unseen by his characters; in the other he is (mostly) Salvador Plascencia, a character who can walk the streets, stay at his mom's house, and go around defacing street tags (111). Therefore, for Saturn as *author* to present the image of a crossed-out EMF tag in the text—using the same image of an EMF tag he has Little Merced introduce earlier in the novel (on page 33)—means he is crossing out his own ink, implying an erasure of himself as author as well as character. Salvador Plascencia's act of vandalism appears to symbolically erase both versions of Saturn. But why?

The answer lies in the later stylistic shifts of the novel. In the first section of the book, Saturn spares his own ink/blood and appropriates that of his characters instead. But after EMF's first win in the "war on omniscient narration" (218), Saturn, now without characters or a town to narrate, introduces *himself* as a character: the writer Salvador Plascencia. In this central, disjointed section, the author, clearly suffering from writer's block, begins cobbling together plotlines taken from his own biography. The commodification of the stories of others seemed innocuous in the case of Frederico de la Fe and the early EMF members, who do not exist

the church of Guadalupe was spared. And every time Saturn came across
one of the tags he crossed it out:

Saturn knew that it was on account of the war against EMF that she
had left. It was impossible to be loyal to a war commander who was always

FIGURE 4. Saturn crosses out EMF tags. Note the X's next to the name, evocative
of the graffiti imagery Grider describes in "Con Safos." (From Plascencia, *The
People of Paper*, p. 112)

outside Saturn's story. Yet when Salvador Plascencia turns toward autobiography, his "real" ex-girlfriend Liz speaks out against being consistently
depicted as a heartless "vendida." In her critique we see Saturn's abuse of
the power to name and create:

> So I have moved house and replaced you with a white boy, but that is noth-
> ing compared to what you have done, to what you have sold. In a neat pile
> of paper you have offered up not only your hometown, EMF, and Fred-
> erico de la Fe, but also me, your grandparents and generations beyond
> them, your patria, your friends, even Cami. You have sold everything, save
> yourself. . . . I have only a request: *You need to remember that I exist beyond
> the pages of this book.* . . . Sal, if you still love me, please leave me out of this
> story. Start this book over, without me. (138; emphasis added)

Liz here distinguishes between people of blood and people of paper, not
to forgive one form of commodification and condemn the other but to
condemn them both in varying levels. "Not only" does Salvador Plascencia offer readers a fictionalized version of his own hometown with a
fictionalized history of its gang and its citizens "but also" he puts on the
page a fictionalized version of real people, alive and dead. Liz calls it all
selling out, but she reserves her strongest censure for his slander, in ink,
against people of blood. In her own version of *con safos*, Liz reaffirms the
connection between the written name and its real-world extension and
asks Salvador Plascencia to honor that intimate link.

Saturn's response to the larger question of commodification that Liz
addresses will take up the remainder of the novel. His response to her

personal request, however, is honored immediately, albeit bitterly.[2] The book starts over on page 141, and Liz's name is never uttered again. Saturn/Salvador Plascencia still speaks of her often, but he obeys her literary "C/S" by refraining from naming her or defacing her reputation. Liz's new boyfriend—a "white boy" not from El Monte—suffers a less noble fate, as his name is consistently scratched out throughout the text. To mark the boyfriend in ink but not name him serves as a superlative insult in a world where names have such power.

Liz's reproach drives Saturn back to El Monte: he renews the war with EMF, seeking to take his wrath out on the "imaginary flower people" whom he can exert power over as an authorial tyrant. In response, EMF members, and other characters from the novel, crowd the page with their thoughts, attempting to push Saturn—who normally occupies at least a third of every page with his omniscient narration—to the literal margins of the page. This offensive is rendered graphically by the addition of multiplying columns on each page to indicate the loss of space.

Saturn finally acknowledges that the war is indeed one of commodification, not just commodification of sadness, as Frederico de la Fe and EMF assert, but also of a place. Saturn addresses his surrender to Liz:

> A whole war for you. To prove that I too am a colonizer, I too am powerful in those ways. I can stand on my tippy toes, I can curl my tongue and talk that perfect untainted English, I can wipe out whole cultures, whole towns of imaginary flower people. I can do that too.
>
> But Saturn was not Cortez; he did not want to trek across the land and stab flags into the dirt and nail royal crests into walls and oaks. Saturn would end the war, tumble all the columns, even if it meant his own destruction. (238)

The book's insistence on its materiality and its innovative usage of space on the page serve as a cue for interpreting Saturn's confession as an admission of the motivations of literary creation. The weight here is given to his own expression, his ability to "curl [his] tongue and talk that perfect untainted English," as it is the *telling* that can wipe out whole cultures. The passage highlights the expressive and minimizes the active, as Saturn turns away from a series of concrete verbs: he does not want to "trek" or "stab" or "nail." The analogy, first to British imperialists, then to Cortez, functions more abstractly, drawing into relief both the egotistical desire to claim something as one's own and the economic impetus to find and cultivate something worth selling. The analogy of the conqueror or colonizer is particularly apt here, as these terms are dependent upon a socioeconomic relationship to a concrete land. Saturn confesses his bind, desiring to dramatize El Monte's "flower people" but aware that doing so is an exploitative and proprietary act. For him to cease telling the story of El Monte means the end of his story, and thus of his identity as narrator, yet he would rather surrender his authorship than colonize his beloved city. And so he abdicates in a way consistent with the town's cultural norms: having first declared war by crossing out EMF's tags, he now concedes that to do so means negating himself as author. After his confession, Saturn "tumbles" all the novel's columns, and lets his two main protagonists walk "south and off the page" (245).

The insertion of graffiti is only one of a number of ways that *The People of Paper* draws attention to the text *as* text: the novel boasts different spatial formations depending on the chapter, the book "restarts," with front matter, midway through, revealing itself as a work in progress, and there are adulterated (blacked out, crossed out, struck through) sentences and paragraphs throughout. *The People of Paper*'s unorthodox physical layout also questions Plascencia's role as creator, but its logic is distinct from the rules that obtain in *con safos*. Plascencia manages to create and then decolonize that creation by exposing the materiality of the text itself. These defamiliarizing tactics highlight the created nature of the work and flout the rules of form of both its genre and medium. This mode, which revels in the created and ignores or even boasts of one's rejection of classic form, reflects a *rasquachismo* that is particular to the neighborhood geography of El Monte.

The Rasquache Aesthetic

In "Rasquachismo: A Chicano Sensibility," Tomas Ybarra-Frausto offers us a description and definition of *rasquachismo*: "Propriety and keeping up appearances—el qué dirán—are the codes shattered by the attitude of rasquachismo.[3] This outsider viewpoint stems from a funky, irreverent stance that debunks convention and spoofs protocol. To be rasquache is to posit a bawdy, spunky consciousness, to seek to subvert and turn ruling paradigms upside down. It is a witty, irreverent, and impertinent posture that recodes and moves outside established boundaries" (155). Examples of the rasquache sensibility range from high art to lawn art, which may combine religious icons with plastic animal statues. It rejects the notion of good taste as being dictated by restraint and instead offers a paradigm where so-called poor taste—the chintzy, the excessive, the cluttered, the garish—is valued for its very rebelliousness against the norm.

Rasquachismo pervades the historically Chicanx sections of contemporary El Monte (see figs. 5–7). A casual walk through El Monte's Mexican American neighborhood provides myriad examples, at the level of architecture and landscape: beautifully kept gardens share space with planks of wood, brightly colored homemade sheds, desk chairs, engine parts, trophies; lawns and homes are decorated in a variety of figurines, statues, or objets d'art; rosebushes are accented by aesthetically positioned clothes hangers; summertime finds a *"feliz navidad"* message written in neon lights, adjacent to a backyard shaded by draped sheets, full of ready building materials and children's toys. The inclination to an excess of materials, the "filling [of] all available space with bold display," the "playful and elemental" juxtaposition of the useful and artistic, the natural and man-made, and the reappropriation of objects for new purposes all evoke a neighborhood rasquache sensibility (Ybarra-Frausto 155–57).

The aesthetic of rasquachismo emerges from a working class that is "making do" with what is at hand. Practitioners trump the aesthetic principle of decorum with the more pressing need to collect and salvage materials, for building, decorating, or artistic projects that are still in process. Faced with limited resources and wary to throw out anything that may be of use, rasquachismo's operating principle is to mend, fix, and

FIGURE 5. The El Monte aesthetic: an artfully cluttered lawn, 2013

FIGURE 6. Decorative plastic hangers for an El Monte driveway, 2013

FIGURE 7. Ready building materials and a brightly colored shed, 2013

alter any and all materials. Things are not thrown away; rather they are reused, recycled, and repurposed for different contexts (157): "Resilience and resourcefulness spring from making do with what is at hand (hacer rendir las cosas). The use of available resources engenders hybridization, juxtaposition, and integration" (156). As Amalia Mesa-Bains asserts, following Ybarra-Frausto, "the capacity to hold life together with bits of string, old coffee cans, and broken mirrors in a dazzling gesture of aesthetic bravado is at the heart of rasquachismo" (Mesa-Bains 158).

Rasquachismo, then, is a sensibility built upon the reappropriation or "recoding" of objects, taking what one has and changing it into what one needs. As a result of this emphasis on making do and remaking, the rasquache sensibility breeds an excess of materials, its "inclination piles pattern on pattern, filling all available space with bold display" (157). Its axiom that "too much is not enough" could be called baroque, except that its tone is "playful and elemental" (155) rather than declaratory or ostentatious; unlike baroque art, "there is sincerity in its artifice" (155). Rasquache art also has a makeshift feel that is alien to the baroque: "Pulling through and making do are no guarantee of security, so things that are rasquache possess an ephemeral quality, a sense of temporality and impermanence" (156). Ybarra-Frausto argues that "a work of art may be rasquache in multiple and complex ways. It can be sincere and pay homage to the sensibility by restating its premises. . . . Another strategy is for the artwork to evoke a rasquache sensibility through self-conscious manipulation of materials or iconography" (161).

This rasquache aesthetic is at work in *The People of Paper* at several levels. In terms of physical layout, the *text*'s "filling of all available space with bold display," its "playful and elemental" juxtaposition of various graphics, narrators, and formatting, imitates barrio style. The novel's form functions as the literary equivalent of an El Monte front yard. The format is visually arresting, even garish, and its neo-baroque collection of unlike items is undoubtedly rasquache. Many of the characters might also be called rasquache, as they make do with what they can find or afford and reconstitute objects according to their own unique purposes. Antonio, the first origami surgeon, is put out of work by bioengineers; he converts his paper organs into paper animals and sells them on the street (Plascencia 13). Little Merced attempts to pass off a typewriter case (purchased at the Papal Pawn & Loan) as a lunch pail so that she can sit with the proper white kids at her school during lunch (40). Maricela uses fire and screwdrivers to create her own tattoos (59). EMF's chief weapon against Saturn are the shells of defunct mechanical tortoises, which they now use as mental shields (57). Once Frederico de la Fe declares war on Saturn, he develops a plan dependent on importation of Mexican culture to function: the army drives to Tijuana, "the city of invention and discovery" (56), to buy goats and roosters; Frederico personally carries with him to East Los Angeles the commonplaces of the farm he has come from, and yet these are now reappropriated to different effect.

The most rasquache character, however, is the author. If, as Ybarra-Frausto puts it, "the use of available resources engenders hybridization, juxtaposition, and integration" in rasquachismo, we can see how *The People of Paper* functions as a rasquache text. We've seen Plascencia's playful appropriation of Judeo-Christian elements, with the retelling of the Garden of Eden and the apocryphal story of Vatican decrees and exiled monks. However, the text also gleefully strays outside Christian tradition, juxtaposing various myths and dogmas. Plascencia as the Roman god Saturn evokes a series of connotations: as a god of agriculture, Saturn is an apt deity for the flower picking community of El Monte; as a Titan who famously ate his children, Saturn reflects Plascencia's tyrannical view of fatherhood; both gods eventually suffer from overthrow at the hands of their own progeny (Hornblower and Spawforth 1360). The novel also references the planet Saturn's connection to lead, when all of El Monte falls ill with "Saturnism," or lead poisoning, after lining their homes with lead to protect themselves from the author, who cannot penetrate the metal.

When, despite their lead poisoning, El Monte succeeds in shutting Saturn out, and the author's set of raw materials—the sadness and subsequent coping mechanisms of his characters—is taken away from him, he must "make do." He uses what he can find left behind: namely, his own personal anecdotes. The desperate grasping of the author to continue the story is palpable in Part Two, as he is starkly limited by the resources at hand: he begins to narrate his own heartbreak, he leans on vignettes about his grandparents and his exes, and he even tries to throw some research on Napoleon into the story to stitch it together.

Yet, although Plascencia renders visible the skeleton upon which the story is constructed, the novel's tone remains playful. Plascencia writes himself into the story as an unwitting author, caught sleeping face down and shirtless, at an utter loss to recognize one of the characters he's created, who has scraped away a hole of sky to meet him (105). Saturn hits his head on a lead ceiling fan as he tries to ascend to an omniscient position, and Little Merced notices the plaster falling as a result (84). If one of the strategies of rasquachismo is to "pay homage to the sensibility by restating its premises," Plascencia utilizes metafiction here for a rasquache feat:

inserting himself and stating his own makeshift appropriation of new construction materials.

Ybarra-Frausto tells us that "another strategy is for the artwork to evoke a rasquache sensibility through self-conscious manipulation of materials or iconography," and *The People of Paper*'s transparency of construction extends from its narrative form to its defamiliarization of its own physical presence. It reminds the reader constantly that it is made of materials. Formally, the departures from the standard form of the printed page recall for the reader that the text is being held and read. In fact, the characters often allude to the text's physicality: Baby Nostradamus, the clairvoyant toddler, "knew the different grips of the readers, how some cradled the open covers" and how others "were intimate with paper" (166); Little Merced "began to feel her own resentment, not only toward Saturn, but also against those who stared down at the page, against those who followed sentences into her father's room" (186). Ralph and Elisa Landin, who fund the book, treat the text's physical and emotional import as equal: "The Foundation and its endowment are not liable for any loss or damage . . . This is inclusive of all paper cuts" (218).

These gestures—the self-awareness of the author and the characters, the experimental layout of the text—are certainly metafictional, yet they are not merely working to make the reader self-aware. *The People of Paper*'s layout innovations tie it to a lineage of radical metafiction that includes contemporaries such as Mark Z. Danielewski and predecessors like John Barth, and Plascencia's insertion of himself as a character is a metafictional move with a long literary pedigree extending back to Miguel de Cervantes. Read as a generic attempt to defamiliarize the reader, to play with form, or to comment on writing as writing, *The People of Paper* might even be considered derivative. Yet in *The People of Paper* these tropes function as an author's attempt to present, without usurping, his adoptive hometown by imbuing his telling with the aesthetics of the town it describes.

Reading the text's construction as rasquache, imitating at the formal level the everyday aesthetic practices of El Monte, reveals the novel to be mimetic of its particular locality. This homegrown cultural form allows *The People of Paper* to escape its own bind, as Plascencia—the author and the character—navigates his role as an ethnic writer attempting to evoke the particularities of place, identity, and culture without merely commodifying them. Rasquachismo is the novel's formal analog to Plascencia's adoption of the principle of *con safos*, to finally erase his own name, and by extension himself as author, allowing his characters to walk off the page. Ybarra-Frausto claims that rasquachismo is inherently Chicanx, "rooted in Chicano structures of thinking, feeling, and aesthetic choice. It is one form of a Chicano vernacular, the verbal-visual codes we use to speak to each other among ourselves" (155). Plascencia's rasquache construction, then, tells a Chicanx El Monte story in an El Monte way, using the "verbal-visual codes" of the local Chicanx community to reflect the spirit of the neighborhood. This aesthetic choice simultaneously implies that other narrations, with their undisputed omniscient narrator and stock form, are written from the vantage point of the outsider, or colonizer. Through these innovative narrative strategies, Plascencia manages to offer us a critique of authorial appropriation without replicating it. Plascencia writes a text that is *of* a place rather than *about* a place by inserting himself and refusing to edit away the signs of his own construction.

Transnational Migrations

In her piece on *domesticana,* a Chicana variation of rasquache artistic production, Amalia Mesa-Bains asserts that rasquachismo is an inheritance from the Chicanx community's ties, both present and past, to Mexico: "Operating as an internally colonized community within the borders of the United States, Chicanos forged a new cultural vocabulary composed of *sustaining elements of Mexican tradition*" (159; emphasis added). Not only the content of this Mexican tradition—corridos, Mexican cinema, *calendario* graphics—but the *form* of integration is crucial to rasquachismo, as these are brought together through "fragmentation and recombination" with contemporary iconography that is vaguely understood as "American" (159). Expanding on Mesa-Bains's description, then, rasquachismo reflects the local and the transnational operating at once, as the Chicanx community's artistic production insists on a very particular relationship to Mexico while also reenvisioning that connection from the perspective of an internal "colony" of the US.[4]

As we have seen, El Monte is indelibly marked by its proximity to Mexico and its history of Mexican immigration. This extends to the names, as Barton tells, and to the botánicas and ubiquitous menudo stands, as well as the city's rasquachismo. In the novel, both immigrants and their country of origin's cultural touchstones migrate and transmigrate across a seemingly permeable border, disputing the now antiquated notion of immigration as a linear process of assimilation. The war against omniscient narration and the colonization it implies would have been impossible to win without the constant importation of goods and cultural practices from Mexico. The text's aesthetic depends on principles of rasquachismo and Chicanx graffiti art that are themselves the product of a neighborhood marked by migrant labor and a blend of generational Mexican Americans and newly immigrating Mexicans and Central Americans. Therefore, while *The People of Paper*'s construction cannot be understood without reference to its locale, the text is also inscribed in a broader transnational social field.

In an interview, Plascencia says of his El Monte that, "like in all immigrant communities, everybody has some of the old country in their backyards" (Benavidez 26). The "backyard" for *The People of Paper* is the barrio it narrates, one marked by irreverence, resourcefulness, and the refusal to throw anything out that might still be usable, one whose "verbal-visual codes" and relationship to names and places is distinct from any other neighborhood. *The People of Paper* does not simply find inspiration in El Monte's particular mélange of Mexico and the US, its peculiar gang history, and its Chicanx modes of naming: it *depends* on these local traits for its very form and aesthetic. However, Plascencia's quote also reminds us of the cultural persistence of that old country. The novel describes the unique relationship El Monte's barrio has to transnational flows, as an outpost of Mexican culture that has also inherited the sociocultural norms of its long-standing Chicanx inhabitants. Starting from the backyard, so to speak, we can see larger hemispheric movements, without losing sight of the particular local conditions that make an experimental work like *The People of Paper* legible.

2

"Earthquakes or Earthmovers"

THE EAST L.A. BARRIO AND HELENA MARÍA
VIRAMONTES'S *THEIR DOGS CAME WITH THEM*

WHILE PLASCENCIA's El Monte enclave is the perhaps unintended victim of the city's attempts to rebrand itself, Viramontes's 1960s East Los Angeles is a barrio explicitly at war with the greater city of which it forms part. *Their Dogs Came with Them* describes a neighborhood under siege by earthmovers, freeway construction, the removal of open spaces, and government quarantine. The novel's literary realism makes the text appear deceptively unexperimental, yet a barriography reveals the numerous ways that Viramontes's text is innovative in its evocation of the aesthetic characteristics and cultural practices of the Eastside barrio. By writing out the journeys of characters on roads about to be forever changed by the unspooling of six freeways, Viramontes builds a paper version of a barrio that is rapidly disappearing under the concrete. Through her use of multiple interlinking perspectives to imitate events experienced by an entire neighborhood, nonlinear narration to mimic oral storytelling and the processes of remembering, and the consistent metaphorical yoking of characters to places and both of these to memory, Viramontes offers up her novel as a container for place memories, delineating the irreplaceable yet replaced streets, stores, houses, and neighbors of East Los Angeles.

Ironically, to preserve the barrio in writing Viramontes must use the very medium of its destruction—paper. As in *The People of Paper*, paper is treacherous, but in *Their Dogs Came with Them*, the focus is on official documents more than official histories: papers prove legality and citizenship, they map the streets, determine new freeway paths, disrupt traffic flows, track neighbors in and out, and variously alienate many Eastside residents. Yet Viramontes works to literarily extend the limits of the barrio to include nonresidents, effectively seeking to ameliorate the barrio's geographic and cultural isolation through written exposure. *Their Dogs Came with Them* incorporates potential outsiders, giving them the communities' memories, anchoring new initiates with extensive place details, so that the reader too becomes a neighbor. Archival work on the novel's manuscript conducted at University of California, Santa Barbara, reveals Viramontes to be in a dialogue with her Anglo editor, attempting to explain the particularities of her Chicanx community and to draw the editor, and future readers, literally into the story, as fellow rememberers.

This chapter demonstrates the specific consequences of L.A.'s urban planning and construction schemes upon the East L.A. neighborhood, using Viramontes to explore the psychological damage of freeway (and cemetery) incursion, with its simultaneous alienating and isolating effects, depicted metaphorically through the novel's "Quarantine Authority," which equates East L.A. barrio residents to second-class citizens who therefore require identification of residence to enter or leave their own neighborhood. *Their Dogs Came with Them*'s response to freeway destruction is to shore up place memories of the neighborhood, the neighbors' experiences of one another and their concrete ties to the Eastside, which cannot be erased, despite the attempts of earthmovers.

Papers and Freeways

First separated from the city by the very interurban railways many barrio residents built, restrictive housing covenants and a neglectful public transportation network left the Eastside barrio unconnected and insulated by the 1960s, when Viramontes's novel is set. *Their Dogs Came with Them* narrates a new phase of aggressive expansion of freeways by the California Department of Transportation. The neighborhood by 1970 is unrecognizable after a series of freeway construction projects that essentially assaulted the Eastside in the 1950s and 1960s: "In the late 1950s the massive construction of freeways linking the Anglo suburban communities with the central business core began. High overpasses and expansive six-lane freeways crisscrossed the east side. Thousands of residents from Boyle Heights, Lincoln Heights, City Terrace, and surrounding neighborhoods were relocated. The freeways divided the neighborhoods without consideration for the residents' loyalties to churches, schools, businesses, or family" (Sánchez 170).

Mike Davis refers to the contemporary clearing out of South Central to make way for the Century Freeway as "a traumatic removal of housing and restriction of neighborhood ties that was the equivalent of a natural disaster" for its close-knit Black community (*City of Quartz* 298); the emotional and physical effects of eviction, earth removal, and freeway construction are no less brutal in the Eastside. Davis relates that once redevelopment of Downtown began in earnest, "established Black and Chicano neighborhoods were losing several thousand [housing] units a year to freeway construction" (168). Multiple freeways now run through East Los Angeles, including I-5, I-10, Highway 101, Highway 60, and I-710; several of their interchanges between one another now occur literally on top of the Eastside neighborhood. The hyperconnectivity of this section of road for freeway travelers ironically—or tragically—results in a bifurcated and hyper-*unconnected* barrio.

Their Dogs Came with Them takes places from 1960 to 1970 and oscillates in that timeframe between chapters and within chapters. We follow half a dozen characters, chief among them Ermila Zumaya, Turtle Gamboa, and Tranquilina Tomás. Ermila, Turtle, and Tranquilina are natives to the Eastside; Turtle and Ermila are next-door neighbors on First Street, who as children witnessed the destruction of that street just to the east of their homes in the face of freeway construction of the on-ramps for the 710 Interstate and the Pomona Freeway (Highway 60). Ermila continues to live on First Street with her grandparents; we follow her destructive relationship with Alfonso, a leader in the local McBride Boys gang, her fraught romantic entanglement with Nacho, her "fresh off the boat" cousin from Mexico, and her deepening friendship with her girlfriends and fellow Eastsiders. Turtle is biologically female but acts, dresses, and is perceived as a boy (though she maintains female pronouns); now AWOL from her gang (the McBride Boys) and homeless since her mother left her and the house on First Street, she wanders the streets of the barrio, attempting to evade detection from the Quarantine Authority, her own gang, and the rival gang, Lote M. Tranquilina's parents escaped indentured servitude in Mexico by crossing the desert illegally, and after starting to raise Tranquilina on the Eastside, they move their ministry to Texas, only to return to East Los Angeles after Tranquilina and her mother are brutally sexually assaulted. They find the neighborhood radically altered, but Papa Tomás and his family continue to seek out new church members.

The freeways take on epic significance for the characters. The novel opens in 1960, with the eviction of Chavela, Ermila's neighbor, from her house on First Street. Through this scene, the chapter alludes to the forced eviction of many Eastside residents as multiple, imminent freeway construction projects consumed neighborhood land. After the opening the novel remains largely in the mid- to late 1960s, with frequent flashbacks to this earlier period. Viramontes gives us multiple perspectives on the building of the freeways as lived by neighbors on First Street, whose block

FIGURE 8. The view from First Street in 2014, just east of the fictional homes of Chavela, Ermila, and Turtle in Helena María Viramontes's *Their Dogs Came with Them*

will eventually live under and between the intersection of two freeways (see fig. 8).

The construction is often described as a malevolent force from the outside: "the bulldozers had started from very far away and slowly arrived on First Street, their muzzles like sharpened metal teeth making way for the freeway" (Viramontes, *Their Dogs* 6). The metaphor of bulldozers as dogs is not idle. The title of the novel, *Their Dogs Came with Them*, is a quote from the Aztec Nahuatl account of the conquest of Mexico, which also serves as the sole epigraph: "They came in battle array, as conquerors. . . . Their dogs came with them, running ahead of the column. They raised their muzzles high" (2). The freeways thus represent a new conquest that will result in "the four-freeway exchange," which Viramontes tells us will "reroute 547,300 cars a day through the Eastside and would become the busiest in the city" (169).

The novel's opening scene with Chavela and Ermila both introduces what is being lost and plants the possibility for how it can be kept, in the face of erasure and change. As we watch Chavela frantically smoke and pack for her eviction, all the while warning Ermila of the dangers of earthmovers, Viramontes scans the house and reports its contents:

The old woman had taped scribbled instructions all over the walls of the house. **Leve massage for Josie. Basura on Wetsday. J work # AN 54389.** I need to remember, Chavela had told the child when the child pointed a matchbox at the torn pieces of paper clinging on the walls. **Water flours. Pepto Bismo. Chek gas off.** It's important to remember my name, my address, where I put my cigarillo down **Call Josie. Chavela Luz Ibarra de Cortez. SS #010-56-8336. 4356 East 1st** or how the earthquake cracked mi tierra firme, my país, now as far away as my youth, a big boom-crack. The dogs and gente went crazy from having the earth pulled out right from under them. **Cal Mr . . . Lencho's tio sobre apartment. Shut off luz.** (7)

Chavela has written her full name, social security number, and address on scraps of paper on her walls, among other reminders and important data. The written words are in bold in the text, and the narrator intersperses the notes throughout the scene, at times midsentence, introducing phrases that at first seem random (**"Cobijas,** one note said; **Cosa de baño,** said another. **No good dreses. Josie's tipewriter. Fotos"** [5]) but eventually make sense in terms of the monologue Chavela is giving the Zumaya child. The memory of the smell of charred flesh after an earthquake precedes the scribbled directive to **"Smoke outside"** (7); when she explains she needs to remember her name and address they follow in bold.

Ermila Zumaya is mute in the scene, but "when the child pointed a matchbox at the torn pieces of paper clinging on the walls" (7), Chavela explains: "I need to remember. . . . It's important to remember" (7). The paper scraps, offset and scattered in bold in the text and scattered throughout the house, serve as Chavela's memory. The novel thus begins by introducing the importance of writing to remembrance. Yet it also gives us an unorthodox kind of writing to remember: the notes combine boring, misspelled, quotidian reminders with crucial, essential facts, like Chavela's full name and address. Paper functions as memory here, but like memory, it does not discriminate between important memories and everyday reminders, and perhaps it even suggests that the everyday reminders, which locate Chavela in time and space, watering plants, shutting off the lights, J's identification number at work (which she writes out twice), are as important as her name. The scribbled notes, while anchoring Chavela in a concrete time and place, also prompt her, in indirect ways, to recount her deeper memories of the earthquake in her former country.

Chavela is not wholly literate; without the narrator to tell the story, her notes are lost. As in *The People of Paper, Their Dogs Came with Them* will enumerate the dangers of paper. In Plascencia's text, paper obscures

Mexican residents with a public history that excludes them; here paper renders barrio residents second-class citizens, fomenting the Eastside's fear of official documents. However, in both works (albeit to different degrees), paper also becomes the solution to the erasure of the community. Like Chavela's strips of reminders, Viramontes's text itself is serving as the Eastside's memory, giving voice to Mexican immigrants like Chavela as well as Chicano/a s like Ermila, because "it's important to remember."

Still, Viramontes must justify her use of paper, as throughout the novel papers are used to restrict and coerce Eastside residents. By 1970, the ostensible present of the novel, the construction that kills the "dead side" of First Street is complete: "Four freeways crossing and interchanging, looping and stacking in the Eastside, but if you didn't own a car, you were fucked" (176). The characters now face a new form of isolation: The Quarantine Authority, a shadowy governmental force that declares an alleged rabies outbreak in the barrio and decrees that access in and out of the affected area—a map which contains the Eastside—be restricted and controlled by police. For the neighborhood, the QA is but a continuation of the assault that began with the freeways: as a young woman, Ermila "will recognize the invading engines of the Quarantine Authority helicopters because their whir of blades above the roof of her home, their earth-rattling explosive motors, will surpass in volume the combustion of engines driving the bulldozer tractors, slowly, methodically unspooling the six freeways" (12).

Ermila and her friends, as well as Turtle and Tranquilina's ministry, all exist inside the geographical limits of a barrio-wide quarantine, an ominous map of exclusion:

> The girlfriends lived within the shaded boundaries of the map printed in English only and distributed by the city. From First Street to Boyle to Whittier and back to Pacific Boulevard, the roadblocks enforced a quarantine to contain a potential outbreak of rabies. Back in early February, a pamphlet delivered by the postman read: *Rising cases of rabies reported in the neighborhood (see shaded area) have forced Health officials to approve, for limited time only, the aerial observation and shooting of undomesticated mammals. Unchained and/or unlicensed mammals will not be exempt.* (54)

The boundaries of the quarantine—First to Boyle, Whittier to Pacific— neatly demarcate the borders of the Eastside barrio. The pamphlet's printing in English only and its distribution by "the city" doubly indicate that this authority is being imposed from the outside. The quarantine enforces a curfew, requiring residents to show an ID card to get in and out of the neighborhood after sunset. The absence of any medical aspect to the quarantine, such as checking entering and exiting patients for symptoms of rabies, suggests that the residents themselves present a danger to the city and that the "undomesticated," "unchained," and "unlicensed" mammals cited here as easily refer to the neighbors as to the barrio's stray dogs. The complete irony of shooting undomesticated mammals without exemption isn't revealed until the final scene, when the QA gun Turtle down (spoiler!). The roadblocks of the quarantine stymie characters throughout the novel. The roadblocks, however, do not affect the freeways, which run above the barrio.

The QA controls barrio residents through the use of checkpoints, which require residents to carry proof of *"valid government documentation"* (55). Failing to get home before curfew because she has to take a bus instead of a ride, Ermila waits in line behind a frantic woman without identification who wants access to her house to get rent receipts for the QA. As she waits, Ermila considers the absurdity of the checkpoints:

> The city officials demanded paper so thin and weightless, it resisted the possibility of upholding legal import to people like herself, her cousin Nacho, her girlfriends and all the other neighbors with or without children who had the misfortunate of living within the shaded designated areas. Didn't the QA know that in the Eastside getting a valid ID was more complicated than a twelve-year-old purchasing a six-pack from Going Bananas [a store clerk's drunk brother]? A neighbor's idea of validity was totally incongruent with the QA's norms or anyone else's, for that matter. Business was done differently on the Eastside. In need of a dentist? Wait for Dr. Padilla from Tijuana the first of each month, home visits with a leather bag full of clanging metal tools and novocaine injections. What about a loan? The lending was done between two men, one of which had a reputation for breaking bones. Need legal status? For those without papers, legal status became a shift in perspective, a matter of dubious demarcation, depending on who the border belonged to.
> *No one in the Eastside believed in paper.* (63; emphasis added)

The neighborhood's notion of identity and validity is different from that of city officials. The thinness and lightness of paper defies the common sense of the barrio, that objects so frivolous could uphold "legal import." "Legal status" in particular in the Eastside is "a matter of dubious demarcation." Viramontes extends the disbelief of paper to everyday financial transactions, as even store receipts are not used. In the Eastside, proofs of transaction are oral rather than paper: the calculations were considered valid because, "of course, your word was your word" (63). So the checkpoints become fraught with wary residents, incredulous toward the power of paper, who lack the proper pieces of it necessary to gain entry into their own neighborhood.

Viramontes's style here mimics the barrio's oral, rather than written, mode of communicating. The manuscript version of the novel, currently housed at the California Ethnic and Multicultural Archives (CEMA) at UC Santa Barbara, shows that Viramontes changed the language here from the draft by removing prior anaphora, making the passage sound more aural than literary (Manuscript 76). The first draft read: "Need a dentist? . . . Need a loan? . . . Need legal status?" (76). Substituting a colloquial "what" for "need" here—"What about a dentist?"—recasts this as a speech or monologue, spoken out loud, as opposed to the more studied feel of repeating the introductory phrase, "Need a." This slight change alters the tenor of the passage, making it read like a conversation among those waiting in line. The novel's construction here imitates the barrio's suspicion of paper, by highlighting the spoken over the written, while ironically using that very medium to convey its alliance with neighborhood customs.

The disbelief in paper turns into a fear of its fragility in the roadblock line: "They fisted gas company bills, birth certificates, bogus driver's licenses, anything to get themselves home. The longer the wait, the larger the nervous obsession with the handled paper" (*Their Dogs* 63). "Fisted" tightly like talismans against the QA, the neighbors' documents, forged and real, are trusted by the "unquestioning" residents as their only key for entry. The nervousness provoked by the "handled paper" makes the neighbors seem like "illegal aliens" attempting to cross an international border, yet while some of the documents are bogus, these residents are not foreign to the barrio: they have cluttered kitchens and beds waiting for them inside the neighborhood (63). Natives treated as foreigners, those in line recognize that their own proof of belonging is a too-thin and too-light piece of paper. The elision of two kinds of legality—are the neighbors undocumented aliens to the barrio or undocumented immigrants to the country, or both?—returns later in the story when Ermila watches the women of uncertain nationality waiting for the bus outside her house: "They sat on the bus bench, canvas bags beside them, filled with the day's essentials: fearlessness scrambled with huevos con chorizo and wrapped in a tortilla *as thin as the documents they carried to prove legality*" (176; emphasis added).

This view of paper as a tool of Eastside oppression foreign to the barrio is both upheld and challenged throughout the text. In terms of legal or financial documents, yes: the Eastside does not believe in paper. However, paper elsewhere in the text carries a lot of meaning: Chavela's scribbled notes for instance. Or Ermila's dream of becoming "an empty wine bottle being jammed with a note and then tossed out into the ocean, rolling on the spume of the sea until someone discovered her" (66). Or Obdulio the butcher's tender regard for the letters from his wife in Mexico, which he rereads so often the paper grows thinner (137). These other kinds of paper, not imposed upon residents from the outside but internal to their community, which are used to communicate and remember, *are* believed in by the Eastside. Viramontes evokes the neighborhood's wariness of paper as an implement used to control and confine but demonstrates how the written can become a positive medium, when the residents themselves utilize it. Viramontes uses a number of literary techniques to produce this other type of paper—paper as a precious tie to distant places or persons, paper as reminder, paper as a note in a bottle hoping to escape to a wider audience.

The Power of Place

In her 1995 book *The Power of Place,* a study of urban landscapes and the preservation of underrepresented histories, Dolores Hayden argues that our criteria for what deserves to be preserved is wrong: architectural achievement, marked by aesthetics and usually by the amount of wealth that went into the building's construction, has been valued over the preservation of buildings that reflect social history, thus creating the illusion that the poor do not actually have a history as told by place. *The Power of Place* advocates for the preservation of not just architectural monuments but the buildings such as tenements, factories, meeting halls, and churches that "have housed working people's everyday lives" (11). Attendant on this reconception of what is worthy of preservation is the recognition that public spaces house memories and that places also house both personal and social *identities:* "Identity is intimately tied to memory: both our personal memories (where we have come from and where we have dwelt) and the collective or social memories interconnected with the histories of our families, neighbors, fellow workers, and ethnic communities. *Urban landscapes are storehouses for these social memories*" (9; emphasis added).

Hayden introduces philosopher Edward S. Carey's definition of "place memory": "it is the stabilizing persistence of place as a container of experiences that contributes so powerfully to its intrinsic memorability. . . . We might even say that memory is naturally place-oriented or at least place-supported" (46). My reading of *Their Dogs Came with Them* supports this formulation of "place memory" and Hayden's assertion that identity is tied to memory. Multiple characters conjure memories through the power of place: Turtle's presence in the Chinese cemetery brings her back to her gang initiation, and a mere glance at the "living" and "dead" sides of First Street send her into a series of extended reveries about her childhood there, including a cast of characters all now absent from the neighborhood; Ermila places a finger in the windowsill notch left by Chavela's cigarettes long after Chavela has gone and is transported to their last night together; Turtle visits the "falls" in Monterey Park and instantly becomes a kid again, absorbed in her last memory at the site. We can see how *Their Dogs Came with Them* delineates a barrio's memory and sense of itself through its neighbors' experiences of the places that have come to define them.

Hayden also highlights the stakes of radical urban development: the potential loss of those storehouses of social memories and their stabilizing container of shared experience. Throughout the novel, characters face the disorientation and sadness of watching parts of the barrio be destroyed, as the freeways become the new, unwanted neighbors in the Eastside. A representative example of both the power of place memory and the threat of loss comes when Tranquilina and Mama find themselves getting lost on their way back to the church:

> The two women struggled through the rain in a maze of unfamiliar streets. Whole residential blocks had been gutted since their departure, and they soon discovered that Kern Street abruptly dead-ended, forcing them to retrace their trail. The streets Mamá remembered had once connected to other arteries of the city, rolling up and down hills, and in and out of neighborhoods where neighbors of different nationalities intersected with one another. To the west, La Pelota Panadería on Soto Street crossed Canter's Kosher Deli on Brooklyn Avenue, which crossed Pol's Chinese Kitchen on Pacific Boulevard to the east. But now the freeways amputated the streets into stumped dead ends, and the lives of the neighbors itched like phantom limbs in Mama's memory: La Señora Ybarra's tobacco smell and deep raspy voice; the Gómez father's garden of tomatoes; Old Refugia, who had two goats living in her cluttered backyard and who took the goats to graze at the edge of the Chinese cemetery before opening hours.
>
> The city of Tranquilina's birth was hardly recognizable. (33)

"The freeways amputated the streets," which had formerly served as the barrio's arteries—both literal and figurative, connecting it to other ethnic enclaves, resulting in the stumped and dead-ended lives of neighbors. However, while the freeways do isolate the Eastside, stopping flows to communities to the west and east, Señora Ybarra's smell and Gómez's tomato garden and Old Refugia's goat grazing practices are still brought to Mama's mind by the streets, even though they are now "hardly recognizable." The simile of a phantom limb is apt, as Mama has a memory tied to a location that she continues to feel even after that specific location marker (the limb itself) is gone. This passage simultaneously demonstrates Hayden's notion that memory is "place-oriented" while showing that even in the absence of a specific place "support"—the grazing backyard, the garden—the memories remain in the landscape. The ability to remember at the site of a place memory despite fundamental changes to the location is one powerful way that the characters maintain their sense of community.

Radical urban planning, however, still threatens to render the barrio unknown, even for its lifelong residents. To counteract this inevitable loss of the physical storehouses of memory to miles of freeway, the novel attempts to become its own place container. Yet to be the right kind of paper, and to produce the right kind of writing, Viramontes, like Plascencia, must respect the rules of naming and representation obtaining in her barrio. The novel itself seeks to endure as a kind of barrio tag, attempting to preserve the place identity it represents in the face of disappearance and destruction.

Viramontes intimates her preservation strategy through an extended depiction of gang tagging. *Their Dogs Came with Them* shows us how Turtle and her former gang, the McBride Boys, combat erasure through the written word:

> Tonight the McBride Homeboys would claim Luis Lil Lizard by searching out the freshly laid cement of the freeway bridges and sidewalks in order to record their names, solidify their bond, to proclaim eternal allegiance to one another so that in twenty, thirty years from tonight, their dried cemented names would harden like sentimental fossils of a former time. The huge slabs of concrete would provide inviting canvases for the boys, . . . and Caltrans would try not to lay cement over the weekend, too many vandals destroying property. (164)

Not only do they assert their own name, and their own territory, the blocks surrounding McBride Avenue that they control, they also assert themselves against the encroachment of the freeways and the California Department of Transportation's construction.

The manuscript version of the novel reveals that Viramontes does quite a bit of revising in the following paragraph to heighten its gravity and to explain the motivation for the taggers to proclaim their names and allegiances to the neighborhood, as well as to the Caltrans invaders. She begins the paragraph stating that "The boys would never know that in thirty years from tonight, the tags would crack from earthquakes, the force of muscular tree roots, from the trampling of passerby," and then in the margins of the draft she adds the damning line, "become as faded as ancient engravings, as old as the concrete itself, as cold and clammy as a morgue table" (Manuscript 207). This is the only time in the text that Viramontes breaks with the chronology she has established and indicates that the omniscient narrator is in the present, *not* the 1960s. She fast-forwards to "thirty years later" (she will repeat the phrase) to highlight the change, the loss of these boys' names, and by extension these boys themselves, to the neighborhood. "Faded," "ancient engravings" immediately conjures the image of old tombstones in an older graveyard, perhaps alluding to the six cemeteries that dot McBride Boys' territory and whose outer walls and sidewalks are today still popular sites for graffiti tags, over forty years later ("On one of the brick pillars [of Evergreen cemetery]," "Turtle saw the old washed-out tag: **McBride Boys Controla**" [Their Dogs 222]).

The conversion of the tag to a tombstone epitaph "in thirty years" foreshadows the contracted life spans of the gang members, as Luis Lil Lizard dies in Vietnam while most likely still in his teens and Turtle will be killed in the closing scene of the novel. Thought of this way, tags and epitaphs both connect the name to the person in order to honor them publicly. The "cold and clammy" morgue table takes on the characteristics of what it carries, becoming as dead as the person on it. This image follows tagging logic: as in *The People of Paper*, the cement "engraving" shares personhood with the name inscribed there.

The metaphorical yoking of tag to tombstone continues in the next lines, to which Viramontes adds the phrase "eternal bonds" in the manuscript (Manuscript 207): "And in those thirty years the cracks would be repaired . . . making the boys' eternal bonds look worn and forgotten. Not even concrete engravings would guarantee immortality" (164). "Eternal" and "immortality" call up Catholic rhetoric of immortal souls and eternal rest. Like a gravestone, these tags are meant to confer a site of memorial, to bestow a qualified immortality to the departed. However, despite the importance of the tags, Viramontes highlights their fragility, indicating that a more secure form of writing is necessary to achieve personal immortality through remembrance.

These engravings are not only subject to the ravages of time and the erasure of Caltrans, but also to defacement by other neighbors, a most grave offense (pun intended):

> She could read, Turtle wasn't stupid. The cross-outs, tags, new gang emblems trashed all over McBride's graffiti on the walls of the bridge—all bad news. Lote M had fingered out the McBride Boys big time. . . . The Lote M vatos meant business and crudely chiseled away at the calligraphic tags . . . Perforating new conquerors over old ones with a blunt hammer, the remaining tags erased, shitted on, with strokes of red runny spray paint. Bold, ballsy headlines, Turtle was thinking . . . That's exactly what the Maravilla vatos planned to do on the bridge, send a dispatch announcing erasure. (217)

The insult of tags being effaced (see fig. 9) is not only grounds for a gang war: Turtle insists on the physical, anatomical nature of the affront, referring to it as "tearing off McBride balls" by "shitting on" "old conquerors." While the bridge still hosts the memory of all the taggers, as once again place memory prevents total erasure in the Eastside, the *threat* of that permanent erasure remains the neighbors' constant fear. Viramontes's surprising telescoping to the future earlier demonstrates that a more concrete (another pun!) form of engraving will be necessary, to protect against both time and rivals.

Viramontes's literary treatment of the tags demonstrates the author's own reverence for the written name and the power of tags to evoke identity, pointing to *Their Dogs Came with Them*'s project: to preserve the place memory and thus the social identities of those who live in the barrio. In the manuscript, she offers a depiction of the tags that comes with specific instructions:

> Too many warning signs that justify menacing threats, more sheriffs patrolling giving the boys a hit-and-run game of tagging, spray-painting all over the signs in laugh-out-loud violation, becoming the Caltrans contractor's worst nightmare.
>
> On a Monday morning the workers would find:
>
> MR SPEEDY x POOR x SIDE; BROOKLYN DIABLOS c/s; RUEBEN, ERNIE, RALPH; EL CHINO JOCKEY x Lote M/ LIL LIZARD, SANTOS X McBRIDE QUE RIFA; RUDE LOVES LA CAT BERNIECE POR VIDA. (164)

FIGURE 9. "Turtle wasn't stupid. The cross-outs, tags, new gang emblems . . . all bad news" (Viramontes, *Their Dogs*): Graffiti tags outside the Evergreen Cemetery on First Street, 2014

Viramontes insisted in the manuscript draft, with bold underlining and two extra-large, circled, all-caps STETs, that these names were to be written *as is,* in bold, in all capitalized letters. Viramontes also continues her education of the editor, offering a definition in the margin: "game of tagging=spray-painting all over the signs" (Manuscript 207).[1] Viramontes feels she needs to explain to her early reader what "tagging" means and suspects the editor will not recognize the x's common to street tags, the "c/s" marker (note the "c/s" or "*con safos*" attached to "Brooklyn Diablos"), or the logic of what is capitalized and what is not. Even in the fictional world of the novel, it matters to Viramontes that these names not be miswritten; her anxiety over their "performance" mimics the gravity of the tags for the boys themselves, who seek to "record their names," to have them harden, fossilize, and remain as a testament to their identities twenty, thirty years from now. Viramontes has found a site safer than cement to proclaim the pride of the neighborhood, and less subject to effacement: we turn now to how the novel functions as its own storehouse for barrio place memory.

As we've seen in her manuscript dialogue with her editor, Viramontes is trying to introduce outsiders to her barrio, to essentially reintegrate an isolated neighborhood: the ultimate goal of *Their Dogs Came with Them* is to make the reader a citizen of the barrio it narrates. Viramontes utilizes two specific stylistic techniques to turn the reader into a neighbor, one spatial and the other temporal.[2] Viramontes walks readers through the barrio with her characters, teaching us street names and landmarks to the point where we feel we know the neighborhood, demonstrating how her characters have developed their identities in symbiosis with where they have grown up and what they are living through there. The text anchors us in the minutia of place detail, weaving moment-by-moment depictions of characters' journeys in the Eastside with their memories of the places they pass. By moving memories out of chronological order and introducing characters and events without context, the narrative manipulates time, creating the effect of remembering for the reader. Along with the characters, we recall images or stories or other characters that have been remembered before in the narrative from other points of view or that will soon be mentioned again when we least expect it. Both the streets and the memories of the barrio begin to become our own.

Eastside Barriography: *Their Dogs Came with Them* as Place Memory

Even though *Their Dogs Came with Them* is a work of fiction, the built environment of East L.A. it depicts is historically accurate: the streets, stores, houses, and cemeteries in the novel are all actual. The reader is constantly located in a specific part of the barrio, and Viramontes always tells us which direction we're headed in and what houses, landmarks, landscapes, or persons are there. The author keeps the reader moored to the barrio by painstakingly tracking the movements of her characters: by learning those street names, landmarks, paths in and out of roadblocks, journeys on foot, by bus, and very occasionally by car, we come to recognize the streets and to remember them as they reappear in the narrative.[3] After following multiple characters on multiple trajectories as they return to First Street, we start to know the Zumaya front porch, its avocado tree, and its unhappy residents. We even feel like we know Chavela's old blue house, long since demolished, across the street. The barrio becomes familiar.

Of the several journeys taken by the characters, Turtle's nightlong mission to stay awake, undetected, and warm is the most detailed and extended. By mapping her steps, Viramontes steeps the reader in the barrio's deep history, as told through its many cemeteries. Juxtaposing the two neighborhood-wide treks—Turtle's and my own four decades later— illustrates the confining nature of the barrio and its resistance to foot traffic and outside visitors; it also excavates the history of a neighborhood essentially transformed into a giant graveyard and freeway for Los Angeles's city center. By the end of Turtle's vigil, which spans five cemeteries and ends with her death, the "dead side" of First Street will take on new meaning.

We first meet Turtle at First and Hastings, scoping storefronts for the possibility of food she can steal after spending the night hiding in a dumpster. AWOL from the McBride Boys, evading both the rival gang and her own for fear of reprisal, Turtle is alone and without a home. Turtle wanders for several hours and then arrives "in the Eastside late" (*Their Dogs* 218): she must cut a path to avoid the QA roadblocks. Deciding it safer to stay with the deceased, Turtle takes Third Street again to walk past Calvary cemetery. From here she turns on Eastern, vaulting over "the short brick wall" into the first Serbian cemetery. From there she "hopped out and jogged across the severed deserted remains of Second Street, and then climbed the wire-mesh fence of the second Serbian cemetery" (219). Second Street abruptly dead-ends at Interstate 710, a six-lane behemoth that almost symmetrically bisects East L.A. The first and second Serbian cemeteries sit across from each other on "the severed deserted remains" of Second Street, nestled between highways, with I-710 marking their eastern border and Route 60 (Pomona Highway) at their northern edge.

Those "remains" of Second Street are part of a landscape much older than the freeways. As Turtle waits for the coast to be clear, she stands "under an ancient Eucalyptus" (219). The Serbian cemetery's trees, and its inhabitants, are foreign to her but have old roots in the Eastside: "she walked in a rumor of lamppost light past the engraved markers with names like Radulovich, Babich, Bezunar, Mijanovich. In a fenced-up country, the names were exotic, safely protected from the outside of the living, from the spray-painted names like Gallo, Spook, Lencho, Fox, BamBam, Wilo x *Con Safos*" (219). While no one she knows currently living in the Eastside has names like these, the Serbian community, at least in death, has been subsumed into the neighborhood: the names are "exotic," but they need no protection from the living, the way the Chicanx names tagged outside do. The barrio under quarantine is as much a "fenced-up country" as the Serbian cemetery, and Turtle recognizes the kinship (see fig. 10).

From the Serbian cemetery, and with "the Interstate 710 below her," Turtle sprints across the bridge and scales another tall chain-link fence, into the Chinese cemetery (219). She has just traveled north from Second

FIGURE 10. The Serbian cemetery at the edge of the freeway, 2014

Street to First Street, over one of the on-ramps built in the early 1960s. She decides that the Chinese cemetery's position half underneath the 60 and 710 freeways makes it low-profile enough for her to rest here a few hours. She leans on the brick crematory chimney and smells the incense and begins to remember:

> This was her neighborhood, the one she grew up in, right across the street from where she stood now, and yet this particular cemetery had always remained a mystery. She touched the crematorium and remembered smoke from the chimney blowing ash over their games of stickball, and remembered too the fireworks and the grieving brassy orchestra playing mournful songs of farewell. The music, the scent, the mystery, had begged for Turtle to press her face against the fence like the other neighborhood kids had done. (219)

Touching the crematorium launches a set of place memories for Turtle. Although the Chinese cemetery is one of the most familiar sights of her childhood neighborhood, it is shrouded in the unknown (the word "mystery" is used twice in three sentences). The cemetery, like the names in the Serbian cemetery, is somehow both foreign and indigenous to her barrio.

Thus, even though the rites of Chinese mourning are alien to her, and she is literally starving, Turtle refuses to eat the food offerings left by families for their ancestors (219–20). After a few hours by the crematorium, remembering her gang initiation and looking out at her old house (221), Turtle jumps out of the Chinese cemetery and heads west (see figs. 11 and 12).

I find what would have been Chavela's house, 4356 East First Street, and I start walking. The Chinese cemetery across the street is still in use. On a Sunday there is a family visiting an ancestor's grave, with incense and offerings. Fresh flowers, clementines, and even an open juice bottle adorn newer graves, most of which are situated in the western part of the cemetery, farthest from the freeway. A pavilion built in 2006, near the cremation chimney Turtle leans against (which is still in use), symbolically marks the oldest part of the cemetery, which contains graves dating from the mid-1800s, when Chinese immigrants first came to the area, up through World War II (Cheung and Chiu). For many years, when the

FIGURE 11. The Chinese cemetery, including the crematorium Turtle rests upon, 2014

FIGURE 12. The view from the crematorium, showing the roofs where Turtle's fictional house would stand, 2014

Chinese were "relegated to quasi-slave labor, in the constructions of railroads, farms, and cities," they were excluded from cemeteries in the area and buried in unmarked fields near labor sites (Cheung and Chiu). The Chinese community raised funds for the cemetery in the early twentieth century and established this site in 1922. At that time the Eastside was still ethnically heterogeneous, with Jewish, Italian, Russian, and Polish residents as well as Mexicans (Romo 65). In the 1920s the diversity of the neighborhood's cemeteries matched the diversity of its surroundings, as the Eastside functioned as Los Angeles's catch-all immigrant neighborhood until the late 1930s.

I head south from the Chinese cemetery, passing over the imposing Pomona Freeway, and reach the first and second Serbian cemeteries. The first, closest to the freeway, is older and appears to be abandoned. It's fenced off, a simple chain-link fence without a lock but empty, even on a Sunday, and there are no new flowers on the graves. Its derelict state suggests that the older Serbians and Russians buried there have not been survived by local families. Conversely, the Serbian Cemetery across the short nub of Second Street has poinsettias and visitors. The main cemetery was consecrated in 1908, and only houses dead from the late twentieth century and earlier, hence the few visitors.[4] Walk south from the Serbian cemetery and immediately at your diagonal is Calvary cemetery. This large cemetery edges both Third and Eastern, but the entrances are only on Downey and Whittier, the south and west corners of the eight-block by six-block area. This means that while you can see Calvary's rolling green hills, well-kept grounds, manicured lawns, and quaint asphalt path, you cannot access it from this part of the neighborhood: a tall, bulky barbed-wire fence lines the north and east sides, contrasting starkly with the elegance maintained within. The names on the graves are visible from Third Street, however. Unlike the Chinese or Serbian cemetery, Calvary boasts a variety of ethnic residents. Spanish, Italian, Irish, and Eastern European surnames rest near one another: Flores, Vasquez, Zapata, but also Ledesma, Sardo, Kriaucziunas, McKinney, Buysens, and Abat. Founded in 1896, Calvary is one of the oldest cemeteries in Los Angeles: its residents recall East Los Angeles's era as a mixed-immigrant community, before the barrio's edges became rigidly defined in the mid-1900s.

Turtle walks west from the Serbian and Chinese cemeteries to Evergreen, along the perimeter of Calvary cemetery. The first three cemeteries lay within three blocks of each other; but reaching Evergreen by foot entails a mile-and-a-half walk. The first half of Turtle's route—across Hastings Street, then the cantinas of First Street, and then past the First Street Store (222)—takes me through one of the Eastside's main drags, as First Street from Gage Street to Hicks Street is a bustling commercial area. Here we find a local department store, El Surtidito (variety) outlet store, El Mexicano shoe repair, various *panaderías,* First Street Burgers, a few dollar stores, Dental Jalisco, and the *tienda de segunda,* the oft-mentioned First Street thrift store. There are crowds of families walking First Street on a Sunday late morning, and even more outside the churches in the area, several of which lie on or just off First. There's a large gathering of parishioners outside of Our Lady of Lourdes Catholic Church on Third Street and Rowan, preparing to go in for the noon service. The only language I hear in the streets is Spanish. I don't know whether the Spanish I hear is Mexican, Salvadoran, Guatemalan, Nicaraguan, or Chicanx—I can't distinguish those accents—but I can say that no English is being spoken in the streets I'm walking, the markets and eateries I'm going into, the stores I browse at, or the churches I pass by. Families are walking the main street, and perhaps it's just the feeling of an outsider, but everyone seems to know everyone else. *Their Dogs Came with Them* conveys the insularity of its barrio, and it is not an exaggeration (see figs. 13 and 14).

FIGURE 13. The stores of First Street, 2014

FIGURE 14. Mexican baked goods for all occasions, First Street, 2014

Once past this busy intersection, First Street takes on an abandoned feel, as I continue walking west. The second mile of the route to Evergreen leaves Turtle, and me, exposed, and even midday on a Sunday the neighborhood makes a solo female traveler uneasy. Here and on neighboring side street excursions, I pass several groups of men, with their pit bulls, talking by their cars and men talking through their car windows to one another, engines idling; the sidewalks and even some houses are graffiti-laced, and whether by virtue of being a woman or of not being of the neighborhood I am the recipient of intense attention from passersby. Turtle has to escape from drunks exiting the cantina as she's attempting to break into the cemetery; I have no such problem, but the fear of exposure and interpellation is similar.

At last, Turtle reaches Evergreen, "the oldest cemetery city-wide" (222). The names in the Evergreen cemetery are different again: "The majority of the names engraved on the mausoleum and on the large marble staffs were those Turtle recognized as street names: Hollenbeck, Lankershim, Van Nuys, Bixby" (236). These kinds of names are as foreign to the present-day barrio as Serbian surnames or Chinese burial customs, yet they are familiar to Turtle not because of their presence in the cemetery but because of their conspicuous stature throughout Los Angeles. These Anglo pioneers came to the area after it traded hands from Mexico to the US in 1848, before the waves of Midwestern settlers came on the railroads in the late 1880s. As L.A.'s first cemetery, Evergreen houses some of these illustrious founders and prominent developers of Anglo Los Angeles, who are now the namesakes for Turtle's own streets, boulevards, and neighborhoods.

After breaking into the cemetery, Turtle heads for the "ancient chapel" that "stood right smack in the middle of the grounds" (222), which she hopes to sleep in (see fig. 15). But the Cremain Garden Chapel is locked (234). She ends up gathering dead flowers from a trashcan near the graves, stuffing them into her leather jacket for warmth, and sleeping in Robert E. Ross's crypt, noting he was born in Clarke County, Ohio, in 1836 and died March 31, 1884, in Los Angeles (236). Ross's crypt does indeed lie just across from the "ancient chapel" Turtle mentions, and his origins and dates are as she relates (see fig. 16). The dates and places of Ross's life puzzle Turtle, and "right before she drifted off, Turtle wondered what possessed this old white man named Ross to die so far from home" (236).

This ending of the chapter is almost humorous. The presence of Serbian and Chinese dead in her Chicanx/Mexican barrio does not faze Turtle, and while the Chinese cemetery holds mystery for her, she thinks

FIGURE 15. The "ancient chapel" at Evergreen Cemetery, 2014

FIGURE 16. Robert E. Ross's crypt and Turtle's resting place, 2014

of it as part of the neighborhood. Yet the "white man" dying "so far from home" gives Turtle pause. Indeed, inside Evergreen, like Calvary, burials reflect an integration no longer seen in the neighborhood outside, with the older graves of Los Angeles's Anglo elite interspersed with newer Japanese graves. The permanent Latinx residents of the cemetery, lying mostly in the eastern corner, have several different visitors on a Sunday; I see a cherry-red lowrider pass and another family with small children at a gravesite with flowers. All the oldest graves at Evergreen, however, are for "white men" who came from somewhere else, many from New York, Massachusetts, and the Midwest. What we learn from Turtle's wonder is that, dead or alive, she is not used to white people in the barrio.

To a reader it seems jarring or a contrivance of fiction that Turtle passes through so many cemeteries on her all-night journey. However, in reality, the Eastside is beset on all sides with dead people. Walking the neighborhood draws in relief the effects on pedestrians of having so many cemeteries close by. Beginning with Evergreen cemetery in 1877, the Eastside functioned as the burgeoning city of Los Angeles's main burial site. A few of these, such as Evergreen and Calvary, were initially for the city's elite; other sites were purchased from the city for various ethnic and religious communities, some of whom lived in the Eastside, including Mount Zion (1916) and Home of Peace (1890s), two Jewish cemeteries, as well as the first and second Serbian cemetery. By the time the Chinese cemetery was built in the 1920s, the Eastside was already housing most of the city's population of immigrant and ethnic dead. *Six* of these are within a few blocks of one another; Evergreen is only a mile and a half to the west. The close proximity of the cemeteries to one another and in turn their proximity to several freeways, including the I-710, the I-5, and Highway 60, result in a very unwalkable neighborhood. The cemeteries are all fenced or walled and often have only one functional entrance gate. This forces pedestrians to walk around the green spaces and to go sometimes several blocks before returning to stores, restaurants, or space used for anything other than burial or vehicle traffic. This isolating effect is compounded by the unavoidability of walking under overpasses, over concrete bridges, or otherwise in the shadows of the freeways. The neighborhood's wealth of cemeteries and freeway exchanges serve Turtle well as hiding places for the same reason they serve poorly as functional spaces for the community: they limit the ability of walkers to move among them or from them to parts of the neighborhood that are literally more alive.

This closeness and confinement of the Eastside is represented literarily by the Quarantine Authority: the sharply demarcated lines of the fictional

QA's shaded area feel very accurate compared to the lived experience of being a pedestrian in the neighborhood. The anchoring in place that Viramontes achieves through Turtle's precisely detailed all-night barrio walk also allows her the freedom to move the reader about in time and space, creating myriad intersections of characters throughout the novel, and crafting place memories for us and for barrio residents in the novel itself. The ease with which a reader can, even forty years later, use *Their Dogs Came with Them* as an accurate map and representation of the Eastside speaks to the success of Viramontes's project of preserving the barrio on paper.

Reader as Neighbor

This spatial anchoring offsets the disorientation of the narrative structure, which moves around in time without warning and which oscillates among the perspectives of over a dozen characters. This experience of reading mimics the nonlinear and decontextualized nature of memory, manufacturing a process of remembering for the reader, which ultimately complements our experience of becoming experts on Eastside space. Viramontes shapes her narrative so that we remember moments and encounter characters before we realize who those characters are or what those moments mean. Then the narrative will return to the moment, or introduce a character, often from the perspective of a different character, and we will suddenly realize that we remember already meeting that person, or already having that memory of an event told earlier and out of context. As we travel streets we now know, encounter characters we've met before, and return to memories of events we now feel as if we've lived through, the neighborhood becomes the reader's own. *Their Dogs Came with Them* achieves a strange prestidigitation, transforming the reader into a member of the East Los Angeles community it is remembering.

To achieve this effect, Viramontes uses what I call literary prolepsis and analepsis. For example, in the first chapter, Chavela warns Ermila that earthmovers, like earthquakes, will make the *gente* and dogs crazy. Ten years later, Chavela's prophecy rings true: "She [Ermila Zumaya] will be a young woman . . . watching the QA helicopters burst out of the midnight sky to shoot dogs not chained up by curfew. Qué locura, she thinks. The world is going crazy" (12). So far this is not too strange: Ermila is looking out the window, thinking that the world has gone crazy, and this reminds her her conversation with Chavela. However, we return to this *exact* moment in chapter 4, with Ermila looking out the window: "Ermila watched the Quarantine Authority helicopters burst out of the midnight sky to shoot dogs not chained up by curfew. Qué locura, she thought. The world is going crazy . . . The wheeling copter blades over the power lines rose louder and louder . . . just like the unrelenting engines of bulldozers ten years earlier when Ermila was a child" (77). The two scenes form a chiasmus. The narrator prophesies forward, from the kitchen scene to "ten years later," and then the character/narrator looks back, "ten years earlier." This structure transforms the earlier vignette into a memory for the reader: we have a nagging suspicion that we know what Ermila is thinking before she says it, because we have a vague recollection of this very brief moment that we read several chapters and dozens of pages ago. This move ties the extreme policing of impoverished Chicanx communities to the negligent urban development that provokes their impoverishment (the authority's copter blades "just like" the bulldozers), and it ties us as readers to Ermila's place memory.

Viramontes creates this literary prolepsis and analepsis throughout the story in myriad small details. Turtle sees and describes Ben before we know who Ben is. The homeless "ubiquitous woman" sees Turtle on the Third Street Bridge before we know where she is and who see is. Turtle does not see the woman back until several chapters later (217). We meet Tranquilina through Turtle's eyes before we meet her. We meet Ermila's girlfriends through Tranquilina's eyes before we meet them. We're introduced to Obdulio the butcher through the Eastside reporter in Ben's hospital room (113). Turtle sees the fruit crate Nacho stacks by the bathroom to peep at Ermila (221) after Nacho tells us of it and before Ermila uses it to escape. These foreshadowings and flashbacks not only place us in the community as rememberers; they also suggest that knowledge of the neighborhood is relative. The neighbors are all inscribed in each other's memories and get stitched between them, but we never get an outside perspective on any of them. Furthermore, our perspective as readers long ceases to be objective, as this literary legerdemain stitches our memories to that of the neighbors as well.

After Nacho's stabbing and Turtle's death at the hands of the QA, we are told that "except for Tranquilina, no one . . . knew who the victims were, who the perpetrators were" (325). Tranquilina knows the truth because she is from the barrio and knows her neighbors, having encountered both Nacho and Turtle before. However, the narrator omits another barrio witness: the reader. The reader has learned the dubiousness of notions like "victim" or "perpetrator" for a person like Turtle, scarred by trauma, trapped in a "rented body" (322), for whom the word "why" has no meaning: "Why? Because a tall girl named Antonia never existed, because her history held no memory. Why? Go ask another" (324). Between Turtle's memories, bar-rio *chisme,* and our own accumulated memories of walking the neighbor-hood with her, we recognize that the motivation for her violence begins over ten years ago with the aggression of the freeways upon First Street.[5]

Their Dogs Came with Them is a difficult text. The novel overwhelms the reader with numerous characters, shifting time frames, and plot encounters that can only be understood with foresight, in hindsight, upon rereading, or all three. To track the characters and their timelines requires mooring them in space; *Their Dogs Came with Them* encourages the drawing of maps, the recalling of street names, and the recognition of landmarks, rewarding such attention to place by revealing other meetings among characters or other vectors of meaning based in the place memories of each location. In short, Viramontes crafts a text that must be *occupied* by the reader. *Their Dogs Came with Them* is inhabited, experienced not by reading front to back but rather by going back and forth within it, inside the text and outside of it, drawing connections between place and persons and memories both real and fictitious. Readers who stay become residents of Viramontes's literary barrio, which stands as a protection, in paper, against the ongoing threat of the Eastside's erasure.

PART II

WEST

Central American Downtown Los Angeles

DISPLACEMENT BY AND AS WAR: CENTRAL AMERICAN L.A. IMMIGRATION, 1980-2010

THROUGHOUT THE twentieth century, the US maintains the unhallowed distinction of being on the undemocratic side of most political conflicts in Latin America. In 2018, "The Caravan" took over US headlines: over 7,000 migrants from the Northern Triangle, mostly Hondurans, with some Guatemalans and Salvadorans, journeyed from Central America to the US border ("Migrant caravan"); these refugees sought asylum, fleeing conditions that the United States helped to create. In the second half of the twentieth century, the US trained and armed soldiers in El Salvador, Guatemala, and Nicaragua throughout their civil wars in order to stem the rise of socialism, and occasionally toppled democratically elected governments throughout the region that posed a threat to capitalist hegemony. Beginning in 1980, with President Carter's Refugee Act, which declared anyone eligible for political asylum (rather than only those fleeing communist regimes), Central American war refugees increased rapidly in number, with immigration from Central America to the US growing faster than any other population group (Brick et al.). From 1980 to 1990, the population of Guatemalans in the US surged from 71,000 to 226,000, Nicaraguans from 25,000 to 125,000, and Salvadorans from 94,000 to 701,000 (and these numbers do *not* include an estimated 400,000 undocumented immigrants) (Gonzalez 129). While the 2018 migrant caravan was particularly large and particularly politicized by President Trump, these Central American refugees are but the latest of decades of immigration to the US from the Northern Triangle.

After a US-backed coup that installed a military regime, the Guatemalan Civil War raged for over thirty years (1960–96), as the Guatemalan government perpetuated a genocide against the country's indigenous, especially the Maya, engaged in a scorched-earth policy, and "disappeared" leftist rebels and dissidents. According to the final report of Guatemala's Recovery of Historical Memory Project (REMHI), in the 1980s alone, over

440 villages were destroyed, over 150,000 people were killed or disappeared (55), and over 1 million fled the country, most for the United States (Siu 95); ultimately, over 400,000 Guatemalans perished. In El Salvador, whose civil war lasted twelve years (1980–92), a military government—supported with US military aid during the Carter and Reagan administrations—participated in death squads and the forced impressment of child soldiers; over 75,000 died and 50,000 were disappeared during the conflict (Alvarado 481).[1]

The trickle of Central American immigration to the US became a steady stream beginning in the 1980s and cresting in the twenty-first century. According to a Migration Policy Institute report, from 2011 to 2015 metropolitan Los Angeles had the greatest percentage of foreign-born Central American immigrants, over twice that of metropolitan New York (the next highest) (Lesser and Batalova). Another MPI report found that California had the largest percentage of Salvadoran and Guatemalan immigrants and a close third of the most Hondurans (after Texas and Florida) (Brick et al.). More than any other US city, Los Angeles is home to Central American immigration spurred on by armed conflict, including not just the civil wars in Guatemala, Nicaragua, and El Salvador, but also regional cartel violence. The Salvadoran community of Los Angeles went from a scant 30,000 in 1979 to 300,000 four years later, settling in the neighborhoods of Pico-Union, South-East, and South-Central (J. Gonzalez 139); by the turn of the century the Salvadoran population of Los Angeles was second only to San Salvador, El Salvador's capital city (147). The Pico-Union neighborhood of Los Angeles was renamed "Little Central America" in 2012, to reflect this established and growing colonia.

Late twentieth- and early twenty-first-century Central American arrivals to Los Angeles (especially those undocumented) form the basis for the city's low-wage workforce. When high-skill blue-collar work disappeared in the early 1970s in the shift to a predominantly post-Fordist economy, the "Frostbelt and Sunbelt dynamics come together in Los Angeles" (Soja et al. 200), combining white-collar tech development with service sector jobs, unskilled labor, and occasionally mass-manufacturing working conditions akin to sweatshops.[2] Dual, polarizing forms of employment arise: exploitative un-unionized low-wage mass-manufacturing jobs and high-skill aerospace/technology jobs. The former relied increasingly on the inner city's economically and politically vulnerable undocumented immigrant labor pool, with workers from Asia, Mexico, and Central America (Rodriguez 122). Older Mexican American and African American neighborhoods (like East Los Angeles, El Monte, South Central, and

Compton), built around union jobs in those areas, were stranded in the 1970s when high-skill blue-collar employment moved overseas. By the twenty-first century, historically Black and Chicanx parts of inner-city L.A. have become predominantly Latinx, as recent immigrants from Mexico and Central America, the often-unseen backbone of L.A.'s industrial economy, have moved in.

In *Magical Urbanism,* Mike Davis explains that Mexican settlement in Los Angeles prior to 1970 follows the "classic Chicago School model" of the North American city, where a given barrio or "ethnic district" forms a single, "simple wedge" (50): this typology is referred to as a "primate barrio with small satellites" (50). The histories of El Monte and East Los Angeles we saw in part 1 bear out this idea. However, by the late twentieth century, Los Angeles's one "primate" Latinx barrio of East L.A. has given way to an entirely distinct urban spatial logic, making it a "case apart" from other major metropolises and even from its earlier self (53). In the 2000 census, there were a staggering 757 Latino-majority districts in L.A., radiating out from the Eastside core but dispersed throughout the city (53). Looking closer, Latino/as have occupied traditional blue-collar sectors, adjacent to "industrially zoned land" along the major interstates. The center of this population is the city's old Central Manufacturing District, "the vast sprawl of aging factories, warehouses and classification yards immediately southeast of Downtown" (53). Within a single generation, Latino/as have taken over the industrial working class of the city, replacing blue-collar Anglo and African American neighborhoods just south and southeast of the city center.[3] As Davis puts it, "Latino succession in Los Angeles is taking place primarily at the base of the post-Fordist occupational pyramid" (56). It isn't *quite* the Latin-American *reconquista* of old Sonoratown (that specific area is now Chinatown), but it's close: Latino/as, at one point reduced to the minority in the city, are once again the majority in the pueblo they founded.

Central American newcomers join a city already at war. As we saw in chapters 1 and 2, there has been a long-standing battle between Los Angeles's local government and the area's preexisting Mexican and Chicanx communities since California passed into the hands of the US. In the twentieth and twenty-first centuries, other ethnic enclaves, including African American and Asian American communities, also found themselves on the wrong side of tracks laid down by the city's forces of urban planning, gentrification, and exclusion. How do newer refugees from Central America fit into Los Angeles's grid of oppositions and alliances? How do these immigrants, victims of forced displacement, create new spaces for themselves, and how does the trauma they carry impact and transform those new spaces? These are the questions part 2 seeks to answer.

"My Country Falls on Me like a Hammer": The Impact of War Trauma in Héctor Tobar's *The Tattooed Soldier* and William Archila's *The Art of Exile*

Central American civil wars entailed the "complete suppression of individual freedoms" (Siu 95), and many of its survivors have been trained in self-censorship to evade government-sanctioned persecution. Susan Coutin notes in her study of gen 1.5 and second-generation Salvadoran immigrants that they feel their stories are needed to "overcome silence" from their parents, who still refuse to speak about the civil war (818). This repression of wartime trauma is compounded by the absence of public accounting, either from the governments responsible for genocide and violence or from the US government, which has yet to fully implicate itself in the political, social, and legal circumstances that have brought scores of Central Americans to this country (818). The postwar years have failed to exact commensurate accountability, as amnesty laws in Guatemala and El Salvador have granted immunity to former soldiers, and Guatemala to date has not issued a formal apology to its citizenry (Rodríguez, "Diasporic Reparations" 13, 42); El Salvador President Mauricio Funes just made a formal apology to victims in 2021. In the face of this public disavowal, "cultural memory work" by transnational Central Americans and Central American Americans, that actively remembers and revives marginalized histories "becomes a form of speaking back and refusing erasure" (Alvarado 478).

Thus, in the absence of justice and the absence of testimony, the authors of part 2 are bringing these civil wars onto the page and into L.A. barrios through narrative. Héctor Tobar and William Archila present two aspects of this late twentieth-century wave of Central American migration. As the child of economic immigrants from Guatemala, as well as a local and international reporter for the *Los Angeles Times,* Tobar is an inheritor of civil war conflict in Latin America who also has the trained objective eye of a journalist: thus, *The Tattooed Soldier* offers a survey of the city's different socioeconomic strata, placing Guatemalan immigration within the context of Los Angeles's ongoing racial and class-based struggles. Archila does not have the advantage of this objective distance: as a refugee fleeing the Salvadoran Civil War as a young teen, his poetry collection, *The Art of Exile,* is raw and close—possibly too close—to its source: as it oscillates between El Salvador and Los Angeles's Lincoln Heights and Van Nuys neighborhoods, the poems reflect the onus upon the poet, as one who got out, to bear witness for those who did not. Tobar can imagine the intersections of the *city*'s past among its present-day Central American downtown locales; Archila's writing feels doomed to see only his own traumatic past everywhere in his US barrio.

If the authors in part 1 were dogged by the dangers of paper and utilized barrio communication codes to let the reader in without selling their neighborhoods out, the authors of part 2 are much more explicit about using paper to expose violence and social injustice that goes largely unseen by the US public. Here the reader is forced to witness what his or her ignorance of (at best) or indifference to (at worst) conflict in Latin America—*and in US streets*—has wrought. While Tobar and Archila come from distinct diasporas, move to different L.A. neighborhoods, and have vastly different writing styles, both works show subjects who see and ultimately project their past country everywhere in their new city. *The Tattooed Soldier* and *The Art of Exile* demonstrate the interconnectedness of the hemisphere, portray the complex and lasting effects of transnationalism tempered by trauma, and, most important, require US readers to acknowledge their country's own role in its current Central American immigration "crisis."

3

"Los Angeles Was the Problem"

THE WAR FOR SPACE IN HÉCTOR TOBAR'S
THE TATTOOED SOLDIER

> He remembered coming across a group of Indian women one day, not
> far from the vacant lots where he and José Juan now lived. They were
> wearing their traditional dress, embroidered huipiles and long rainbow-
> striped skirts. He watched them, these ancient people of the corn, as
> they walked through a canyon of brick tenements, their leather sandals
> scraping along the oil-stained sidewalk of Bixel Street. What were they
> doing here, in this place where not a single stalk of corn could grow?
>
> —Héctor Tobar, *Tattooed Soldier*

THE TATTOOED SOLDIER hinges its chief argument upon Los Angeles's
use of space. In his tale of revenge and immigration set during the Rodney King riots, Tobar takes great pains to show how survivors of the
Guatemalan Civil War are only one of many groups, including the rioters, the homeless, and other immigrants, attempting to make space for
themselves in Los Angeles. The homeless occupy Crown Hill, a forgotten,
undeveloped grassland on lucrative downtown real estate, and then the
tunnels, vestiges of a public transportation system from a bygone era that
the city abandoned in favor of freeways. Central American and Mexican
immigrants turn MacArthur Park and Pico-Union into echoes of their
old *aldeas y barrios,* with the languages and customs of their pasts. Finally,
the Rodney King rioters burn and destroy their own South Central city
blocks, recognizing how these urban spaces cordon and curb their movement. The novel demonstrates how Los Angeles, perhaps most aggressively of all US cities, sharply juxtaposes claimed and unclaimed spaces.

Neither kind of space is safe from the past; the narrative is drawn back
repeatedly to the war in Guatemala that has brought both the protagonist and antagonist to L.A. Given the absence of justice for past crimes,
whether the impunity of Guatemala's war criminals or the US's continued
systematic oppression of African Americans and immigrants,[1] the invisible spaces of Los Angeles become differential spaces[2] that make justice

possible by virtue of their very position outside the social ordering of the city. Tobar's novel traces how claiming space can serve as an act of justice, as Los Angeles's unseen places become sites for enacting retribution for violence that remains unpunished.

The story follows two Guatemalan immigrants to Los Angeles who have fled the war in Guatemala. The first, our protagonist Antonio, escapes death at the hands of the soldiers who have marked him and his family as leftist provocateurs; his wife, Elena, and son, Carlos, are murdered in their home, and Antonio carries this tragedy with him as he struggles to find a place for himself in Los Angeles, eventually becoming homeless and unemployed. The second, our antagonist Guillermo Longoria, is the sergeant who killed Antonio's family. The proud tattooed soldier of the title, forced into service as a peasant child, who fell in love with the army and trained in the US, Longoria has moved to L.A. out of a misguided idolization of the United States' sense of order. When these two men meet by accident in MacArthur Park, a hub of Central American L.A., a revenge tale unfolds. However, since Antonio is undocumented and penniless and Longoria is immune to prosecution for war crimes committed in Guatemala, the justice Antonio seeks is personal and far outside the legal system. Justice becomes another unclaimed territory that must be seized through violence—just as the Crown Hill homeless encampment will be leveled and erased, just as the Rodney King riots will reclaim South Central streets.

Most scholars writing on *The Tattooed Soldier* avoid the antique trap of equating physical migration with psychological or emotional migration. However, there is less scholarly consensus on the role of memory, especially traumatic memory, in the lives of migrants to the United States. Dale Pattinson, for instance, argues that L.A.'s forgotten spaces provide what historian Pierre Nora calls *lieux de mémoire* that allow the protagonist to process his traumatic past, claiming that "in order to access his repressed memories from Guatemala," he must negotiate these "sites of memory" that require subjects to remember an overwritten past (126). Yet the Pico-Union neighborhood the characters inhabit is not one of these "memorial" spaces, and traumatic Guatemalan memories still spill into both characters' lives in Los Angeles. Rather than being *prompted* by their environment, they both share, with all migrants, a propensity to *project* upon their new locations the spaces of their own past experience.

Ana Patricia Rodríguez's interpretation of transnational trauma processing comes closer to the manner in which memories are depicted in the text. Using theorist Ruth Leys's concept of the experience of genocidal trauma as intrusive memories that refuse to be represented as the past but rather are reexperienced constantly in the present, Rodríguez claims that for Guatemalan refugees "the recent past cannot be forgotten for it will return in some shape, form, and fashion. The past must be recalled, reli(e)ved, recovered, and recorded in order to overcome the lagging traumatic effects carried by many, especially when they have been silenced and hidden for so long" (*Dividing the Isthmus* 128). This description of "intrusive traumatic memories" that "refuse" to be represented as past but are instead incessantly "reli(e)ved" in the present, is an apt description of the narrative effect Tobar creates in *The Tattooed Soldier,* for both his protagonist and antagonist. But how do these relived memories impact *space?* We must add Pattinson's worthwhile intervention regarding the use of place memory to Rodríguez's elegant articulation of how memory functions in the text.

My analysis interrogates the relationship between these two crucial narrative aspects: the depiction of memory and the focus on place setting. The structure of *The Tattooed Soldier* suggests that the clichéd and spurious "new life" promised to immigrants is even less attainable for refugees of war, regardless of which side they fought on. While the narrative moves seamlessly and often between L.A. and Guatemala, the second section pulls the narrative entirely to events in Guatemala that predate both the first and last sections. In fact, the third part begins exactly at the moment the first part ends: with the surprise chance encounter between Antonio and Guillermo in MacArthur Park. This jarring and prolonged dislocation in time but more importantly in space does several things: it reflects the impossibility of forgetting or building a wholly new life in Los Angeles for either protagonist or antagonist, as a character deceased by the present of the novel offers her history and we are shown how it reverberates in the lives of both Antonio and Longoria; it indicates that immigrants and perhaps especially refugees will bring their former countries with them into the spaces of their new host country; finally, despite depicting the tattooed soldier's cruel murder of Elena and her son, the Guatemala section humanizes him—he is literally given a name afterwards, going from "the Sergeant" to "Guillermo." Humanizing Longoria demonstrates that while he and Antonio are antagonists, they also share the hardships of displacement and the impossibility of remaking themselves in a new land.

In addition to the novel's structure, its narrative form also mimics the manner in which Antonio and Longoria carry their past into their present, as Los Angeles scenes are continuously interjected with Guatemala memories. Told linearly, the narrative would move definitively from one nation to the other, resulting in a traditional immigration story. *The Tattooed Soldier*'s structural dislocation of both time and space rejects this model of assimilation and approximates the subjective experience of contemporary transmigration: the nation of the characters' births does not exist in the past for them but persists in Los Angeles. In turn, these persistent pasts shape and ultimately transform the spaces of Los Angeles.

The journalistic detailing of specific locations of Los Angeles in *The Tattooed Soldier* suggests the use of the city's excluded spaces not only as containers of memories, or *lieux de memoire,* but as sites of possibility for unclaimed justice. Thinking the narrative aspects of memory and space together reveals how Central American immigrants, shunted into the unclaimed or excluded spaces of Los Angeles, impose the pasts they cannot forget upon their new landscape, deploying their own spatial logic. This chapter will begin with the novel's depiction of memory: the achronological narrative intrusions, as well as the oscillation in point of view between the story's hero, his foe, and the key victim of violence (the hero's wife), and all of these perspectival positions trundling between Guatemala and Los Angeles, demonstrate formally the persistence of the past for contemporary migrants, especially those scarred by war. Then a barriography of MacArthur Park, Crown Hill, and the tunnels, all linked to the eruption of the L.A. riots in the novel, will demonstrate how the new place identity forged by the marginalized communities of the city—its homeless, its immigrants, its dispossessed African Americans—is capable of transforming space and potentially seizing, as Antonio does, vigilante justice.

The Persistence of the Past: Guatemala in Central L.A.

There are myriad instances of both Antonio and Longoria being drawn back into their memories of Guatemala. However, an examination of one representative example demonstrates the impossibility of these immigrants fully assimilating into their new nation. Longoria is approached at El Pulgarcito Express, a small Central American shipping company where he is a clerk, by an old Cachiquel Indian woman who recognizes him from Guatemala, exclaiming that he murdered her son Demetrio. Longoria's reaction to her attack, despite suspecting he is guilty, is to slap her so hard she loses a tooth. The act of violence transports him to Guatemala: "But no one moved or spoke, and for an instant Longoria felt like he was in Guatemala and he had this control over people again" (161). Just after this revelation, he immediately regrets his actions, thinking, "But he was trying to make another life now. His violent reactions belonged to a distant, black past" (161). Longoria tells himself that he is no longer the soldier who committed that killing.

The past, conjured by the old woman, continues to haunt him as the days go on. He insists to himself that he didn't know Demetrio (168) with such intense repetition and anxiety that it is clear he likely did "cross paths" with him. As he obsesses, Longoria finds himself back in Guatemala, remembering his many operations to eliminate "the union leaders, the writers, the lawyers, the anthropologists" (168). Much later, Longoria, still shaken by the encounter, seeks out a fellow Jaguar in L.A. to calm himself and reassert his moral rectitude (185). The accusation of being a murderer creates "confusion" for Longoria, who is unaccustomed to viewing his actions at a remove from their original context. In this sense, Longoria is *not* "trying to make another life," since who he is in his new nation conflicts with who he *was* (in his eyes). To settle his mind, he needs to reassure himself that he is in fact the same tattooed soldier he was in Guatemala. Longoria claims "his violent reactions belonged to a distant, black past," but the Guatemalan Civil War justifies them; consequently, Longoria needs *more*, not less, of who he was before coming to Los Angeles to be visible in the person he is now.

This rejection of "new life" rhetoric characterizes the majority of late twentieth-century/early twenty-first-century transnational narratives, which contest anterior immigration narratives, where the individual or family builds a brand-new life in a brand-new country. In transnational narratives, the possibility of a wholly "new life" is almost always called into question and ultimately denied. Additionally, while it is true that Longoria's migration has placed him in a legal no-man's-land that exempts him from punishment, Antonio's resolution to hunt and kill him demonstrates that, with increasingly global twenty-first-century migration patterns, no one can escape their home country or their pasts.

The Tattooed Soldier uses migration, specifically immigration to Los Angeles, as a pivot for character development. The main characters' inability to escape their pasts, yet their lack of recourse for either asking forgiveness or seeking justice for the acts in that past, lead to the book's violent climax. The middle section of the novel shows us that in Guatemala Antonio is a poet and a pacifist, a man who is only reluctantly radicalized by Elena. Even when Elena and their son are murdered in their home, Antonio fails to act when the tattooed soldier who killed them is pointed out to him in the town plaza (18). In Guatemala, Antonio is not a confrontational man. The audacity of Longoria getting a second chance in Los Angeles is what ultimately motivates Antonio's turn toward violence: "The soldier's life, *his living steps in Los Angeles,* were a violation" (183; emphasis added).

There is no formal mechanism for criminal justice, in either the US or Guatemala. Antonio knows that "the police couldn't care less about international politics" and that his status as homeless and Latin American marks him as unworthy of their protection (210). Nor is there recourse in Guatemala: "In my country there is no one to punish the army for their *barbaridades*. No court will do it" (177). Antonio feels keenly the absence of any legal justice, which obligates him to seek justice himself. Antonio discovers that his Guatemala life requires him to remain in Los Angeles as, if he returned to his home country, there would be "no one to stand and say he was a killer. No one would know about the soldier's crimes" (182).

Indeed, Los Angeles provides ample justification for vigilante justice. Longoria has seen the *cholos*, or "army of painted children," gang members who man the stoop of his tenements, holding their ground and marking their territory just as his own Jaguar battalion might (199–200); they even end up in an armed battle against the LAPD after one of them is shot by police. When Antonio takes his revenge plot to the Major and Frank, two Black homeless men, they assert that many have been killed in the city for less and endorse the plan (177). Antonio reasons that "in this city of vicious madness people did much worse things. . . . if people could commit such horrible crimes for no good reason, then Antonio could bring himself to kill the soldier" (183).

Ironically, the city that creates the vacuum of moral justice Antonio must fill also creates the cover of anonymity Antonio needs to become a vigilante. Antonio's failure to build a new life in L.A., as Longoria has, within downtown's colonia, allows him to transform into a rogue avenger. This transformation begins on Los Angeles's Crown Hill and completes in the forgotten tunnels of downtown. Ultimately, to succeed in avenging the soldier's war crimes, Antonio must force Longoria from his provisionally claimed space in Central American L.A. into the marginalized and forgotten areas of the city.

Downtown Barriography

For this chapter's *barriography* I was lucky enough to have Héctor Tobar himself escort me on a tour of the Los Angeles locations of the novel. As I ran the tape recorder (so to speak), we strolled MacArthur Park and the Westlake neighborhood together; then in classic L.A. fashion, we drove to the other sites: Crown Hill, the tunnels (which Mike Davis had in turn shown *him*: I could not help but geek out at the thought of being initiated into some kind of L.A. urban landscape writing legacy), a few locations he covered during the Rodney King riots that made it into the story, and, finally, his own childhood neighborhood in Little Armenia. On the tour,

I learned about Tobar's extensive history covering the Central American beat for the *Los Angeles Times*, including a foreign correspondent stint covering Guatemala from the region. While Little Armenia is his hometown, he has adopted Westlake and Pico-Union, gravitating toward the Central American community there. Like many children of immigrants (his mother immigrated when she was pregnant with him), Tobar both was and was not a part of the Guatemalan diaspora of his parents: he was proud to be part of the only Guatemalan family on the block he grew up on, and he visited Guatemala every Christmas and kept up his Spanish (Tobar, personal interview), but I suspect Tobar would agree that the desire to be closer to his ancestral homeland and to speak his parents' native language was part of his motivation to take on Central American downtown, and Central America period, as a reporter. We will return to Tobar's philosophy of journalism and his rationale for incorporating reportage into fiction at the end of the chapter.

MACARTHUR PARK AND WESTLAKE

Immigrants' pasts exist not just in memories but also in the new spaces they create, and the MacArthur Park neighborhood reflects the spatial logic of its inhabitants and users,[3] who have transplanted their Central American modes of spatial organization. MacArthur Park was and is ground zero (as much as L.A. can be said to have centralized foci) for the Central American diaspora. The neighborhood that encloses it has been home to Latin American refugees and newly arrived immigrants since the 1980s, and the crumbling tenements and newer but still crumbling apartment buildings continue to house many first-generation immigrants (Tobar, personal interview). Longoria lives in the Westlake Arms, a tenement building inspired by this area's housing. Tobar located the fictional Westlake Arms a few blocks from the park, in an empty lot across the street from the *rescate* center where he first heard the story that inspired *The Tattooed Soldier*.[4] The streets surrounding MacArthur Park's south and east side are lined with vendors who perch on the sidewalks of 6th and Alvarado, between the street curbs and the storefronts, funneling pedestrians into a narrow path that ensures perusal of the merchandise, sometimes laid out on blankets or tarps, which on a recent Sunday includes Latin American CDs and DVDs, clothing, and street food. Tobar pauses to check out a row of CDs before we turn onto South Bonnie Brae, the side street with the empty lot. We head to the apartment building next door, which also makes its way into the novel: Tobar once covered a fire at this building and saw a gang of young tattooed cholos outside, the blueprint for the "army of painted children" in the book. We are eyed by renters entering and exiting, as we sneak our way into the lobby. Back out front, as he's telling me the fire story, two cops literally *run* past us, chasing a suspect on foot. "This is like my fucking novel!" Tobar exclaims. "When do you ever see a foot chase? Cops on a foot chase in *L.A.?!*"

Back at MacArthur Park, I see how the park now functions as a kind of plaza—the heart of any Latin American town, where you'll find the church, the town hall, and any other crucial building for civic life, directly abutting a park or green area, often full of bustle. MacArthur Park lacks those civic anchors (since it is, after all, not a pueblo but a town-within-a-town), yet its users manage to re-create the central meeting place or main thoroughfare of a Latin American town or capital. Latin American music blasts from stores facing the park on Alvarado, Wilshire, and Sixth and Seventh Streets, which sell calling cards or mail packages internationally. In the park, groups of men gather at picnic tables to play a game of chance, a

FIGURE 17. The Latin American sidewalks of Westlake, 2017

soccer game is being played by young boys, lovers pair off and nestle on the northern lawn, and families stroll by, talking in Spanish. While the eastern hill of MacArthur Park is occupied by the homeless, who Tobar tells me have long camped on this site, the rest of the park is "owned" by Latino/as. The bandstand at the northeast corner serves as the neighborhood's political center: several protests were held here in the 1980s and 1990s. Tobar says back then demonstrations and marches against Latin American dictatorships or US intervention were "a routine thing." A speech Tobar heard here from a female former commandant protesting the war in El Salvador even made it into the novel (Tobar, *Tattooed Soldier* 66–67). To me, the sidewalk vendors, the cacophony of competing stores' music coming out of opened doors, and the variety of street food and *pastelerias* is reminiscent of downtown Mexico City (though I've never been to Guatemala City or San Salvador). The unmistakable Latin American character of MacArthur Park demonstrates how its inhabitants shape space according to their own communal logics. The immigrants of this neighborhood have essentially projected the spatial organization of their countries of origin onto Los Angeles. In so doing they have claimed the neighborhood (see figs. 17 and 18).

FIGURE 18. MacArthur Park as a gathering spot for residents, 2017

CROWN HILL'S VACANT LOTS AND TUNNELS

Crown Hill was one of Héctor Tobar's neighborhood beats for the *L.A. Times*. The area captured his imagination: "It was such a dramatic place back in the day, because you'd be standing right across, half a mile, from the towers of the financial district, and it was all open land. It was a metaphor for devastation" (Tobar, personal interview). In a story for the *Times*, Tobar described the ironies of Crown Hill: once an upscale neighborhood at the end of the nineteenth century, the land just outside the downtown financial district was razed to be sold off to developers, many of whom planned to build offices and mixed-use buildings ("Homeless Camps"). The steep economic downturn of the late 1980s stymied new construction and left other lots unsold, resulting in a stretch of over eight acres of land that remained vacant. Construction on the purchased lots was for high-rise office buildings, at a time when over 20 percent of downtown's offices were empty (Tobar, "Homeless Camps"). The same depressed economy increased the number of urban poor, and an estimated 177,000 people were homeless in L.A. County in 1992. With over a thousand housing units razed to make room for new developments downtown, the market for housing soared while the market for development stagnated.

The result: a massive homeless encampment on Crown Hill's vacant lots, on a large hill overlooking the downtown skyline. The homeless took over a vastly expensive and yet unclaimed portion of the city. Tobar interviewed a resident who wondered "What can $341 (from a monthly welfare check) do for you but keep you in poverty?" while standing, ironically, on land that was worth $900 per square foot (Tobar, "Homeless Camps"). The men and women camped on the hill occupy parcels that were sold for $24 million four years prior. The homeless encampment had its own rules and a different code of conduct from the more violent Skid Row closer to the center of the city. Tobar interviewed a Vietnam veteran and Crown Hill homeless resident who claimed, "It's a whole other society with its own code of ethics" (Tobar, "Homeless Camps"). Tobar's fictional "Mayor" of Crown Hill, the encampment's unofficial spokesperson, echoes the sentiment: "Here we all got our little piece of earth. I guess you can say we've got a small investment in the community" (*Tattooed Soldier* 47). The Mayor goes so far as to claim that "the Man, he leaves us alone"; "He's afraid because this is our territory. It's like a liberated zone" (47).

In the present, Crown Hill still serves as a powerful geographical metaphor for the contrasting logics of space simultaneously at work in the city. As extremely valuable but unclaimed space, Crown Hill was an anachronism: an eerily undeveloped grassland in the middle of down-town Los Angeles's financial district. In a testament to the power of place memory, even now, several years after the hill was turned into a very well-protected and monitored high school (the perimeter of the school, with intimidatingly high fencing and mounted cameras, reads more like a prison than a place of learning), a colony of homeless still live stretched out on the street than runs down its slope. The decision of the commu-nity to line up along this sidewalk seems confounding—why not a park or an underpass?—without knowing the history of the area. Crown Hill remains a site where two different temporalities and their structures of space chafe against one another (see figs. 19–22).

This real-life no-man's-land serves the novel as both "metaphor for devastation" and training ground for our protagonist's growing invisi-bility as a marginalized resident of Los Angeles, despite its jarring loca-tion in the heart of the city. On why he chose to write about Crown Hill, Tobar referred to Los Angeles's stark temporal and geographical uneven-ness: "What really makes L.A. interesting is there are all these cultures and subcultures that overlap with each other, and they mix a lot, but also

FIGURE 19. A photo taken from what is now Vista Hermosa Natural Park, directly across from Crown Hill's old homeless encampment ("the blank slate in the center of the city"), 2017

FIGURE 20. Old Crown Hill's homeless encampment is now a very well-guarded high school

FIGURE 21. The somewhat menacing exterior of the high school

FIGURE 22. Homeless still reside along Crown Hill's steep edge on Emerald Street, next to the site of the 1990s hilltop encampment, near the defunct trolley tunnels, 2017

they seem to move according to their own logic, and sometimes they do cross" (personal interview). Crown Hill is one of those sites of crossing, where the homeless, addicts (Tobar says this area was "crack and heroin central" in the 1980s), and immigrants, undocumented and not, coalesce and develop their own society, literally facing the social ordering, represented by downtown L.A., that has pushed all of them to a vacant lot at its edge.[5] In the novel, Antonio is thus placed in a tribe within a city, with "its own code of ethics," shared by others who operate at the fringes of the mainstream system. Crown Hill transforms Antonio simultaneously into an anonymous migrant and a member of the community of homeless who have claimed one of Los Angeles's unclaimed spaces.

Antonio describes Crown Hill as "some sort of geographic anomaly, a lush knoll of wild plants and grasses in the middle of the city" (Tobar, *Tattooed Soldier* 12–13), with skyscrapers "so close he could almost make out the faces of the janitors inside" (13). For Antonio this "geographic anomaly" comes to reflect his own identity as a transplanted Guatemalan seeking justice for past crimes in Los Angeles. Having failed to pursue his political asylum, Antonio becomes undocumented when his tourist visa lapses; aside from the occasional under-the-table jobs far below minimum wage, he has slipped below legal Los Angeles (52). Just before the homeless encampment is razed in the novel, Antonio refers to it as "the blank slate in the center of the city" (227), recognizing that its citizens are as unmarked as the vacant lots they occupy. Antonio's own blank slate refers to both his status in the city system—homeless, unemployed, without any ties to "visible" Los Angeles—as well as his status as in between countries: until he avenges Guatemalan war crimes he will not be able to claim a new life in L.A. Ironically, Antonio's position within a "geographic anomaly" gives him the invisibility he needs to carry out his act of unsanctioned justice: Antonio's current location on the social (if not physical) outskirts of L.A. also provides a tool for securing retribution.

When the Department of Sanitation comes to destroy the settlements, Antonio perceives it as a vindication of his plan for revenge against Longoria, further identifying himself with his location: "Obstacles would be crushed, smashed and destroyed, in the same way the buildings on Crown Hill had been flattened. There would be an evenness to the world again, land empty for a new beginning" (266). Antonio echoes the hackneyed hopes for immigration as a "new life" in an "empty" land yet believes that, in order to start over, the land must first be emptied of its past. Antonio then imagines "bulldozers," literal earthmovers, "converging" on Longoria, implying that the tragedies he experienced in Guatemala are still too intertwined with the spaces he inhabits now. Only by taking Longoria's new L.A. life can Antonio get his own: "Antonio would kill him, and then walk and breathe in the *open city* as a *free man*" (258; emphasis added).

After the homeless settlements in Crown Hill are destroyed, Frank and the Mayor guide a small group of homeless "down the steep drop of Bixel Street" (233) to another place they know to camp: "an open lot surrounded by a chain-link fence, a vast concrete floor, V-shaped, like a funnel, enclosed by two concrete walls that converged towards a tunnel entrance" (233). Like Crown Hill, the tunnel "had not been used for years, at least not for its intended purpose" (234). Left behind when the Pacific Electric Red Car Trolley line shut down in 1953 and cars officially replaced trolleys downtown, the tunnels become a forgotten landmark of Los Angeles's past. Like Crown Hill and "so much else in this corner of the city, it seemed to belong to another age" (234). Antonio thinks of the entrance as a "concrete temple," furthering the metaphor of the tunnel as belonging to a different time and space than the urban center it hides inside (234). This temporal disparity persists in the description of "the crumbling staircases and ancient palm trees of Crown Hill" (234), just above the tunnel archway. Crown Hill is unmarked but still physically visible, sitting in the midst of the city; the tunnel is both invisible and unclaimed, running underneath the city *as well as* outside its social logic. The abandoned tunnel thus continues Antonio's training in invisibility and eventually provides the literal cover Antonio needs to fulfill his act of vengeance.

The only users of the tunnel since it ceased functioning as a trolley station are graffiti artists, who have covered every inch of the entrance with spray paint, a "vast canvas shimmering like an acrylic rainbow sea" (234). Elsewhere in the novel, graffiti marks territory, as on the steps of Longoria's Westlake Arms: "To mark their position, their sacred ground, they had covered the black asphalt of the street with a huge graffito announcing the name of their gang, Bixel 13" (200). As in Salvador Plascencia's *The People of Paper* and Helena Maria Viramontes's *Their Dogs Came with Them*, graffiti is used by inner-city residents when their spaces are under contestation from rival groups or larger forces (urban planners, outsiders, Caltrans), as a way to claim pieces of the neighborhood. In fact, gang tags in Crown Hill function as place memory: one local gang, started, incredibly, in the 1940s, is named after Diamond Street, once a main part of the neighborhood, long since demolished (see fig. 23). While the

FIGURE 23. The "Diamond Street Gang": note the use of a diamond icon; the "13" may refer to collaboration with Mara Salvatrucha 13, a transnational gang with Central American ties, 2017

FIGURE 24. The tunnel, now sealed up and gentrified, with a visual gesture to its storied graffiti past, 2017

graffiti artists here turn the tunnel into their own "private gallery" (234) rather than a more public display of ownership, the acts of vandalism are still acts of claiming space. The "army of manic graffiti artists" (234) has kinship with the "army" of cholos Longoria sees tagging the corner and fighting the police (201).

The tunnel, like the vacant lots on Crown Hill, is geographically and historically accurate (see fig. 24). As I mentioned, Tobar was introduced to the tunnel by Mike Davis, L.A.'s preeminent urban geographer, as part of a story about the area's subcultures, since graffiti artists and homeless coexisted in this clandestine space (Tobar, personal interview). On our visit to the site, which is now in the midst of gentrification—the tunnel entrance has not been demolished, but maybe fifty feet away are the manicured back lawns of the new condominium building "Belmont Station," a linguistic gesture to the former trolley stop, the neighborhood's own anachronistic blight—Tobar tells me the story of the tunnel, which he has the Mayor recount for the reader in the novel: "Over there, in the old financial district at the bottom of bunker hill, pretty close to the grand central market, underneath a building, was the end of this rail line, and there was a subway station there. So this went all the way through. Except that, when they built the big towers of the financial district, when they built the parking garages, they destroyed the tunnel, so when you walk to the end of the tunnel, there's a huge concrete wall" (Tobar, personal interview). Tobar said the combination of Crown Hill's homeless encampment and the dark tunnel to nowhere directly underneath it made him picture Dante, "souls living on top of purgatory." Tobar did not need to invent a location that could hide Antonio's act of vengeance; in fact, the realness of the place increases the emotional impact of the story, itself also based on a real-life encounter between a former Guatemalan soldier and his former Guatemalan victim. Choosing to remain faithful to geographic details closes the gap between fiction and truth.

Using the actual locations of Crown Hill and the tunnel also exposes the absurd realities of structural inequality in L.A. The tunnel as a metaphor is almost too perfect: if it were fictionalized, it might strain credibility. When Antonio and Frank head deep into the tunnel for target practice (Frank takes Antonio to the Eastside to secure the gun), they find rainwater dripping down and stalactites that have formed. Frank tells Antonio that "It's all that rainwater from Bunker Hill. All that rain that falls on stockbrokers" (267). Deep in the tunnel, they are directly under downtown, subject to the runoff and remainders of the financial district. The scene symbolizes how Los Angeles foments violence borne of inequality, housing a literal underground connected to the core of the city in unseen ways. Yet the tunnel is *not* a symbol but the reality of L.A. Tobar calls attention to the very real uneven development of our contemporary cities, rendering visible what those who dwell outside these "undergrounds" are blind to. Given this motive, *The Tattooed Soldier*'s setting during the Rodney King riots is apt. The riots demonstrated the confluence and eruption of multiple L.A. undergrounds or subcultures of invisible, undervalued, underrepresented communities, exposing the disparate spaces of the city and warning the reader against the consequences of persistent marginalization.

THE RODNEY KING RIOTS AND SOUTH CENTRAL

The Tattooed Soldier provides the experience of the riots from the Central American perspective, detailing how conflicts in Central America become reanimated in the Rodney King verdict and the city's response. Tobar briefly recounts the initial reaction near the Civic Center, from rioters and homeless who are protesting racial injustice, where the riots are viewed positively, referred to alternately as a "war," a "historic battle," a "revolution," and "when the people got theirs" (275). The novel's focus, however, is on Latin American immigrants who become looters not in solidarity with King but rather as a release valve for exploitative working conditions and their traumatic war-torn pasts in countries of origin that they continue to carry with them. The chapter covering the riot scenes alternates between Antonio and Longoria in L.A. Longoria witnesses the riots as both undignified disorder and a battle he doesn't understand; he is thrown back into his memories of war and held accountable for his role in that war by Central American looters. Antonio witnesses the riots as just, interpreting them as a dispensation to pursue his rogue vendetta. Tobar shows us how the urban disorder is promulgated by a coalition of those unseen armies of Los Angeles that are part of both Antonio's and Longoria's communities.

While Antonio and Frank conduct shooting practice, Longoria and his coworkers watch the Rodney King verdict on TV at El Pulgarcito Express in Pico-Union. Longoria's boss, Duarte, a right-leaning anticommunist Latin American like Longoria, cheers the verdicts of "not guilty" (270). Then they watch as the riots unfold in South Central and downtown near the Civic Center (271–72). The violence onscreen feeds Longoria's ongoing equation of the war in L.A. with the war in Guatemala and forces him to remember: "Memories rushed forward, taking hold of him by the chest. Fire and laughter. . . . To see this here in Los Angeles, . . . was to remember the names of villages turned to ash: San Miguel, Nueva Concepción, Santa Ana" (272). Longoria is proud of his conduct in the war and claims elsewhere that he turned villages to ash so that they might be rebuilt, in the image of order he has learned from his military training in the US: "The new Guatemala would be a place like Fort Bragg, like the United States" (292). His position is precarious: as a former agent of fire and destruction, he should be aligned with the rioters; however, his right-leaning, racist politics (even against his own Latin Americans) cause him to condemn the riots in favor of law and order. His suspicion that these rioters too are burning in order to rebuild forces him mentally to acknowledge either that he himself was an agent of disorder or that the rioters have just cause. Neither suits his image of himself, and so Longoria is caught between two wars. As a result, he will slide further and further back into his past during the riots.

Whether or not Longoria knows where he stands, fellow Latin Americans will decide for him. A group of young Central Americans storms the shop, transformed into "a platoon of looters." These looters are joined later by a "thin grandmotherly woman" who may or may not be the "grandmother" who had confronted Longoria. The onlookers are interested in revenge for packages that were lost, stolen, or adulterated by the shipping company; the Central American and Mexican witnesses consider it justice against a business that takes advantage of transnational circumstances. Yet in addition to being cheated, the rioters also share an ideological stance in response to the politics back in their countries of origin:

> A dark young man emerged with several posters in hand, portraits of El Salvador's right-wing presidential candidate. . . he made a show of tearing them in half, throwing the pieces to the ground, and stepping on them in a little jig. Another man joined him. The grandmother clapped.
> "¡Así!" she shouted. "Get him, *muchachos!* Stomp him!" (289)

Despite the rioters being from different Latin American countries, they are united in their anti-right-wing sentiments and conflate their protests of their old country with protests in their new one. Government-backed battalions like the one Longoria led have decimated settlements and forced the migration of many Central Americans who now find themselves in Los Angeles. The riots become these displaced migrants' opportunity to protest the wars they have fled. Longoria very rightly sees the fires onscreen as a continuation of the fires he set in Guatemala.

Longoria erroneously equates two seemingly similar spaces, but he stumbles upon a truth about Los Angeles. He considers the Rodney King riots an *effect* of the war in Guatemala: "the infection had followed him to Los Angeles. . . . Children were all around him now, their bodies painted like his, a guerrilla army of tattooed cholos" (292). Not only is Los Angeles more chaotic and less militaristic than he expects, it is also overrun with Central Americans and Chicano/as, veterans of dirty wars. The collective memories of these traumas, like his own, are "spilling" from "head[s] unto the streets." Longoria realizes that the displacement and transplantation of thousands of Central American war refugees and thousands of impoverished migrants must also result in the transplanting of the conflicts that have generated these massive migrations. In turn, the character of the city of L.A. transforms these conflicts and adds to them its own endemic wars. What the cholo army and the rioters teach him about space is that it is not static and not an empty container; it is created and projected upon by its inhabitants and users.

During the second day of rioting in Central-South-Central L.A., it is not protesters angry about the Rodney King verdict but exploited Central Americans who have turned to looting. When Antonio says to José Juan that the looting is "because of that *negro* who got beat up," José replies, "What *negro*? They're Latinos. They don't know any *negro*" (281). These rioters, like the rioters in Watts and downtown, are also reclaiming spaces that are denied them: "Housekeepers, garment workers, bus boys. Mexican, Honduran, Costa Rican, Nicaraguan. And of course his countrymen, the Guatemaltecos. It was a day without submissiveness, a day without coffee to pour or strangers' babies to feed or the whir of sewing machines in a factory. It was a day to liberate toolboxes and diapers from their glass cages. A day when all the pretty objects in the store windows would mock them no longer" (283). The underpaid and largely unseen workforce of Los Angeles—housekeepers, bus boys, garment workers—becomes visible and revolts against unjust working and living conditions. The "liberation" of "toolboxes and diapers" suggests that this eruption of disorder stems from the rioters' inability to purchase even essentials for their families. The image of "glass cages" that mock again points to the stark, uneven development at work in L.A., the spatial juxtaposition of an upper-class elite and the underclass of unprotected and undocumented workers who serve them. The power of their numbers allows the rioters to boldly throw off the submissive posture they've had to adopt to make lives for themselves in the US: "The waddling looters laughed and ran . . . *No one will catch us because we are hundreds*" (281). Tobar offers the symbol of the rocks young men are carrying: "How did they get rocks in the middle of the city? Antonio looked closer and saw they were just chunks of concrete and brick, pieces of crumbling walls. There were plenty of crumbling walls in this neighborhood and thus no shortage of ammunition" (283). The very conditions of living provide the "ammunition" for the rioting; the city has abandoned the neighborhood and left it to deteriorate, and this deterioration literally fuels the rioters to take back the space.

Antonio recognizes the riots as a time, and a space, to seek justice: "Someone had declared this the municipal day of settling accounts, a day for all vendettas, public and private" (283). He repeats the phrase, "municipal day for vendettas," suggesting it is city-sanctioned, and realizes that with "no authority or order of any kind" (284) in charge, a different spatial ordering is possible. Upon arriving at Longoria's apartment to shoot him, Antonio sees potential witnesses but is spurred on by the "municipal" character of the riots, describing the shooting as "something like a public execution" (294). Los Angeles's real history serves again as plot device, as the riots generate the space for unauthorized justice Antonio needs to kill Longoria.

Antonio has been living in unclaimed, invisible spaces, which allow him to become a killer: to get a gun, learn to shoot, meet others who know how to secure firearms, kill, and help plan an attack. Antonio has to be homeless, unemployed, and undocumented; unless he is outside the system, he will be punished for this sanctified crime. Yet Longoria exists in claimed space, as a functioning member of Los Angeles's society, and his context protects him (*"They can't see what the soldier is"* (295), Antonio says of Longoria's neighbors). The riots provide the cover Antonio needs for the initial shooting, but to get away with the crime, he needs to take away Longoria's visibility. Antonio must force Longoria out of L.A.'s claimed spaces and into its unseen ones, and so the story will end in the tunnels. By tracing Longoria's slow death as he is dragged from the Westlake Arms to the tunnel, Tobar again uses the space of Los Angeles to effect the former sergeant's transformation from city citizen to unknown soldier.

After Antonio shoots him, Longoria begins to realize the reverberations of his military actions in the war he is now in. Though wounded, Longoria slowly follows Antonio, whom he recognizes from the first attack in the park, when he was struck with a metal pipe: "He would be persecuted by men with pipes and guns and old women with sharp teeth until he caught up with the shooter and found out who he was" (297). The past that Longoria is proud of but has left behind will continue to haunt him until he is held accountable to his victims. In the extended slow-motion chase that follows, Longoria is displaced in both time and space as part of his penance: he retreats in his mind further and further back toward Guatemala, eventually arriving at his rural childhood, and he crosses into Los Angeles's unseen spaces. Accounting for his crimes requires Longoria to give up his Los Angeles citizenship, to be recognized as a man who has acted outside the system of justice and who should thus be barred from the city's social order.

As victim pursues shooter over the long distance from Bonnie Brae to the tunnels (it is over a mile on foot), Longoria progresses away from visible Los Angeles. He passes a Vons supermarket stocked with army soldiers; then "he finds himself stumbling into a barren area of the city, a place with fewer and fewer buildings, fenced-off fields of green" (299). The crest of Crown Hill, with its unmistakable empty grasslands, continues to function as a metaphor for the unseen inhabitants of Los Angeles, yet now Longoria is among them: "Longoria has the strange feeling that the missing buildings have floated up in the air like balloons, *in the same way his head is floating now,* bobbing somewhere above his body and *leading him deep into this empty land*" (299; emphasis added). Unmoored by the city, Longoria is dislocated, "floating" and "bobbing" away like the buildings "missing" from the center of L.A.

The title of the chapter, however, is "Below Crown Hill," and Longoria must be carried even further. Antonio proceeds to carry and then drag the tattooed soldier toward the tunnel. At the tunnel entrance, Longoria again wonders at this "missing" part of the city: "they are at the foot of a green mountain, wild plants and shrubs all around them. . . . Are they still in the city? Surely Longoria is hallucinating now" (300). He is dragged into the anonymity of the tunnel. Only now, in this space, does Antonio ask if he remembers Elena and Carlos in San Cristóbal, but the soldier does not reply, having converted the space into the Guatemala of his peasant childhood: "there is a burst of light. Growing golden in the darkness of the tunnel is a cornfield. Stalks rise from the black mud and push against the cement walls, fleshy leaves shining" (301). Longoria's final thought before dying is of this countryside and of his mother greeting him with the Quiché word "*balam*" (301).[6] Longoria thus projects his past onto his present even with his dying breath.

Longoria must die in this no-man's-land in the heart of the city. The act literally steals Longoria's life: his existence has become unknown and undiscoverable and thus achieves Antonio's hope to create "land empty for a new beginning" (266). If the past persists for these traumatized victims of Latin American wars, and Los Angeles both excludes certain of its citizens and then provides the forgotten spaces to siphon them off to, it is inevitable that these places will serve as containers for those pasts. In the darkness of the tunnel, Longoria leaves L.A., returning to Guatemalan cornfields (301). In turn, Antonio takes Longoria's visibility, and with it his L.A. life: he leaves the former soldier in the tunnel and walks to his new house in South Central, his new job, and his new burgeoning community of Latin American immigrants. Having resolved his personal vendetta, which trailed him from his country of origin, Antonio can *now* begin to claim space in Los Angeles.

Antonio's new life still contains memories of Guatemala, but they are tempered by the justice sought for the murder of his wife and child:

> Would he ever forget. . . the face of a man at the moment he reached for his last breath? . . . He would carry this memory next to the image of Carlos and Elena on the steps of their home in San Cristóbal. Twin images, emblazoned on the front and back of a book filled with his wanderings. The blood of Los Angeles was colorless in the black-and-white light of the tunnel. The blood of Guatemala was crimson under a tropical sun. The blood of Los Angeles might soon begin to fade. The blood of Guatemala was indelible.
>
> A park in Guatemala and a park in Los Angeles. (304)

The passage traces Antonio's revenge but also his migration trajectory, from San Cristóbal (where he and Elena fled from the capital) to the L.A. tunnel: that the soldier's dying face is the "back" of the book suggests that the story of his Guatemalan past has come to an end. Los Angeles's violence is black and white, colorless, hidden, and quick to fade; Guatemala's violence is bright, colorful, tropical, and impossible to erase. The violence of Los Angeles is metaphorized as the darkness of the tunnel, suggesting that the tunnel itself—the urban forces that build it, abandon it, and retake it—is a symbol of unseen or bloodless violence. Conversely the violence of Guatemala's civil war was visible, government sanctioned, and in the open, "under a tropical sun." The final line's juxtaposition of the two parks syntactically makes them equal: here again, as with Longoria's scenes of "fire and laughter," we have the equating of two dissimilar spaces. Yet it is the immigrant's refusal or inability to see the new space of Los Angeles as distinct from the space of his former nation that allows Antonio to seek justice: he shrinks geography and time (seven years have passed) because his lived experience belies the idea that his new country has given him a new life.

Yet if every immigrant of Los Angeles carries her past country, and projects those memories upon her present, how is the need for justice or resolution achieved? There are not enough tunnels! *The Tattooed Soldier* thus closes with uncertainty, with a hint of silent menace. As Antonio walks to his new home in South Central, "an army of people with brooms materialized" (305). The former "army" suspects Antonio of looting: "All the Mexicanos and Centroamericanos stared at him with contempt because he looked like a brazen thief and brazenness was something that belonged to yesterday. Today, their eyes said, we are a different people. . . . We do not take things that don't belong to us" (305). The act of sweeping demonstrates the Latino/as' custodial relationship toward the shared spaces of Los Angeles and reads as an act of contrition for their rioting. Yet the eruption of this "army" was caused by the exploitation of their submissiveness, as "housekeepers, garment workers, bus boys" (283), a submissiveness they now voluntarily embody again: "The sweeping and the sweeping, strangers meeting to collect a treasure of simmering shards. We are cleaning now. Here is the true brotherhood of the city. But the brooms could not do their work without the fields of broken glass, without the soggy ashes that covered the sidewalks" (306). "The true brotherhood of the city" includes the sweeping as well as the "fields of broken glass." This closing image implies that as long as this community of exploited immigrant workers remains relegated to custodianship without ownership, their potential as an army with the power to upturn claimed spaces lies in wait.

Coda: Little Armenia

The question remains: why write a fictional narrative with so much real-life place specificity and so many real-life scenes? If the goal is a political statement about Los Angeles and its unseen communities, why not write nonfiction? The answer lies in Tobar's own biography. Tobar was born and raised in what is now called Little Armenia in Hollywood, about four miles northwest of the action of *The Tattooed Soldier.* He grew up in an ethnic immigrant neighborhood notable for its diversity, with classmates from other nations like Uruguay, the Philippines, and Lebanon, as well as from Texas. His family anticipated by a few decades the great influx of Guatemalans to L.A., so he found himself the only Guatemalan American in his neighborhood: "nobody knew where Guatemala was. Everybody thought it was part of Mexico" (Tobar, personal interview). Despite general ignorance about Central America, this immigrant community cultivated in Tobar a shared sense of identity as newcomers, who ironically belong by not belonging elsewhere; Tobar tells me that "everyone was from somewhere else, and so everyone was equal."[7] Rather than being shy about his family's origins, Tobar's childhood encouraged him to be proud of it: "I felt it [being Guatemalan] was a private and cool part of me. I thought it made me special. My father and mother always spoke of Guatemala in these tones of respect. . . I think if you can't go home, you have a different relationship to a place, but I could go home all the time and so I loved it" (Tobar, personal interview). Tobar thus felt a unique connection to the country of his parents' births, which was burgeoned by his role as seemingly the sole ambassador of Guatemala in the neighborhood.

As a lifelong Los Angeleno, and a decades-long reporter and columnist for the *L.A. Times,* Tobar also saw dramatic changes to the landscape he grew up with. This unique vantage point, as inhabitant and then documentarian, deeply inflects his aesthetic choices in *The Tattooed Soldier:* "The central dramatic truth to me of my life in L.A. is that I had grown up in L.A. as this incredibly affluent city of limitless opportunity. I was born in the L.A. where the freeways were still being built. And then becoming a reporter and discovering this city of incredible inequality, homelessness, anger—you know I witnessed the '92 riots. And so I wanted to write a novel that got at the unease that informed me as a writer" (Tobar, personal interview). As a reporter on the immigration and homelessness beats for the *Times,* Tobar learned about the Central American communities that his family arrived too early to be a part of and recorded the effects of their migrations upon their own present and the city of L.A. Witnessing the dissolution of that "incredibly affluent city of limitless opportunity" spurred him to remember and record the downward turn of L.A. (we'll see in the next chapter how William Archila feels similarly about experiencing L.A.'s decay). As a transnational who returned often to Guatemala and who worked the Latin American Office for the *Times*, Tobar also saw the degeneration of his country of origin to civil war. Thus, witness to two homes that had turned violent and hopeless, Tobar sought out narratives that would expose the conflicts and mark the changes: "I wanted to write about the war in Central America and the war here at home, and that [*The Tattooed Soldier*] was the story that brought them together" (Tobar, personal interview).

Once Tobar decided that he wanted *The Tattooed Soldier* to be a political novel, real-life accuracy became an integral part of the project. When asked if he feels a responsibility to the actual source material of L.A., Tobar replied, "Oh, absolutely. I know you can be a political novelist and write like Jose Saramago or George Orwell, and I love that work, but in this case, . . . It's using real-life stuff. It's this emotional, intellectual, linguistic exercise, to try and re-create—no, not re-create, but create—an understanding of the time" (Tobar, personal interview). Tobar's perhaps intentional slip—between "re-create" and "create"—speaks to how seriously he takes the mandate to capture actual Los Angeles on the page, to document the series of forces that caused not just the L.A. riots but also the invisible or marginalized subcultures Tobar spent years reporting on for the greater Los Angeles community. His training as a journalist had taught him the power of truth-telling: "Journalism is an amazing teacher of what the world is. . . Truth has this incredible power. And the harder you work to get closer to the truth . . . people respond to that. People respond. I seek that kind of authority" (Tobar, personal interview).

As we will see with Junot Díaz in chapter 5, Tobar deploys real-life detail to intensify the impact of his fiction. Yet unlike Díaz, Tobar is not using autobiography to create this effect: instead, he uses the tools of the journalist, providing precise place descriptions and windows into the different communities that constitute inner-city Los Angeles. *The Tattooed Soldier* is an act of archiving in order to "create" "an understanding of the time." In addition to exposing such rifts in the city's communities to a reader, the novel is a personal exercise: Tobar's attempt to track how the "city of limitless opportunity" he knew from childhood could become so broken. The extent of the change the city undergoes in such a short period of time and the city's propensity to try to erase its own past create a sense of urgency to get an era of L.A. on the page accurately before it transforms. This personal motivation to write necessitates felicity to the source material, as Tobar's allegiance to his city makes fictionalizing seem like betrayal. That even in a work of fiction Tobar feels compelled to be faithful to the streets and alleys and neighborhoods of L.A. is a testament to the power of place his hometown has over him.

4

"The Blackouts of a Tiny Country"

THE ART OF WILLIAM ARCHILA'S SALVADORAN EXILE

THE SPEAKER of the semiautobiographical poems within William Archila's *The Art of Exile* has fled trauma and war, arriving to the US as a refugee.[1] This makes the poems operate somewhat differently from the writing of authors whose families leave their countries for economic reasons, aligning Archila's project more closely with the world of *The Tattooed Soldier*. Los Angeles becomes a place to forget and to escape memories rather than to nostalgically reminisce. Yet Archila also desires to honor those he has lost and returns to El Salvador, in poetry and in person, to record their fates. While the characters in *The Tattooed Soldier* similarly wish alternately to forget and to remember as tribute, *The Art of Exile* manifests a distinct relationship to place that comes from experiencing Los Angeles as a refugee and *writing as* a refugee.

For Héctor Tobar and for many of the transnational writers in this book, there is often a personal stake in claiming their parents' immigrant story: demonstrating knowledge of the country of origin confers authenticity upon the author, making him or her more Dominican, Cuban, Mexican, or Central American. Yet Archila's poems set in the United States are largely devoid of this anxiety about identity.[2] Where several writers in this book try to conjure the country of their parents, Archila calls to mind his *own* past life in another country, seemingly against his will. His lived experience of war in El Salvador inoculates him from the specter of not being Latinx *enough* that we see preoccupy authors like Richard Blanco, Junot Díaz, or Angie Cruz.

Two important differences distinguish Archila's writing from the other works in *Walk the Barrio*. The first is that, because there is not the same urgency to prove identity that often fuels the performance of neighborhood expertise, the poems' relationship to Archila's US neighborhood is more tenuous. Archila's work proves, through absence, one of the central theses of this book: that transnational subjects connect place identity to personal identity and use the neighborhood to fulfill their desire for a sense of authenticity. *The Art of Exile* does not incessantly lay out the exact street names and landmarks of Van Nuys, opting for a far more abstract depiction.[3] The poems set in Los Angeles focus on the natural landscape, another departure from other writers in the book, who generally reserve rich, sweeping landscape description for their country of origin, as a contrast to the gritty and specific ordering of their US barrios. The distinction indicates how different the experience of immigration is as a war refugee: we cannot consider Archila's work as transnational in the exact same way. Thus, my barriography is slightly more abstract, following the collection's aesthetic.

The second difference of note is that with Archila, we have our first (and only) instance of a writer as a witness. *Walk the Barrio* includes writers who want to assert their connection to a place of origin outside the US or who establish their identification with a place to establish their own sense of self; *this* speaker feels obligated to write about his country of origin, not as a way of coming to know himself but as a mandate to respect the dead. He does not specify family members or personal loved ones who have been lost but rather the anonymous "bodies" killed in war. These two distinctions ultimately dovetail, as the poems' marked *absence* of US place detail, reflecting the lack of attachment the speaker seems to feel for his new home, allows him to reaccess more completely his country of origin.[4]

Form of the Collection

William Archila is born in 1968 in Santa Ana, El Salvador. In 1980 he moves with his family to escape the civil war when he is twelve, and they settle in Los Angeles. William Archila will go on to get an MFA in poetry at the University of Oregon before resettling permanently in Los Angeles. After the civil war ends, Archila returns, as an adult, to El Salvador. *The Art of Exile,* his first collection of poetry, recounts his childhood in El Salvador, his adolescence in Los Angeles, time spent in New York City, and then his journey back to El Salvador. The title (and its eponymous poem in the collection) is a clear play on words, signifying both the mastery of being an exile and the art produced as a result of exile. As intimated by the allusion to Elizabeth Bishop's "One Art," the poet will show us how this "art" is still becoming, that exile is never fully mastered, and how poetry at least allows the writer to craft meaning from the process of sorting through the experience.

The collection is in four parts: the series of poems in section 1 take place in El Salvador when the speaker is a child and preteen; the poems of section 2 are mainly in Los Angeles but also other US points of contact; section

3 consists of a single poem ("After Ashes") in multiple sections; section 4 gathers Archila's poems about his return journey to El Salvador after the civil war has ended. The collection's structure at least initially follows a linear trajectory, echoing more traditional versions of the "Immigration Story": beginning in the home country and then describing the process of assimilation in the new host country. However, the third and fourth sections adapt the form to be in line with more contemporary transnational iterations of immigration: the poems end back in El Salvador, ten years and more after the opening section, as the speaker has returned to rediscover his home and to realize that it is no longer his home.

The opening poem sets the stage for the poet-speaker's exile. "Radio" places us in the midst of two "civil" wars: the Salvadoran civil war, fought in the countryside of the speaker's hometown of Santa Ana, and the civil war of Archila's family, mother and son feeling abandoned while their father and husband relocates to Los Angeles to work. It is not a stretch to say that a third civil war is subtly waged between languages: the title, "Radio," is the same word in English and Spanish, and the bilingual poem, which inserts untranslated snippets of Pablo Neruda's verses, holds a tension between the speaker's native language at the time the poem is set (Spanish) and his native language at the time the poem is written.[5] Regardless of the language it is in, poetry is the speaker's lifeline: left behind by his father and caught in a brutal war, Archila finds a new father in the beauty of poetic language, connecting him to something outside his immediate experience of danger and suffering.

The poem begins with two lines of Neruda in Spanish: "I can write the saddest verses tonight."[6] Neruda's poem, the twentieth from his work *Veinte Poemas de Amor y Una Canción Desesperada*, goes on to lament, as this poem does, a night that is empty with the absence of a former loved one. The speaker is ten; his mother wakes him up to listen to the voice on the radio. Most of the figurative language and imagery in the poem is marshaled to describe this voice. While the radio only "throws" a "half-yellow light," Neruda's voice is "reaching the darkest corner/of the house." The voice is hyperbolized as being distant using various metrics— "ancient," "full of rain," and "from a foreign planet"—that contrast with the quality of distance in the father's voice later in the poem.

Archila settles on the conceit of the poems as "fat waves," "lapping at my bedside" (*Art of Exile* 10): the bed becomes a "prow / reaping through the waters," making "a sound / like the whoosh of pine trees bending." The heft of the waves and the sound of pine trees are two allusions to a different Neruda poem in *Veinte Poemas* (which will be directly quoted in a later stanza); Archila demonstrates the power of poetry to color his reality by seamlessly incorporating the poetic imagery he hears into his remembrance. Archila spends six full stanzas describing the voice from the radio before describing his immediate surroundings, a deliberate choice of focus that demonstrates how Neruda transports him from his current situation. These waves rock against the boat that holds the speaker, his mother, and the radio, and will be "ignorant" of the speaker's father trying to call.

The imagery eventually moves on because of that same radio, which has a "rusted gun" concealed inside to protect from the war outside. After the speaker's brief depiction of the present circumstances, awareness of his surroundings prompts a consideration of who is missing:

> ignorant of my father on the phone,
> calling long distance from Los Angeles,
>
> his voice, a buzz and a click, clipped
> by the tiny blackouts of a tiny country.
>
> Who knows what kept
> my father in the north? Perhaps
> it was the city lights of a woman,
>
> long snouts of avenues
> clutching their tongues, unrolling
> the drunken dollar flat on his hand. (4)

The father's voice is dwarfed by the powerful sounds of the poetry crashing into the bedroom. In contrast to those "fat waves," his father's voice, "calling long distance from Los Angeles," is curtly described as "clipped," "a buzz and a click" (26–28). While Los Angeles enters the world of the poem, El Salvador demonstrates dominance, its blackouts cutting off the sound of the United States, its radio waves "ignorant" of the father's voice (25). The sound is ironically described by its absence or interruption, "buzz" and "click" and "clipped" all being ways the voice on the phone is distorted or eliminated. While the voice on the radio is also described as far away, its distance has an organic and even magical cast—it is "ancient" and "from a foreign planet"—and despite having to span time and space it is *still* transmitted clearly to the listener. In contrast, the distance of the father's voice is marked by interference with its reception.

Splitting the nuclear family to make financial gains is of course a common transnational strategy, and El Salvador's contemporary immigration follows transnational trends. However, when a parent is "kept" "in the north" during a civil war, that absence can be perceived as abandonment rather than sacrifice. The speaker's tone in this section reflects keen resentment that his father has left the family behind in the midst of armed conflict, ruefully positing that the father is detained by the lure of the city, or alcohol, or women, rather than by the need to make money to send home. In these lines the poem travels to Los Angeles, but only briefly. The speaker attempts to describe the "long snouts of avenues" (32) that might tempt his father to stay, but the language is overwhelmingly figurative: the ten-year-old can only dimly imagine this unknown country and his father's unknown life.

Ungrounded in first-hand knowledge of the city, the speaker quickly gives up imagining what the father stays away *for* and starts imagining what the father is staying away *from:*

> Perhaps it was the vertebrae of broken bodies
> caught in the gutter. Who knows
>
> if he knew that wind flew
> around our house, howling like a dog?
>
> That his wife came to bed
> as if rejected by the moon once again,
>
> Radio in the crook of her arm
> tuned to the dark shade of pines,
> "lento juego de luces, campana solitaria." (35–43)

The focus on "vertebrae" intimates the potential lack of spine, or cowardice, of the father who stays away from the war, fearful for himself. The repetition of "Who knows" and the interrogation marks to follow make the father's position anonymous, distant, and uncertain. The almost absurd assonance and alliteration of the lines, "Who knows / if he knew that wind flew / around our house, howling like a dog?" highlights the father's ignorance of the conditions the boy lives in, which are clearly too loud to be dismissed, if one is present on the ground. To complete the picture of the father's distance by situating the speaker firmly in his Salvadoran location, the poem moves from the gutter to the wind to the moon, which rejects not the mother but "his wife."

The juxtaposition between the father and the radio is solidified by the way the imagery of the transmitted poem injects itself directly into the room: the "dark shade of pines" is "tuned to," and the levels of mediation, of the voice of the speaker through the radio, of the pines as a metaphor in the poem, are erased. The reference to pines alludes to poem 3 in *Veinte Poemas* ("Ah vastedad de pinos"); the second line of that poem is directly inserted into Archila's stanza, eliminating the distance between the poet's voice and the speaker's setting. Referencing the "buzz and a click" of the father's voice, the radio voice "crackle[s]"; however, the sound of *this* technological failing is quickly transformed into an organic sound, as the crackle of a fire that "glow[s]." This voice, unlike the father's, is stronger for the speaker than the mediation that seeks to diminish it. The simile of the radio as "a boatman standing in the mist" (49) turns the ship into sound, passing through the poem's waves of poetry. The boat*man*, already possessing agency, is "pulling" the speaker. It is the poetry and not the father's voice that will help the speaker "through the slow nights of a small war" (5).

The power of poetry—enacted by the unmediated opening lines of Neruda, the figurative description of the verses as waves rolling and pine trees bending, and the figure of the radio as boatman carrying the speaker through war—is marked by its presence in the speaker's life in contrast to the absences he experiences. The poetic inspiration the speaker feels as a young boy transforms into the poetry he utilizes now to enact that experience in verse as a poet. "Radio" thus demonstrates how the journey of the refugee cannot be captured without recourse to figurative language— and in Archila's case, figurative language in two languages.

The poems of part 1 of *The Art of Exile* are firmly set in El Salvador and in the speaker's childhood. Aside from the occasional highway or school-house or tin shack, the poems avoid man-made settings: nearly every poem in this section has a natural landscape description, of the earth, the sun, black mud, and "coffee mountains." These are not overburdened with adjectives or adverbs; often the natural elements get a simple simile or metaphor, and they frequently have the power of personification, lording over the fates of the protagonists—soldiers, victims, schoolyard friends, and the speaker himself. There are several poems where the speaker personally encounters dead bodies, seemingly strewn about the landscape.

Indeed, the people of El Salvador become organically woven into the place in part 1. The dead are "eating wet dirt" (14), dead bodies are "a reflection in a vulture's eye" (15), black mud and disintegrating hyacinths share a stanza with open graves and coffins (16), the sun finds a slumped body on the ground (18), the neighbors' figures are "almost baked in clay" (22), "stiffened bodies" are "now dust" (22), and the dead "wither into the earth" (21). Human death and violence in this section are inextricably linked to the natural world. Archila appears unable to describe El Salvador without describing its dead, and vice versa. He tells us, "Every morning, I think about the war" (21). As Karina Alvarado astutely notes, "the poet exists in relation with the dead as a perpetually living memory" (482).

The final poem of part 1, "This Earth," presents us with the poet-speaker's rationale for the graphic and macabre character of these first eleven poems. The poem takes place on the cusp of the speaker's exile, remembering earlier moments from a teenaged vantage. Archila's childhood friend Memo is found dismembered by the shore of a lake as a teenager. Many months and many burials later, the speaker realizes that all these dead persist in the landscape: "Somewhere in the mist, I know the earth, / cold and damp with rain, belongs to them" (Archila, *Art of Exile* 22). Not only does the earth belong to the dead, the moribund landscape saps life from those still alive in it.

Throughout the section the mountains, sky, and earth have menaced the inhabitants, but in "This Earth" the threat becomes explicit. Archila sees the dead in the living, imagining Memo among the workers coming home. However, instead of this making Memo seem more alive, it makes the workers seem more dead:

> behind the mountains, I watch the neighbors,
> all soiled, figures almost baked in clay,
> come back from the greasy stacks of factories.
>
> This could be Memo,
> trudging across a charred city,
> crumbling into the street, hungry (22)

In the stanza just prior, we are told that the dead own the earth; this transforms the significance of the neighbors as "all soiled": instead of literally meaning they are dirty, the line suggests they too are already covered by earth. This darker reading is reinforced by the depiction of them "almost baked in clay," which turns them from animate to inanimate. In the next stanza the deterioration of people into the landscape becomes complete, as Archila imagines these neighbors, and Memo, "crumbling into the street." After "so many buried / under stones" (22), those left behind become weighed down and swallowed up by the growing death toll. War here permeates everything, even the bodies of the living, and especially the land where these atrocities take place.

His urgency to capture this war-soaked landscape comes from his felt need to be a witness. In "This Earth," as young boys, Archila and Memo learn about their own war from their surroundings and from the newspapers and about the war in Vietnam from the TV and their textbook. United by youth, poverty, and war, the globe they are taught to memorize in school becomes a "plastic soccer ball / we kicked in the streets with unknown children, / hot soil burning the bottoms of our feet" (21). Yet despite sharing "hot soil," the war in Vietnam is distant: the "TV news played images," but Archila has no sense of the people in those neighborhoods or the dead. However, while those killed a world away in Vietnam are only abstractly known to him, those buried in his neighborhood are not. *His* earth he is intimately familiar with, and if he is to honor the dead in *his* ground, he must transform his remembrances into memorials.

The closing lines of the closing poem of the section indicate that despite the terror of this Salvadoran landscape, Archila will spur himself to remember it and to remember those who died in it:

> I pull the string from the lightbulb,
> remember my geography book,
>
> the bombed-out walls of my school,
> neighbors closing doors, nailing their eyes shut,
> Memo under my feet, how I love the smell of wet dirt,
> how I will cup my hands, carry this earth in my pockets. (22)

His "geography book" has taught him that conflicts like the one in El Salvador happen everywhere in the world; but he does not want this war to be abstract and faceless. He takes literal and figurative possession of his own surroundings, "my book," "my school," "my feet," "my hands," "my pockets": this land is his and these memories are his inheritance. Through his "skillful reconjur[ing]" of the dead, Archila "transforms the testimonial witness to a collective experience now integrated into cultural memory" (Alvarado 484). To "carry this earth" means to mark the specificity of his own homeland, to never forget what it was like there in that corner of the globe, and to recount his experiences so that El Salvador becomes human for his readers, for those who have not smelled its dirt themselves.

This mode of perception—where the landscape becomes human, and the humans become landscape—borne of bloody conflict, will persist when the poet moves to Los Angeles. The line between animate and inanimate remains blurred. The boundary between past and present, and between the US and El Salvador, will also become unstable. While *The Art of Exile*'s two sections that take place in El Salvador stay set there, the US section moves constantly back to El Salvador. The movement between countries is common in transnational literature, but here, as in *The Tattooed Soldier*, the speaker is seemingly compelled to return to traumatic memories from his country of origin against his will. Having exited the monolingual prelapsarian state of part 1, the speaker undergoes a linguistic transformation: English, at first a daunting obstacle to belonging, becomes more natural than Spanish: by the time of his return to El Salvador in part 4, the poet is doubly displaced from his country of origin, both geographically and linguistically.

The opening poem of part 2, "Immigration Blues, 1980" (25–26), demonstrates how the blending of the human and natural both continues and is changed by a new environment. The speaker has arrived in Los Angeles and is walking the streets, disoriented. As in part 1, nonhumans are anthropomorphized, and humans become inhuman. However, the character of these transformations shifts dramatically in the speaker's new setting. Unlike the prior section, man-made things proliferate and begin to take on life: cars become people, "lungs rusting" as they groan (18–19), and the streets become the "carcass of a dead cat" (2–4). The dead of El Salvador turn into inorganic and inanimate things in L.A.

The dead become "items for the evening news" and "documents from another small-foot country" (22–24), indiscriminate and vague objects, characterized by being one of many, "another" in a series of tiny conflict-ridden countries. After existing in a place where the dead were under his very feet, the dead now can only reach Archila "in letters," as "blue ink that stains" (28) hands that once cupped the sacred dirt of El Salvador. The United States turns the humans of El Salvador (the country itself anthropomorphized in the poem as a scratch on the knee of the isthmus) into disposable man-made things. The dead are highly mediated now, divorced from Archila by his spatial displacement.

This loss of connection to the earth and to the animate is matched by and linked to the speaker's displacement in language. The bodies have turned into letters he reads in English, but the Spanish syllables are still caught in his throat (14), and new "words" are "locked in a dictionary"

(15). A "foreigner everywhere I go," and "a war away from home," the speaker is caught between worlds and words. He finds himself lost

> among buildings downtown,
> pronouncing the sound of their names
> in the hollow roof of my mouth,
> spelling them over
>
> and over again, till they mean
> nothing, nothing at all.
>
> My country falls on me like a hammer. (29–35)

His past experiences were unified by a single language and a single country: now his experiences are split or doubled. He finds his new location inscrutable, and his new words are incapable of meaningfully connecting him to either the animate or inanimate things around him. They themselves are things without referents. The buildings will remain unnamed and thus unknown. In a poem that has exclusively trucked in metaphor until the final line, the use of a simile is striking: the speaker loses control of language, and its power wanes, as it can no longer transform things, but only compare them.

Yet the terror of a world without meaning is less than the fear for what this new language and place do to his memories. Archila deploys enjambment so that "I'm lost" refers both to how Salvadoran bodies have become letters that arrive to him midsentence and to his wandering downtown. The simplest interpretation is that the written letters that point to home still mean something, while the names and sounds and spellings of "buildings downtown" mean "nothing, nothing at all" (39). However, the enjambment builds a deliberate confusion about whether the "they" of the poem has shifted from "bodies" to "buildings": whose names are being pronounced and whose names are being spelled? Is it the buildings around him, or is it the names of those he now reads of, which come to him in a strange new language? If the cramped bodies of the war that he knows so intimately can become items and ink, his very past is at stake in his new home.

If the new words are incapable of pointing to *either* animate or inanimate things and they can inform Archila's understanding of both his present and his past, then the speaker's own agency is also at risk: he too may become a thing without referent here in Los Angeles. As the "I" of the poem—which has been present throughout in concrete statements,

"I walk," "I'm a war away," "I'm a man," "I think," "I'm lost"—is forgotten in the syntax of the gerunds "pronouncing" and "spelling," and in the repetition of phrases to indicate that these words simply do not work, the speaker's status as an actor falls away. This loss of self is reinforced by the structure of the lines, which abandon the poem's steady quatrains, diminishing to a couplet and finally to a single line left orphaned.

Ultimately, Archila becomes a grammatical object. The transformation of the speaker into a thing, like the dead, like the buildings, becomes complete with the final line, which turns him into a nail—to be hammered, violently, into his current surroundings. The possibility exists to read "my country" as El Salvador, but the use of an inanimate object in the simile points to the US as it has been described in the poem. Still, the presence of El Salvador's violence throughout the poem, and its intrusion in the speaker's new life in the US, suggests that perhaps it too "falls on" the speaker. A phrase like "my country" appears to be evacuated of meaning for the speaker, as he feels disconnected from both the US and El Salvador.

Parts 2 and 3 of *The Art of Exile* will track Archila's journey to belong in this new place and language, as it continues two of the techniques established in "Immigration Blues, 1980": to correlate the man-made to the US and the natural to El Salvador, and to oscillate rapidly between home and host countries, as well as past and present, in its imagery. The trauma of living through civil war profoundly impacts how the speaker experiences Los Angeles: Archila's mode of perceiving space, hewn in a landscape of death and fear, colors his perception of his new setting, transforming the city in unexpected ways. *The Art of Exile* must develop a new language to reconnect to the past, to learn how to express memories in a new place, to translate them so as not to lose them. And yet the more Archila feels at home in English, the further away he feels from El Salvador. Throughout the collection, and especially in part 4, we will see how interpretation and translation require the poet to sacrifice his sense of belonging to the original language.

Most of the poems in part 2 move between El Salvador and the United States. Very rarely does Archila separate the two national settings by stanza: El Salvador usually encroaches on the L.A. scenery, taking over a stanza in its final lines and moving us to El Salvador with no notice. This fast shifting creates the effect of interruption, of unintentional movement from El Salvador to the US. This disorienting mode—what I call a "displacement effect"—is significant in several ways: It implies these memories of the past are returning against the speaker's will, it shows how

Archila is caught in his sense of belonging between places, and it enacts how the poet carries and projects his traumatic past upon his present, ultimately transforming his perception of Los Angeles.

The poet's desire to find grounding in his new environment climaxes in "Bird" (29–30), which shows the sharp juxtaposition between the natural power of El Salvador and the manmade character of Los Angeles. While "Drinking Beer in East L.A." and "This Is for Henry" both reference Los Angeles's Eastside, "Bird" is the only poem in the collection that deploys explicit L.A. landmarks. It begins, "On the bus to Lincoln Heights": The speaker faces a young boy with a backpack on the bus, "stroking the veins" (4) of a map in the geography book on his lap, praying or reciting in Spanish over them. The geography book, which recalls the lessons he and Memo had in school, and the prayer "so simple and slow I could recognize / every word from my childhood" (7–8), reminds the speaker of his own boyhood imaginings of Central America. He muses that before the conquest, "Central America / must have been a quetzal, a young bird" (11–12). The poem goes on to contemplate the deep past.

As occurs repeatedly in the collection, Archila returns his imagery seemingly instantly to Central America from the US. What is different in "Bird" is that the speaker forces the reader to also experience Central America—on an L.A. bus. The stanzas shift to a pair of commands to the reader. First, we are told to "Look at the fold out map" (15) and see the quetzal in the image. The speaker confidently asserts, "you can see its beak" (17). The map becomes the bird, and we are set back in time, "before Christ," "before Columbus" (9–10). Then we are commanded to "Study the topography" (21). In doing this, the map becomes the *place*:

> Study the topography
> and the land rises out of the water,
> names of rivers, roads sprawled
> over the graphs. You can follow the train
> on rails of night, around coffee mountains,
> through dark fields of corn, cane,
> along rooftops burned red,
> away from the soft lights of a brick house. (21–28)

The graphs and names and roads dissolve as the stanza continues, as the speaker again asserts with certainty that the reader can experience the place on the ground, in the present. All that is required is to "look" and to "study," to recognize the existence of this region from one's seat on a

Lincoln Heights-bound bus, or one's seat while reading the poem. Archila utilizes prepositional phrases to move us quickly through the country and from the deep past to the present, demonstrating how easily one
can inhabit the space if one would only try. The combination of senses
involved in the journey—the visual images of red rooftops and soft lights,
the taste of corn and cane—embody the experience of this place.

The "young bird" the speaker first sees is a quetzal from pre-Columbian
times. In the next stanza however, we meet a bird who is pierced by the
"black ball" of a shotgun, symbolizing how the isthmus is currently torn by
war. The stanza hinges on this death, exhorting the reader, again, to "imagine / that before insects, before the slow crumble / of bones," the region's
"legs stretch out, back curves, / beak rises as though in flight." The use of
"its" allows the reader to imagine that the bird that has just been pierced
is flying again, to equate the present bird to the mythical one. Once more
we are commanded to "Search graves and ruins" for the pyramids and
"ancient stones" of pre-Columbian Central America.

Having begun on an L.A. bus, the poem has taken the reader to ancient
Central America, then contemporary Central America, then ancient
Central America again. Now we return to the present and to the first-
person voice of the speaker (having forgotten where we are):

> I go back to the boy, black hair,
> long brown nose, silver cross around his neck,
> books closed, zipped in his backpack.
> He holds a sugarcane stick,
> stripping the peel with his teeth. We sit
> for another minute or two
> while the great city cranks ahead.

The description is devoid of the figurative, vivid language that characterized the earlier stanzas depicting Central America. The stanza moves
from the boy's hair to his nose to his neck to his teeth, in almost a parody
of the two descriptions of the quetzal, which move first down and then
up the bird's body. Despite the straightforward language, the description
carries symbolic weight. The boy reflects the Native American features
of pre-Columbian Central America, but his objects point to the *conquis-
tadores* as his other forebears. His books in his backpack, metonymic of
knowledge, though importantly they are "zipped in" and "closed," and a
sugarcane stick in his hand, which he holds and is "stripping," evocative
of centuries of colonization, plantation economies with their cash crops,

and slavery, transform the boy into both Spanish conqueror and Native Central American. In short, it is the description of a mestizo.

This boy is representative of the isthmus, but his displacement here in L.A. is decidedly unpoetic, dwarfed by "the great city" that "cranks ahead." The present in the United States is concrete and matter-of-fact, far less evocative than the present of Central America we were asked to witness. Yet the poem has returned to the first-person point of view it opened with, when it was firmly set in Los Angeles. This syntactical shift suggests that this location, on the bus, is far more real to the speaker than the geography he is literally commanding the reader to experience. The pronoun and subject change indicate the speaker's potential desperation in getting the reader, and perhaps himself as well, to "imagine" that place so far from his current location.

That current location is precisely given, as the next stanza tells us that "At Broadway and Daily [*sic*[7]]," the boy gets off the bus. The speaker's eyes follow him, as he runs, spreading his arms wide, "before I lose him from the yellow window of my seat." The boy moves past a crowd returning home from work, around a corner store and past a mailbox: again, the descriptions are nouns without adjectives, devoid of sensory detail, focusing on the objects in the landscape. We are still moving quickly, but the richness of that first journey through the Salvadoran countryside is lost.

Then the boy, "arms spread apart, / chest forward," like a bird, calls to the speaker's mind a figure that is exploring, discovering:

> He had the same gaze that glides
> over the ocean, same bearing of a flight
> over a sailing ship breaking waves,
> a lookout manning a crow's nest.
> For miles, you can hear a voice calling out,
> "Bird! Land at first sight."

The poem crafts deliberate confusion about what the "same gaze" and "same bearing" refer to. The anaphora of "over," when added to the boy's posture as flying, at first suggests he has become the quetzal of the poem. The third and fourth line converts the image, as "a lookout manning" makes the boy a sailor and explorer. The juxtaposition of "manning" and "crow's nest" further separates the boy-as-explorer from the bird imagery he was associated with just a line or two before. We seem to have returned to the moment of conquest and first contact, merely imagined in the second stanza. There it was devoid of characters, but here it is "manned." The speaker is able to see the history of Central America in the bearing of this boy.

The poem returns to the second-person command to the reader in its last stanza, calling into question the speaker's vision. The final lines offer the third and last reference to a bird: "For miles, you can hear a voice calling out, / 'Bird! Land at first sight.'" The phrasing allows the possibility for the lookout to recognize Central America as an exotic bird, yet his position as watcher, the ship as one of conquest, and the earlier descriptions of the times after Columbus suggest we take this "bird" ironically, as the harbinger of *La Conquista*. The generic "land at first sight" erases the specificity of the isthmus—any land will do, and "first sight" obviously ignores the vision of the land possessed by its current inhabitants. Two ways of seeing Central America will soon clash. Yet the speaker can still imagine both points of view.

Or can he? The poem switches in the last two lines to "you," which throughout the poem has indicated the speaker's uncertainty or his desire to will an image into existence. He tells us, "For miles, you can hear a voice calling out," but why does the speaker distance this voice from his own first-person narrative? The dislocations of the speaker and the boy, both displaced from their homelands, both on a bus heading toward the "great city," have interrupted their versions of history and the speaker's narrative of the isthmus. The "you" of the poem is an Anglophone reader and most likely an Angeleno, familiar with Lincoln Heights, but unfamiliar with the geography of Central America. The speaker needs this reader to imagine his former home, yet he also needs to imagine it again himself, to capture it as it grows more tenuous.

By placing the mestizo boy in the role of conqueror, and the speaker as the reader's tour guide for a Central America now extinct, the poem demonstrates that both histories—the indigenous prehistory, and the Columbian "modern" history—persist within these L.A. Central Americans. The setting, on a bus heading into one locus of immigrant Latinx L.A., Lincoln Heights, suggests that this trajectory of conquest, and, perhaps more crucially, the internalization of the perspective of the colonizer, has led both the man and boy to their current home, which indeed, as they acclimate and transform the spaces around them, informed by their imaginings of the pre-Columbian Central America that is *also* their inheritance, they might experience as a process of colonizing.

Figurative language offers Archila a method for attempting to conjure his former home, which he recognizes is under erasure in the face of his adopted city but is still seemingly powerless to stop from fading as he gains belonging in his new country. Two poems set in the Eastside, "Drinking Beer in East L.A." and "This Is for Henry," develop the poet's slow path to becoming part of this manmade, concrete landscape. "Drinking Beer in East L.A." is full of evocative (if stereotypical) imagery of East Los Angeles—low riders, hot pavement, smog, Latinos sprawled on a car hood like "lions in the heat"; Archila appears to have gained the capacity to describe his new setting with imagery approaching the richness he normally reserves for the isthmus. However, the poem is in the third person, indicating that the speaker as a lyrical "I" is uneasy at this point in the collection with treating his new city as an object of poetic language.

"This Is for Henry" (34–35) takes on the first person, and we have the poet remembering the past *in* L.A., thinking back to his teen years as a grown man. Still, the speaker is unable to connect people to Los Angeles's natural landscape: they continue to be tied to the inorganic aspect of the city. The boys of East L.A. are leaning and rising above trash cans and beer bottles and their own baggy clothes (18–20). In the speaker's present he has become a teacher, and here too he is linked to the material world: with "fingers of chalk, papers piled around me" (57), he has dissolved into the manmade elements that dominate his day-to-day life. His shift in belonging to his new environment—Los Angeles—and to a new language—English—is complete.

Yet while Archila captures the quintessential L.A. barrios of Lincoln Heights and East L.A., home to a historic and vibrant Mexican/Chicanx culture, Archila did not grow up there. In fact, he grew up in "the Valley," a smoggy stretch of northeast Los Angeles marked by the absence of a cohesive neighborhood identity. How, why, and *when* his own neighborhood appears in his writing is the focus of my barriography. In the enterprise I am aided by Archila's own thoughtful descriptions and remarks on his childhood hometown, as well as the parts of L.A. he has elected to call home.

Van Nuys Barriography

Given his poems about Lincoln Heights and East L.A., I was surprised to learn that William Archila actually grew up in Van Nuys, just down the street from my own home away from home. Most breaks from teaching find me there, staying with my sister, a longtime Angeleno (Angelena?), her family, and our mother. Van Nuys, now a somewhat down-in-the-mouth L.A. neighborhood in the San Fernando Valley, is more accustomed to being the punchline of a joke than the subject of poetry. Yet my Van Nuys is quite different from the one Archila grew up in. The poet was kind enough to send me a "mini memoir" describing his experience of this adopted hometown growing up:

> In the early eighties the San Fernando Valley in LA County had an air of success with its hundreds of square miles of low-rise commercial establishments and its straight, broad boulevards. Every corner had a gas station or a mini mall, equipped with a liquor store or burger joint. Each sidewalk was a path of cement, nicely cut. The lawns were green and well-manicured. . . . Each ranch house, often with its rustic shake roof and broad porch, its citrus trees and sparkling swimming pools, conjured the feel of a perfect neighborhood in a modern world. Even up-and-coming Hollywood Stars featured in horror movies lived in Van Nuys. The valley seemed to me a slight version of the many suburbs I had watched in TV shows like *Adam 12*. Kids rode their skateboards or bikes from school in their ski jackets. Their parents came home in the evenings in cars big as boats. Through the curtained windows, the yellow lamps went on. Around eight or nine the streets were almost empty, maybe a few cars here and there going home, maybe a kid or two in the back with a Rubik's Cube. (Archila, Electronic correspondence)

Coming from a small city in El Salvador at twelve years old, the modernity and promise of Van Nuys must have been striking. In reality, Van Nuys had been a town since 1911, when real estate developer Isaac Van Nuys sold off lots of the land in an afternoon auction (Van Nuys Neighborhood Council). The neighborhood evolved into a booming residential area, lined with tract homes, after World War II, when airplane manufacturing gained momentum (Van Nuys airport today is still a busy general aviation hub), and General Motors opened their Chevrolet factory in Van Nuys in 1946. In the early 1980s the town was predominantly Anglo and fairly middle-class: just the image of the American Dream Archila had seen on TV as a little kid.

Van Nuys today is a study in uneven development and the fraught pursuit of that American Dream. When my sister moved to Van Nuys in 2017, it was because it was the only place her family, like many aspirant middle-class Angeleno families, could afford to buy a house in the city. Data indicates that Van Nuys home prices are significantly lower than in the larger city of Los Angeles: in 2013, the median housing value for homes in Van Nuys was at $407,621 compared to Los Angeles City's

$513,618 (Miguel and Chhea[8]). Van Nuys's housing market also has twice the number of homes within the $300,000–399,999 price range than the city of L.A. (Miguel and Chhea). The old suburban-yet-still-urban L.A. dream Archila describes, with a backyard, a ranch-style layout, a pool, and a garage, is still within reach for some in Van Nuys.

Yet these pieces of real estate are in the midst of an urban decay that Archila began to experience in the 1990s.[9] For the poet the change to his neighborhood felt stark and swift: "the cold autumn chill of the 80's had vanished, and an intense, oppressive heat had settled. It seemed as though the cold wind and soft rustling of leaves of the 80's had become nothing but traffic, smog, crowds and the perpetual heatwave" (Archila, Electronic correspondence). Archila describes a demographic shift and notes that, in response to "the changes in race," "the city government was no longer concerned with infrastructure and building regulations and development, public health, and other community services. Dilapidated apartment buildings in Van Nuys became the norm and the Valley slowly resembled a community in economic and demographic decline and I was part of it" (Archila, Electronic correspondence). As "one of the new residents, with a new language in my pocket," Archila is compelled to become part of this urban landscape that has already lost the promise of the American Dream.

Along with the ample number of single-family homes, the poor air quality, noise pollution, crime, vagrancy, and concrete squalor keep prices less inflated than in other housing markets in the city. The real estate market is markedly mixed: starter homes are sprinkled throughout a community of apartment complexes, a few which take up entire city blocks. Apartment residents will lay out goods for purchase in the front yard or leave out goods to be disposed of on the sidewalk. Street vendors with food carts take up the corner across from the elementary school, the high school, and the church on Sherman Way. On our street (Valerio), delivered packages left in sight are imperiled. My mom began sorting the recycling so that a separate bag with aluminum cans sits on top, to save the homeless who come by the night before trash pickup the time spent riffling through garbage to collect cans to turn in for coins. My sister pulls up the outdoor couch cushions every night to prevent the neighborhood's feral cats from sullying them. My infant niece (or really, all of us) sleeps with a white-noise machine on to drown out the nighttime sounds of helicopters, fireworks, car backfires, and dogs barking. Even still, property values increase.

Mike Davis's description of "post-liberal" Los Angeles's "obsession with physical security systems" and "the architectural policing of social boundaries" applies easily to Van Nuys, where this "master narrative" of urban restructuring has been at work since the 1990s (223). The elementary schools and high schools (Van Nuys High School, Fulton Preparatory, and Valerio Street Elementary, where *abuela* walks my nephew to preschool) resemble prisons from the outside: few windows, tall chain-link and barbed wire fencing, concrete slabs for recess. Those middle-class starter homes are generally kept behind iron gates and walled perimeters. When architecture fails, the LAPD come in. Homeless encampments, such as at the intersection of Valerio Street and Van Nuys or lining the bike path that runs along the Orange Line Busway, are periodically swept by police.

East from the house on Valerio Street, that small homeless encampment lines the sidewalk,[10] across from a 7-Eleven, a Salvadoran *pupusería*, and Ay Papá Que Rico, a Cuban restaurant (manned by Dominicans). Nearby is the Super King, a grocery store with Latin American, Armenian, Persian, and Asian staples: spoken languages proliferate. The market fronts Sherman Way, a main thoroughfare lined with people waiting for the bus, and the occasional pair of Latina Jehovah's Witnesses, sitting in folding chairs by the curb, with pamphlets in Spanish they are ready to show you. South on Kester, near the Busway and Orange line, there's a designated corner for Latino day laborers to be picked up. I once jogged past that corner later in the day and found instead a small group of young Black men rapping and dancing.

My sister found a YouTube video that captures the feel of Van Nuys. "Van Nuys Tourism Video" is a 2010 parody of tourism ads by a local man (from nearby Canoga Park), "Dr Jedly." An intentionally off-key song about the attributes of the town is paired with video clips of graffiti, homeless and teenagers pushing full shopping carts, Latin American immigrant families crossing the street, a park full of kids' parties (a "moon bounce battleground"), men on corners holding up advertising signs, the ubiquitous strip malls with gold shops and fast food, food cart vendors ("eat corn sold on the street!"), sidewalk and lawn sales, and stolen police cars. The landscape is full of battered, abandoned, older cars; busy streets; unkempt vacant (yet fenced) lots; and pedestrians engaged in sidewalk commerce, selling and buying clothes, food, sundry items, to fill a plastic bag or a purloined shopping cart. This is not the picture of the "American Dream" as it is generally conceived.

Technically, Van Nuys is a barrio, as close to a majority of its residents speak Spanish as their dominant language (according to the 2018 American Community Survey for Northwest L.A. County, which includes North Hills, Sherman Oaks, and Van Nuys). As of 2018, Latina/os make up 65.7

percent of the population of Van Nuys (Statistical Atlas). As of 2013, of the 47 percent of the neighborhood that is foreign born, 71 percent come from Latin America: 32 percent from Mexico, 18 percent from El Salvador, and 12 percent from Guatemala. Greater Los Angeles conversely only has a 39 percent foreign-born population. Only around 5 percent of the Latino/as in Van Nuys speak English only, and over 50 percent speak English "less than very well" (Miguel and Chhea). The neighborhood reflects Mexican and Central American spatial ordering in its use of sidewalks and public recreation areas, and the prevalence of Spanish spoken, of Latin American restaurants and businesses, and of Spanish-language churches all contribute to its character as a barrio. Lincoln Heights' proportion of Latino/as is barely higher (70 percent versus 66 percent), and Echo Park's is actually lower (at 52 percent) (Statistical Atlas). So why does Archila's poetry eschew his hometown for other barrios like Lincoln Heights and Echo Park?

The answer is because of the deep history of the Latinx neighborhoods on the Eastside. As we saw in chapters 1 and 2, places like El Monte and East Los Angeles (which is a whopping *96.4 percent* Hispanic/Latinx [Statistical Atlas]) have had sizable Mexican populations since their beginnings. Other areas of L.A. County, including Lincoln Heights, Echo Park, and Boyle Heights, were shaped by the same forces of gentrification and labor exploitation that compelled Mexican and Chicanx migration out of Sonoratown[11] and into the city outskirts and brought thousands of workers from Mexico to build railroads and trolley lines. The poet describes his time in Van Nuys as being "stuck," "without a sense of culture, identity, or center" (Foster), so, upon returning to L.A. to teach after graduate school, he gravitates to East L.A., which "always held a sense of history and culture that the San Fernando Valley lacked" (Archila, Electronic correspondence).

Van Nuys, by contrast, is a newer barrio. In just thirty years, from 1980 to 2010, Van Nuys went from being majority white to majority Latinx. According to the 2010 Decennial Census, in this time frame the Latinx population practically tripled, while non-Hispanic whites went from 70 percent to 25 percent of the neighborhood, making them a minority in the region for the first time since its founding (Colvin). By 1980, barrios like East L.A. were already well established, having become majority Latinx as early as World War II. Van Nuys' Latina/os were also not monolithic: about half hailed from the Northern Triangle, as opposed to Mexico; in contrast, the original Latinx populations of Eastside barrios were almost wholly Mexican, so that newer Salvadoran or Guatemalan immigrants to those neighborhoods in the late twentieth century *join* a preexisting Latinx community rather than establish it.

The *Los Angeles Times* reported in 1991 that "the increase in the ethnic diversity of the San Fernando Valley during the 1980s was remarkably widespread, with minorities moving in greater numbers to virtually every block of every street in every community" (Colvin). The article cites multiple causes for the white flight: the construction of thousands of new apartment units and affordable housing projects that drew the nonwhite working class from their "traditional enclaves" in the northeast Valley, the frustration with failing schools, and the increasing displeasure of Anglo valley residents with crowding, traffic, smog, crime, and high housing prices (Colvin). Donald Schultz, the Van Nuys Homeowner Association vice president, is quoted as saying that many Valley residents "would move out if they could," blaming what he saw as the deterioration of the neighborhood to "overdevelopment, overcrowding, too many apartments, and far too many undocumented, illegal aliens"[12] (Colvin).

Archila lived through Van Nuys's precipitous demographic change. When his family first arrive, they move into an apartment building where they are the only nonwhites, along with a single Mexican family. Yet "suddenly a Guatemalan family followed." By the late 1990s, Archila notes, "the Valley had become a multi-racial community with immigrants from faraway places such as Mexico, El Salvador, Guatemala, Iran, Israel, Armenia, Vietnam and other Asian countries. . . . Suddenly, the white population was decreasing, and a non-white majority moved in. The Hispanic and Latino population had become the majority" (Archila, Electronic correspondence). The closing of the GM factory in 1992 further accelerated white flight, and the continued construction of new housing units encouraged more recent immigrants to make the Valley home.

By the mid-1990s, Van Nuys has become majority Latinx. Yet while Archila is part of the diaspora, he does not identify with his new landscape and his fellow immigrants within it—not yet. The very newness of the neighborhood, and its residents, reinforces the rootlessness Archila feels as a refugee. To be around others who have fled war and persecution turns the neighborhood into a shelter, a haven seemingly marked by its temporary nature. Van Nuys also lacks the cohesiveness of a barrio because its residents are part of multiple diasporas. Like Héctor Tobar's Little Armenia in the same time frame, too many displaced cultures inhabit the same space for a unified Salvadoran or even Central American community to emerge. Furthermore, Archila is encouraged, even compelled, to assimilate to a greater extent than are Latinx transnational populations who maintain economic ties to their country of origin: "Going back home meant death, so assimilation was the only answer" (Archila, Electronic correspondence). His family's status as undocumented only compounded this pressure to forget and rebuild; Archila tells an interviewer that "since we had the fear of being deported," "it was very very clear that we had to learn the culture, learn the language, and basically burn bridges, forget about what happened back there in El Salvador, and just move on" (Archila, Interview by Mariano Zaro). Although he is grateful to be in the US, his experience of the educational system further alienates him from his own status as an immigrant: "In the process of my Americanization, the cultural cleansing, and institutionalized education, I literally went numb" (Archila, Electronic correspondence).

When Archila does put down roots, he seeks out the oldest and most established Latinx neighborhoods in the city: Archila moves to Echo Park and begins his first teaching job at Lincoln High School in Lincoln Heights. In his as-yet-unpublished memoir, he describes immersing himself in "the oldest neighborhood outside of downtown": "Many attempts were made to connect with the Eastside, a community with the highest Latino population in Los Angeles County. Many, many trips were made to Self Help Graphics, a community arts center that has long nurtured noted Latino artists. I was there for some Chicano art, for the annual Day of the Dead festivities, murals that harken back to the days of Diego Rivera and Frida Kahlo. It was my personal struggle to relive the glory days of the cultural renaissance that accompanied the Chicano Movement" (Archila, Electronic correspondence). In the *Los Angeles Review of Books,* he details the scenes of his commute from Angelino Heights to Lincoln Heights, full of Chicanx touchstones: "the walking mother and child . . . old men in their cowboy hats and buckles, mama from Shang-Hai already walking home with her bulging plastic bags from the grocery store, young men in baggy pants and black shades, wearing black sweaters with the letters RIP, In Memory of My Primo Payaso, and girls with their thick, heavy red lips, long curly strands of hair" (Foster). The barrio offered an anchor of Latin American culture and the potential promise of belonging for Archila. Indeed, he gives his first poetry reading at Onyx in Echo Park, becoming part of the artistic community he yearned for.

These barrios found their way into Archila's poetry. In "An Empty Classroom in Lincoln Heights," a poem anthologized in *Another City: Writing from Los Angeles,* the poet describes his students' parents bent over sewing machines or laying bricks and imagines how these young bodies will curve into those same shapes as Los Angeles funnels them into its exploited labor class (Ulin 257–58). Three of the poems in *The Art of Exile*, "Bird," "This Is for Henry," and "Drinking Beer in East LA," are written while the author is living in a 1930s bungalow in Angelino Heights and are set in the Eastside. We saw in "Bird" how the speaker saw the faces of Latin America on North Broadway; "This Is for Henry" and "Drinking Beer in East LA" both capture glimpses of the barrio cholo culture of baggy pants, tricked-out rides, and outdoor posturing.

Yet the history of Mexicans in L.A. is not Archila's history. The poet muses in our interview that he had "too much Central America" in him to claim East L.A.'s Chicanx roots as his own. When he returns to the city in 2010 after his MFA in Oregon, he seeks out his fellow Central Americans. Although he settles in Tujunga, near Highland Park, a formerly Chicanx but fast-gentrifying part of northeast L.A. (where the Archilas were able to buy a home), his new teaching job is in Westlake, the part of downtown L.A. where Antonio and Longoria live in Héctor Tobar's *The Tattooed Soldier*, the contemporary epicenter, along with adjoining Pico-Union, of Central American immigration. Archila notes that in 2016 at Belmont High School in Westlake (right next to the tunnel entrance from *The Tattooed Soldier!*) 40 percent of the one thousand students enrolled were of Central American origin, and a majority of those were unaccompanied minors (Foster). As someone who described himself as "somewhere in between, disoriented in the middle, navigating through a dual liminal space" (Archila, Electronic correspondence), for whom Van Nuys was a symbol of homelessness but East L.A. was ultimately *too* rooted, the stories of Archila's Central American refugee students resonated. He says that "over the last two years I have found myself writing about these students, their struggles, their odysseys to find a home" (Foster), as he relates his own search to belong and his own displacement to this next generation of Salvadorans, Guatemalans, and Hondurans. He again takes on the role of witness, remarking that "these kids' journeys are heroic, and their courage is a virtue necessary of recognition" (Foster). Yet in taking up their histories, he is also in effect honoring his own.

Perhaps as part of this claiming of his own immigration story, Archila is slowly returning to his first hometown of Van Nuys. When I asked why he doesn't write about Van Nuys in *The Art of Exile*, Archila responded that "at the time I did not see a great narrative in Van Nuys. I did not see the poetry in it. I think it was too personal and too painful." As a place linked to a prolonged sense of uprootedness and the pressure to become "American," the area was left behind somewhat in Archila's quest for belonging. Van Nuys certainly doesn't offer the sense of historic community that East L.A. does for its Latinx residents, nor does it have the monocultural majority necessary to form a colonia like Westlake. Van Nuys is also, simply, ugly. Bereft of the charms of old Victorian housing (like Angelino Heights or Crown Hill) or community-oriented public parks (like Echo Park or MacArthur Park), pockmarked with freeways and cut up by massive thoroughfares (Van Nuys Boulevard itself runs eight lanes of traffic through the neighborhood), the neighborhood can offer neither cohesive ethnic solidarity nor aesthetic relief for a poet seeking both. Perhaps unsurprisingly, Archila find himself "gravitating towards Van Nuys and my American upbringing" in his "attempts at writing prose" (Archila, Electronic correspondence). It may be that prose's freedom from a requisite level of beauty allows Archila to come back to the area. Or that now, having forged belonging through writing, he feels sufficiently healed to look back upon a painful place in his past.

Archila's true home, however, is not Van Nuys or Lincoln Heights or even Tujunga (though that last is the closest): as *The Art of Exile*'s epigraph tells us, "Language is the only homeland," and, as we will see, Archila finds his place through poetry.

"Language Is the Only Homeland"

In the next section of the collection, we see how the inorganic character of American life gives the poet the distance from personal experience he needs to be able to write about the past. The third section, "After Ashes," is the longest poem of the collection. Each of the first three sections contains multiple dedications: "for my immigrant father, . . . for my uncle, . . . for my mother" (Archila, *Art of Exile* 59), "for Father Martínez" (61), "for this earth" (62). As elsewhere in this portion of the book, many of these persons and things are transported back to El Salvador, as past imagery interrupts the descriptions of present surroundings. It is unclear what is being dedicated to these entities—the ashes? the poems themselves?— until the fourth and final section, which begins with a single line: "This is exactly where I want to be" (63).

Given all the displacement of the past three sections, this statement is intentionally ambiguous. The stanzas go on to emphasize this exact and suitable "where." "Here" begins in the United States, characterized by the personification of metal pipes and the train that "pulls across the city" (5). But by the fourth stanza, "here" is El Salvador. The "here" of the speaker, then, is *not* the "here" of the lines he is writing. In fact, "here" is devoid enough of intrinsic characteristics that the speaker can fully return to his homeland from his house in the US. "Here" is "where" inanimate things are personified but voiceless: the wind blows, the walls cough and groan, the train outside whistles, but none of these sounds quite approach language or spoken words. "Here" is "between the opening and closing / mouth of night": a personified object related to speech but not saying anything. This wordlessness allows the poet to transform his own words on the page into a place. The next anaphoric repetition of "it's here" achieves the transformation: free from language around him, the poet-speaker travels in his writing to another country.

The poem succeeds in arriving us in El Salvador. Now we see "all the bodies." Then, with the fulcrum of "They're mine," a strikingly offset and right-justified line standing alone, the bodies in El Salvador go from dead to alive. The final stanza refers to them in an active present, "the women and men who wear," "gather," and "learn." That the dead might revolt by raising "sticks and stones" calls to mind the playground taunt, "sticks and stones may break my bones, but words will never hurt me": these ghosts *will* harm the speaker if he does not use his words to relate their experiences. As a survivor, the speaker has a responsibility to these men and women. They have paid the physical penalty with their lives, and they threaten the poet-speaker with vengeance for not writing the words that will "give them back." The urgency of the task is cinched by the closing line, "before I am old and no longer here," which returns us to the writer's room. The speaker's mandate is clear: to use his distance from the war and the acquisition of a voice that his distance makes possible to speak of those who were left behind.

By this point in the collection, geographic displacement has become positive, and not just for ensuring the speaker's escape from war. The distance between former home and new home is *artistically* productive. It allows the poet the space needed from the land and its conflict to become a witness. However, this voice comes at a cost: the very distance that allows him to translate, literally and figuratively, his experiences of the past in El Salvador also attenuates, even severs, his closeness to that first country and culture. The writing is made possible by the poet's belonging to the world of English and inanimate objects and mechanical things that allow his imagination to go elsewhere. Archila gains the power to evoke, but only by losing his complete belonging to the place he seeks to capture with foreign words.

The final section of the collection draws in relief this double edge of being able to bear witness but becoming a stranger to one's original home. The speaker returns to El Salvador for the first time since fleeing as a refugee, ten years after the civil war. Finally back in the country that has haunted the collection, the poet-speaker seems distant from his country of origin. The opening poem of this final section, "The Art of Exile," is written in second-person singular, in the future tense, which creates space between the first-hand experience of the poet and the speaker. The title suggests the poem will serve as a primer on how to be a successful exile, and the structure of the poem imitates a manual: you will "come across," "you'll watch," "you'll curse," and then you will finally reach "the place," "when" "you have begun to speak like a man," arguably achieving the type of exile you desire: where you can return to feeling like a native in your former home.

Other elements in the poem subvert this purported distance, indicating the tension the poet-speaker feels between his expectations of return and its realities. A series of negatives intrude in the middle stanzas of the poem, revealing what was once there for the speaker, now highlighted by its absence. The stack of negative events, "no friend," "no drive," "no one," become very specific, compared to the earlier stanzas, which contained general, universal visions of the country ("a coast," "a boy," "an old woman," "on the Pan American Highway"). These negatives are just specific enough to point to the speaker's memories, demonstrating how he has drifted back into nostalgia in the face of a solitary present.

The distance between the speaker's personal experience and his academic advice to a student of exile collapses by the end of the poem. While the poem maintains its second-person singular syntactical distance, the poem slips from the future into an active present: "By nightfall, drag yourself back to the bars, / looking for a lost country in a shot of Tík Táck" (68). The phrase "lost country" indicates that Salvadoran memories are all that remain. The extended simile in the last two stanzas, where the "you" of the poem feels "torn, / twisted," and "blown / from city to city" like "an old newspaper," does not inspire confidence in the new exile's success. Print news is made in El Salvador but is highly mediated: it presents an "objective," not personal, account of the goings-on of El Salvador, and such news is published within urban centers but then circulates broadly and indiscriminately outside of the cities. The exile as newspaper thus highlights the speaker's remove from the country, his position as bystander, and the failure of his Salvadoran assimilation.

The closing lines similarly raise doubts: the speaker tells us "you have reached the place" once "you have begun to speak like a man / by the side of the road, barefoot" (68). A "torn, twisted" newspaper blown around ceases to become legible; the barefoot roadside man is perhaps illiterate: he is marked by his speech. Together, these images suggest that reaching "the place" mean abandoning the written word (or being abandoned by it) and learning how to speak aloud, to take on the voice of the country rather than the words as printed letters that circulate around it. If this is the price of reintegration it is clear the poet cannot pay it: "The Art of Exile" is a written poem, written in English, and a poem that references an "art"—a mastery of a trained skill. Thus, ultimately the notion of arrival, of being at home in one's former home country, remains elegiac.

In an interview with *Poetry.L.A.*, Archila explains that he doesn't begin writing about the war until 1992, after he returns from his trip to El Salvador. He is spurred to expression by the experience of dual exile:

> I expected to go back to my own native country, and to feel comfortable at home . . . And just feel like one of the natives. It was the complete opposite. I felt like a stranger in a strange land. . . . I felt so out of tune. Everything had changed. The landscape had changed, the people that I once knew, an entire generation was gone . . . So when I came back, I couldn't cope with those feelings. These feelings of exile, of feeling alienated, of feeling like I don't have a home, this sense of loneliness and abandonment, began to surge in me, and that's when I began consciously writing about the war. (Archila, Interview by Mariano Zaro)

The poems reflect Archila's sentiment of being "out of tune" (nod to Wordsworth there: certainly, this allusion to "The World Is Too Much with Us" is productive!), of having one's difference emphasized rather than erased, and, most crucially, the feeling of seeking a home. He adds in our own conversation together that when he went back to El Salvador he was looking "for something that no longer existed," not just lost landscapes and friends but also "a quality remembered from my childhood, a sense of belonging to a country and a language that had changed" for him when he became an immigrant. Thinking that his nation of origin was his home, and realizing it was not, compelled Archila to poetry.

Archila says he realized ultimately that "homelessness and its loneliness is the identity of the exile writer" (Electronic correspondence). To convert the isolation and longing to belong becomes the poet's raison d'etre. He returns from his alienated homecoming to Los Angeles, which for him "represent[ed] homelessness," and to his neighborhood in Van Nuys, that place "without a sense of culture, identity, or center." He felt "not quite at home" and "realized that home is neither here nor there": "I began to write, and the goal was to find a homeland" (Archila,

Electronic correspondence). The belonging Archila finds is not in El Salvador, or Lincoln Heights, or Van Nuys, but within language itself. As we
see through the journey of *The Art of Exile,* which begins in a remembered home, pushes through displacement and translation, recaptures
and remakes the past, and ultimately accepts a present that is steeped
in liminality, what home the poet can create must be built with his own
craft. "Of course," Archila says he discovers, "there is no homecoming,
except in words, phrases, the very sentences I was putting together. The
poems themselves became my homeland."

With this epiphany came kinship, as he saw in the lives of the immigrants around him, whether students at Belmont High School or fellow
commuters in Echo Park or the fearful silent undocumented of Van Nuys,
his same yearning for a place to call home, and the same need to find
words to express the state of transnational exile. He began to feel that his
words "had a strong connection with other people who had gone through
the same experience, other immigrants like me" (Archila, Interview by
Mariano Zaro). The ability to write his displacement, and to harness the
power of poetry, became both his calling and his responsibility. As a survivor, immigrant, exile, witness, and artist, he says: "I'm condemned to write
about everything that was lost" (Archila, Interview by Mariano Zaro).

PART III

EAST

Dominican New York City

"THE ONE FROM THE OTHER LIFE": THE PARTICULARITIES OF DOMINICAN TRANSNATIONALISM

In 2014, Dominicans surpassed Puerto Ricans as the largest Latinx group in metropolitan New York.[1] Today there are approximately 800,000 Dominicans in the city, over half of them living in the Bronx and Northern Manhattan; in contrast, the Dominican Republic's capital city of Santo Domingo has 965,000 people. Over half of all Dominicans in the US are foreign-born, a staggering number compared with 33 percent of other Hispanics (López). From 1990 to 2013, the number of Dominican-born US immigrants has tripled, growing 174 percent (López). By 1980, 73 percent of all Dominicans in the US lived in New York City (Hernández and Rivera-Batíz). Today, almost half (42 percent) of all US Dominicans live in New York, and next-door New Jersey is the runner-up at 15 percent (Noe-Bustamante et. al.). So how did Dominican New York, and *Dominican Yorks*, come to be? While the Dominican Republic shares a history of colonization, unwanted US and foreign interventionism, aggressive exploitation, and corporate expansion with many of its Caribbean neighbors, a combination of social, political, economic, and legal circumstances has made the Dominican diaspora begin later and go on longer and stronger than the rest of the Hispanic Caribbean.

The Dominican Republic's diaspora[2] is often held up as *the* global exemplar for "narrow" transnationalism (Duany 169). Of the three Spanish-speaking countries of the Caribbean islands, it has received the most attention from migration scholars as the representative example of a transnational nation-state (3). The Dominican Republic offers its own unique paradigm of Latinx transnationalism, as Cuba disallowed return for decades and Puerto Rico's status as a protectorate of the US makes it a distinct case politically. In contrast to other Latin-American immigrant groups, "Dominican migrants exemplify a more institutionalized and habitual engagement with their country of origin"; this means that Dominicans in the New York metropolitan area call home, travel, and especially send money more frequently than all other Latinx groups

(231). In turn, the level of remittances received by the Dominican Republic is extremely high, compared to other Latin American and Caribbean
nations: in 2009 the DR was the sixth-largest destination for remittances
in the Americas (212). The Dominican Republic legally acknowledged
this economic dependence with its approval of dual citizenship in 1994.
Dominicans in the US also have one of the lowest naturalization rates
among recent migrants, at 48.2 percent (83). These trends lead Jorge
Duany to assert: "the Dominican Republic is a full-fledged transnational
nation-state, encompassing its diaspora to a much larger extent than
either Cuba or Puerto Rico" (170).

This "narrow" transnationalism can be partially explained by the
history of Dominican immigration to the United States. While there
have always been Dominicans in New York City—the first documented
immigrant is Juan Rodriguez, an Afro-Dominican who arrived in Hudson Harbor in 1613, when the area was still New Amsterdam (Lissardy)—
the diaspora was spurred in the late 1950s and early 1960s by General
Rafael Leónidas Trujillo's dictatorship, his assassination, and the political fallout. The Dominican Republic pattern of immigration initially followed broader Caribbean trends, joining other diasporas of the Hispanic
Caribbean as part of a post-1965 migrant wave to the US from Latin
American, Caribbean, and Asian countries, spurred on by an increasing
demand for cheap labor in northeastern US cities and changes to US
immigration policy such as the 1965 Hart-Cellar act, which abolished
national origin quotas (Duany 38).[3] However, Dominican immigration
increased in the 1970s, 1980s, and 1990s, when immigrations from other
countries in the Hispanic Caribbean had slowed considerably. More
than 400,000 Dominicans legally immigrated to the US between 1961
and 1990 (J. Gonzalez 117), about 10 percent of the country's entire population (Atkins and Wilson 161). Compared to Cubans and Puerto Ricans,
Dominican population movements are relatively recent, with more than
98 percent of Dominicans being admitted to the US after 1961 (174).
The Dominican diaspora thus outstripped and outlasted other waves
of Caribbean immigration, even despite worsening economic conditions: "Although historically net immigration has often slowed, or even
reversed direction, in times of economic distress, the number of documented Dominican immigrants admitted to the United States rose" by
almost 35 percent from the 1970s to the early 1990s (Hoffnung-Garskof
202). Dominican immigration to the US peaked during the 1990s and
then leveled off during the early twenty-first century. These late waves of

immigration mean the majority of Dominicans in the US are still members of the first generation, which presents a different paradigm for the Dominican diaspora and helps explain why they maintain such "strong transnational attachments" (Duany 174).

Immigration laws further strengthened these attachments. The US's 1965 Immigration Reform Act restricted new Latin American immigration, creating a backlog for visas in Santo Domingo, as new immigrants needed sponsorship by US employers. However, the restrictions exempted immediate family members of already admitted immigrants: this provision "unintentionally put [Dominicans], with their recent surge in settlement in the United States, in a relatively privileged position to apply for now-scarce Western Hemisphere visas" (Hoffnung-Garskof 91). As a result of their later waves of immigration, Dominicans were in a unique situation to benefit from transnational ties, and the law's family exemption resulted in transmigrants expanding the definition of family, broadening kinship networks to maximize economic and social gains. Already inclined to maintain ties to the island as a result of more recent immigration, racial discrimination in the US, and the possibility of pronounced social and economic advancement back in the Dominican Republic, transmigrants now also had a legislative incentive to build extended kinship networks across national boundaries (91).

For Caribbean immigrants, especially those of African descent, the oppressiveness of the US racial paradigm reinforces transnational processes, and this shared burden encouraged early alliances between Dominicans and Puerto Ricans in New York City (J. Gonzalez 124). As new immigrants of color relocating to a country plagued by institutional racism, "they face the very real prospect of having their educational or economic achievements dismissed or devalued by inhabitants of the host society" (Pessar 4). As a result, the "continuing racial ordering of the United States" often deters Afro-Caribbean immigrants from fully severing ties to their nation of origin, as transmigrants continue identifying with a home nation whose racial paradigm is more conducive to social mobility (Basch et al. 234). Hoffnung-Garskof asserts that racial discrimination profoundly influences Dominican migrants' national identifications, citing as evidence a 1980 *New York Times* survey showing that five out of every six Dominican New Yorkers considered their "home" to be in the Dominican Republic (195).[4] Another key to the social impetus for continued transnational movement among Caribbean immigrants is thus the desire to evade the US's xenophobia and racial prejudice.

Diasporic Gender Norms

Dominican transnationalism has produced undeniable effects upon gender norms both on and off the island. In their study of three generations of Dominican female immigrants, Rosie Soy and Stefan Bosworth find that, historically, women in the DR were rigidly limited in their opportunities for education and employment: "The patriarchal ideology of the culture did not encourage women to work outside the home but find work that relatively limited them to the home environment and maintained their family obligations. In Dominican culture the mother and other female relatives had traditionally been responsible for child-rearing and taking care of *la casa,* the home" (3).

However, due to a gendered disparity in job opportunities abroad, and a contemporary trend toward matrifocal households (where mother and children form the nuclear unit), Dominican women immigrate at a higher rate than men (Soy and Bosworth 11). A 2006 study found that the ratio of female to male migration was 0.70 in the Dominican Republic, much higher than the 0.30–0.39 of Mexico or Costa Rica: "Indeed, within several marital categories, female householders are actually *more likely* than their male counterparts to migrate to the United States" (Massey et al.). Hoffnung-Garskof has argued that this migration to the United States profoundly impacts the dynamics of gender relations in Dominican homes, as "migrant women often had the freedom to work, travel unescorted, and make household and financial decisions for the first time" (168). In his case studies of Hispanic Caribbean households in New York City, Jorge Duany found that, while Dominican women were more likely to fulfill traditional gender roles such as the "emotional, caring, and ritual work required to maintain kinship bonds between home and diaspora communities," this entailed less traditionally female activities such as frequent travel unescorted to the island, incorporation into a paid labor force, and increased individual autonomy to make decisions on behalf of the family, often as the head of a single-person household. Dominican female authority becomes greatly amplified in the US: from the late 1980s to the mid-2000s Dominican women headed 56 percent of all households, with or without husbands present, and barely half of all Dominican households were nuclear families; the rest were extended families or single-person households (Duany 205). In many cases, wives and mothers were temporarily separated from their husbands and children. In 2009, Dominicans had the highest proportion of female-headed households in New York City, at 39.1 percent, higher than All

Hispanics (28.7), Non-Hispanic Whites (7.2), and non-Hispanic Blacks (32.5) (Duany, table 8.2, 178).

The perception of the shift in Dominican family structure in the US divides fairly cleanly along gender lines and can be seen in male and female Dominican transmigrants' differing stance on repatriation. Multiple studies find that Dominican women are far less likely to desire to return permanently to the island, whereas Dominican men are generally in favor of return. Hoffnung-Garskof argues that for many migrant men "the loss of status in the family was part of the nostalgia for home, the return to a 'Dominican family,'" whereas "migrant women told researchers in the 1980s that they resisted their husbands' plans to return to Santo Domingo because they did not relish a return to a traditional home life" (Hoffnung-Garskof 168). In his 1991 study on reverse migration from the US to the Dominican Republic, Luis Eduardo Guarnizo found that a full one-quarter of women, compared to just one-seventh of men, reported that they would have preferred to stay abroad rather than resettle in the Dominican Republic (Guarnizo 27). Milagros Ricourt's research shows that while the majority of Dominican immigrants who identified as either fully Dominican or fully transmigratory are men, only five women out of twenty-five considered themselves to be temporary residents in the United States (22). In decisions to repatriate, "more than nine of every ten males took the initiative themselves to go back to the island, compared to fewer than half of females" (Guarnizo 28).

This resistance to return on the part of women is generally interpreted as their desire to maintain the increased freedoms and the "more egalitarian relations between men and women" they achieved in the United States (Duany 205). Sociologists universally agree that men are more likely than women to plan to return to the Dominican Republic to reestablish conventional patterns of male authority, whereas women are loath to relinquish the social and economic gains made by immigrating to the US.[5] Upon return to the Dominican Republic, traditional household structures are often implemented, which points to the primary male impetus for repatriation. In his study, Guarnizo sees a "stark contrast" in the way household economies function in the US and at home, finding that even though the chief strategy for Dominican households abroad was resource pooling, when transmigrant families returned to the republic, "husbands recuperated their primacy as the dominant breadwinners in migrants' households (54.2%) and resource pooling became the second most common practice (31.3%)" (Guarnizo 38). When women *did* decide in favor of repatriation, the reasons for their return were markedly different: "23.6 percent of women found family obligations to be the principal factor affecting their decision, whereas half that proportion of men did so. Conversely, whereas 43.2 percent of men felt driven primarily to their own personal preference in their resolve to return, only 25.5 percent of women did so" (Guarnizo 28). The studies find that, in contrast to men, women generally repatriated *despite* individual preference, rather than as a result of it.

Diasporic Identity

The diaspora's close ties to urban New York City, the uncontested center of Dominican immigration (Hoffnung-Garskof 5), create an additional cultural idiosyncrasy of Dominican transnationalism. While generally Caribbean transmigrants are greeted positively by their community in their country of origin, in the late twentieth century, Dominican gains abroad translated back on the island with a loss of *cultura,* lack of patriotism, and even participation in the drug trade: "many Caribbean immigrants must await resettlement in their countries of origin before their economic gains and social advancement are generally acknowledged. The Dominican case, however, diverges from this pattern. . . . Rather than being lauded and welcomed, returnees are frequently stigmatized as un-Dominican, nouveau-riche, and drug dealers" (Pessar 4). After the Dominican Republic's severe economic downturn in the 1980s, transmigrants went from being perceived as the plucky and resourceful rural "path breakers" and "quasi-heroes" of the 1970s to becoming stereotyped as explicitly urban (and thus already tainted by US acculturation): Santo Domingo barrio residents who migrated to achieve speedy capital accumulation, abandoning the republic during its economic crises (Guarnizo 46). The term *"Dominican York"* became a pejorative on the island, insinuating that Dominican migrants to metropolitan New York become more American than Dominican and were more loyal to the US.

Transmigrants often repatriate to their countries of origin to gain social capital. However, as transmigrancy took on negative connotations in the Dominican Republic, Dominican migrants found themselves stigmatized in *both* places: "[W]hen Dominican New Yorkers turned home seeking refuge from their low social status in New York, they found an ambivalent welcome. Dominican New Yorkers thus faced the question of their belonging in the Dominican Republic simultaneously with the question of their racial and class status in New York" (Hoffnung-Garskof 164). Dominican transmigrants found themselves in between identities, "perceived as foreigners in both societies: Dominican in New York, *dominicanyorks* in Santo Domingo" (Guarnizo 52). As a result of this dual alienation, Luis Eduardo Guarnizo proposes that Dominican migrants construct a "binational social field," consisting of "multiple cultural discourses and identities," in order to cope with the exclusionary practices at work in both settings (Pessar 5). This "accommodation strategy" helps Dominicans navigate the negative reception of both receiving and returning societies: "when in the United States, their Dominicanness is magnified; upon return, migrants emphasized their Americanness" (Guarnizo 40). These hybrid cultural discourses and accommodation strategies become representative of a new Dominican diasporic identity, one marked in part by its very exclusion from both the Dominican Republic and the US. Metropolitan New York thus indelibly shapes new interpersonal dynamics and evolving constructions of Dominican transnational life, and Dominican-*American* identity for a second generation caught between cultures: the subsequent instability of relationships that we see in the work of Junot Díaz and Angie Cruz is predicated on these particulars of Dominican transnational immigration to the city.

"Learn to Trust Your Men": *Dominican Yorks* and Toxic Gender Norms in Angie Cruz's *Soledad* and Junot Díaz's *This Is How You Lose Her*

"A lot of the Dominican girls in town were on some serious lockdown," Díaz's ever-unreliable narrator and alter ego Yunior tells us in *This Is How You Lose Her*, "since most families knew exactly what kind of tígueres were roaming the neighborhood" (32). Aware of the threat from sexually predatory Dominican male "tígueres," Díaz suggests that Dominican families double down on the surveillance and "lockdown" (a not insignificant synonym for incarceration) of their daughters rather than curtail the behavior of their sons. One of these Dominican daughters comes home in Angie Cruz's *Soledad* and shows us firsthand just who roams her neighborhood and what effects it has on *las vecinas*. Taking in the men catcalling, the lack of privacy, and the role of female family members as wardens, hypervigilant of the reputations of their daughters and nieces, Cruz's chief protagonist Soledad relates that, for her, "time in Washington Heights is like a prison sentence" (3). What are the stresses placed upon Dominican and Dominican American women enduring "lockdown" to prevent their shaming in the community? How do Dominican American men escape a culture that expects them to be *"tígueres"*? And finally, where do these neighborhood dynamics—of highly gendered norms of surveillance and performance—come from?

Part 3 explores two sides of the Dominican diaspora, the male and the female, as well as two generations: the first and the second. Junot Díaz's collection *This Is How You Lose Her* and Angie Cruz's debut novel *Soledad* depict the pressure upon transmigrant men and women to adapt culturally, and the profound consequences of these changes upon interpersonal and intergenerational relationships. *This Is How You Lose Her* and *Soledad* explore the implications of oscillating yet semipermanent settlement in two places on male/female heteronormative relationships, familial ties, and individual identity construction.

The site for these contestations over gender roles and Dominican American identity is greater metropolitan New York City, with narratives taking place in Angie Cruz's Washington Heights barrio of Northern Manhattan and Junot Díaz's London Terrace Apartments in Parlin New Jersey. The Dominican American cultural insecurity and toxic machismo so prominent in the work of Díaz and Cruz is rooted in the history of New York City's Dominican diaspora, as transnational displacement impacts the creation of familial and romantic ties in the US neighborhood.

In the stories "Otravida, Otravez" and "Invierno" Díaz narrates the effects of transnational strategies upon gender roles for Dominican women who come to the US to work or reestablish nuclear families, focusing on the experiences of first-generation migrants to the US from the island. The rest of *This Is How You Lose Her*'s stories are from the perspective of Yunior, a machismo-addled Dominican American man. In these narratives, especially "The Cheater's Guide to Love," we see the effects of transnationalism upon the second generation: Yunior's preoccupation with the role of infidelity in performing Dominican manhood peaks in this final story about obsessive cheating in the Dominican American community and its consequences. The key to Dominican male identity, according to *This Is How You Lose Her,* is the performance of hypermasculinity, with a concomitant, often lurid, objectification of women.

Díaz hints at the difficulties for first-generation Dominican women, yet largely ignores second-generation women as subjects. *Soledad* remedies these lacunae, tracing the intergenerational inheritances of the diaspora for Dominican American women, as well as providing deep interiority into the experiences of being working class, female, and Dominican both on the island and in the US. Cruz shows us three generations of Dominican and Dominican American women who are haunted by sexual violence, cultural surveillance, and a dearth of options for building an identity in the neighborhood outside the prescribed roles of breadwinner, mother, or "slut." I argue that the paradigm of hypermasculinity presented in Díaz's work is a response to the altered gender norms attendant on Dominican transnationalism. In turn, Cruz's novel demonstrates how this toxic masculinity requires a new approach to female relationships and new spaces for female subjectivity.

5

"No Promises Can Survive That Sea"

DIASPORIC IDENTITY IN JUNOT DÍAZ'S
THIS IS HOW YOU LOSE HER

Junot Díaz's 2018 piece for the *New Yorker* titled "The Silence" is a startling account of his own history of sexual assault. The nonfictional story, categorized as "personal history" by the magazine, was released on the eve of the accusations launched concerning Díaz's inappropriate conduct toward female graduate students and seemed to preempt criticisms of the author's sexism and his misuse of gendered power dynamics.[1] Addressed to an anonymous "X" who approached him after a book tour reading to ask him directly whether he was a victim of sexual abuse, "The Silence" describes Díaz being raped by a trusted grownup as an eight-year-old boy and goes on to recount the effects of this trauma upon the author's identity, especially in terms of his romantic and sexual relationships with women. Written as a confession, as well as an apologia to "X" and other readers who sought confirmation that the sexual abuse in his books had seeds in his personal experience, the story reveals Díaz both asking for forgiveness for his personal conduct and explaining the autobiographical roots of several aspects of his fiction.[2]

This *New Yorker* story dissolves the already razor-thin line between writer and protagonist that Díaz has carefully crafted over his career. By speaking as himself, contextualizing his fiction and his characterization of Yunior as both "the perfect cover story"—"someone who couldn't stay in any relationship because he was too much of a player"—and a stand-in who works through Díaz's own misogynistic tendencies and compulsive cheating, Díaz explicitly connects his own grappling with norms of Dominican masculinity and fear of intimacy to Yunior's. "The Silence" even references a real-life bound book of the evidence of Díaz's cheating that was made by his fiancée—that event appears in *This Is How You Lose Her* as the fiancée's final salvo (it bears the inscription, "Dear Yunior, for your next book," a rich meta-moment). This autobiographical detail suggests that the heartbreak that destroys Yunior in the final story of that collection has also destroyed the author, who claims in "The Silence" that *his* fiancée's "heartbreak" "took out her world and mine." Díaz explains that Yunior's double life in *The Brief Wondrous Life of Oscar Wao* and *This Is How You Lose Her* mirrored his own double life and the double life of his father (which that man lived to Díaz's "family's everlasting regret"), claiming that both author and character were "playing out the patrimonial destiny."

Díaz goes on to tell his anonymous reader, and us, that the cheating and the misogyny of his characters hid a truth in plain sight: "since us Afro-Latinx brothers are viewed by society as always already sexual perils, very few people ever noticed what was written between the lines in my fiction—that Afro-Latinx brothers are often sexually *imperiled*." Ethnic stereotypes about black and brown men buttressed Díaz's "perfect cover story" and allowed the characterization to pass unnoticed by readers who were expecting such a performance: to, in effect, let Díaz "rewrite the truth away." That "Afro-Latinx brothers" might be imperiled indicates not only the possibility of sexual assault but also the psychological threat of those same stereotypes, which hopelessly intertwine sexual identity with Latinx cultural norms and one's jockeying for a secure sense of self. Both Yunior and Díaz are hyperaware of what being a "real" Dominican man supposedly entails. For Díaz, rape meant his status as a *dominicano* was revoked: "'Real' Dominican men, after all, aren't raped. And if I wasn't a "real" Dominican man I wasn't anything. The rape excluded me from manhood." These insights into Díaz's past and its effects upon his conception of self strengthen interpretations of his fiction that center on authorial insecurity about genuineness and masculinity that play out at the narrative level.

However, Díaz's explicit autobiographical confession, though powerful, is somewhat redundant. Díaz's decision to "out" himself in his *New Yorker* piece, pointing to the autobiographical referents for fictional characters and plot points, merely makes explicit a tightened relationship between truth and fiction that the author has always cultivated. *This Is How You Lose Her* already reveals the complexity of navigating ethnic authenticity, *sexual* authenticity, traditional Dominican gender roles, misogyny, and family trauma. His published personal essay will now form part of his corpus, but even without his explicit connecting of autobiography and fiction, it is clear that the themes of processing Dominican male identity and living through the consequences of toxic masculinity haunt the author as well as his chief protagonist. In the essay, Díaz sets the worst of his conduct in the deep past, over ten years ago, asserting that he now takes responsibility for his actions. Yet the author admits that "repair is never-ceasing"; indeed, the overcoming of trauma, and the overthrowing of inherited patriarchal norms, is a lifelong process. Looked at in this light, *This Is How You Lose Her* is an act of therapy,[3] which returns to the site of the violation and exorcises the demons of its fractured, hurtful, insecure, and macho protagonist. "The Silence" only intensifies the claim that Díaz's work is ceaselessly interrogating the burdensome inheritance of Dominican male, and specifically Dominican male *diasporic,* identity.

Many readers will be uncomfortable considering the real-life inspirations for Junot Díaz's fiction, for fear of succumbing to the biographical fallacy or of oversimplifying the tie between an author and his or her work. However, Díaz deliberately deploys his biography as a literary device, and his oeuvre pushes us to align his recurring narrator, Yunior, who shares most of the author's personal biographical details, with Díaz himself. Much new scholarship on Díaz engages with the author's personal history and public persona as part of his aesthetic project. Most notably, the editors of *Junot Díaz and the Decolonial Imagination* (rightly) felt justified in rejecting decades of New Critical boundaries and incorporating biographical details of the author in their framing of his work and in several essays in the collection.[4] The current critical work on Díaz attests to how his writing *requires* the critic to engage with his personal history. By creating a narrator who shares his name (Yunior, like Junot, is a variation on "Junior"),[5] shares his vocation and his personal history, lives in the neighborhoods that Díaz grew up in, experiences many of the life events that Díaz experienced and has spoken publicly about, and who speaks often in a first-person voice that is as inimitable as the voice of Díaz's own public persona, Díaz very consciously urges the reader to consider the function of autobiography in his writing. In an interview, Díaz admits, "It's true I play with autobiography. I love to play with it. It's like a medium" (Céspedes and Torres-Saillant 906).

However, while many scholars catch the autobiographical play, and several eminent critics have argued that Díaz's work expresses a diasporic identity,[6] the link between Díaz's transmigrant authorial identity and *place* has yet to be fully theorized. Díaz anchors *This Is How You Lose Her* over and over in its US settings. The role of actual neighborhoods in his oeuvre and the relationship between these and the author's own self-fashioning as a Dominican American, is vitally productive and yet largely unexplored. *This Is How You Lose Her* delineates the myriad ways that transmigrancy shapes Dominican immigrant communities, particularly in metropolitan New York and northeastern New Jersey.[7] What emerges in the collection, through its presentation of place identity, gender, and the role of the written, is an authorial identity defined by the very uncertainty of its position between Dominican and Dominican American cultures. Born of Luis Guarnizo's binational social field,[8] this instability creates the counteractive hybrid cultural identity he describes, where transmigrants oscillate among multiple discourses and identities to navigate being foreign in both home and host country.

As an immigrant to the US at age 6, who experienced continual movement to and from the Dominican Republic and the living across borders of his nuclear and extended family, Junot Díaz exists in the midst of a transnational social field. His writing reflects a minute attention to real-life locations, which, when coupled with his decision to purposefully deploy autobiographical details, functions as a method of more firmly stitching authorial identity to place in reaction to the social dislocations of the Dominican diaspora. In contrast, the work's more hesitant, less veritable style of describing locations in the Dominican Republic demonstrates the narrator's, and author's, own uncertain status as a transnational Dominican American man.

My barriography illustrates the twin legacies of unstable gender roles and bicultural identity upon first- and second-generation Dominicans. Reading the plot of "Otravida, Otravez" in terms of the movements of its female characters within New Brunswick reveals the city functioning as a geographic counterweight and results in a far bleaker reading of the story's ending than its ambiguous closing lines indicate. In "Invierno," as well as "Nilda," Díaz/Yunior performs his knowledge of the architectural specificities of London Terrace apartments to defend his ethnic authenticity; the real as well as fictional contamination of the landfill next door symbolizes his inheritance of a toxic Dominican masculinity. This masculinity is tangled up in authorship, Yunior and Díaz's method of self-fashioning. The collection's conclusion, "The Cheater's Guide to Love," depicts how Dominicanness, manliness, and authorship intersect for the second-generation Yunior. His insecurity about all three must be exposed—in writing—in order to be rectified.

Another Life, Another Time in New Jersey

Heterosexual cheating dominates *This Is How You Lose Her*, appearing in literally every story, but only in "Otravida, Otravez" do we see infidelity from the perspective of a woman. This is the only story in the collection with a female narrator, and the only story not told by Yunior. In it, the Dominican protagonist Yasmin finds herself in the midst of a transnational social field that encompasses both transmigrants and permanent settlers.

Hoffnung-Garskof found in his study of Dominicans in Santo Domingo and New York City that the effects of transnationalism in both cities were felt throughout the population: "Not everyone in the Dominican Republic or Dominican New York regularly participated in transactions across the national boundaries. Yet even those who never moved across a national border, or rarely left their barrios, lived within a world of shared relationships and expectations that spanned the border" (Hoffnung-Garskof 198). The story's title, "Otravida, Otravez," evokes this liminal social space between nations: the title bifurcates its meaning and can be read as either "another life, another time" or "an *other* life, an other time."[9] The uncertainty of the title emulates the characters' ambiguous positions, demonstrating how transnationalism penetrates ostensibly stable local lives in the US, transforming the traditional roles of wife, daughter, and mother.

The ambivalent title emulates Yasmin's ambiguous position, as she is unsure if her life in the US with her partner Ramón is part of a new, different life or just a portion of the other life he already has back on the island. When she refers to Ramón's Dominican wife Virta as "the one from the other life," we hear her fear that she and Virta are in fact sharing the same life and occupying the same position in a romantic relationship; the field of transnational ties Yasmin is inscribed within terminally undermines the possibility of beginning "another," different life. A barriography of the text, which plots the story on the ground in New Brunswick, one of Junot Díaz's former homes, reconfigures the relationship of Yasmin, her friend Ana Iris, and Ramón to their home and host countries in light of their local residences in the US. Specifically, my literal retracing of Yasmin and Ana Iris's final walk in the story allows me to resolve the story's ambiguous ending: despite establishing themselves in New Jersey over years and even decades, both women find their US lives are still inextricably bound to their former lives on the island.

Yasmin immigrates to New Jersey from Santo Domingo when she is twenty-three years old, leaving behind her mother but no husband or children. Yasmin shares an apartment with Ana Iris, a slighter older woman, also an immigrant who left three young sons on the island seven years ago. Several younger female Dominican immigrants stay in the apartment temporarily while looking for long-term lodging. Yasmin lives and works with young girls who are "sent to the States by their parents. The same age I was when I arrived; they see me now, twenty-eight, five years here, as a veteran, a rock, but back then, in those first days, I was so alone" (Díaz, *This Is How* 55). The transnational strategy of splitting the family to make financial gains continues, with parents sending their children abroad to secure employment and send back remittances. The women in the house are either sent by their families to earn money to send back or emigrate to earn enough to bring the rest of their family over. Ana Iris, the stalwart of US assimilation, insists to Yasmin and to the other newer female Dominican immigrants she lives with that they must forget the Dominican Republic to make a new life in the States.

At the story's onset, Yasmin has been dating Ramón for three years. Back "home" on the island, Ramón has his wife, Virta, a house in Villa Juana, Santo Domingo, and a son who died young. Yet Ramón wants to buy a house with Yasmin, but she is convinced he'll "never move me there" (58). Yasmin reads the letters Ramón's wife sends him—he claims he stopped writing, but Yasmin sees new letters under his bed every month—and knows that he hasn't told her about their relationship. The letters from the island, kept in the closet or under the bed, continually remind Yasmin that Ramón has a fully formed life already in the Dominican Republic. Ramón tells her to not be stubborn and to "let go" and "leave alone" his wife and dead child, but Yasmin admits to herself, "I have not stopped watching for signs that he misses her" (67).

Ana Iris tells Yasmin she must "learn to trust your men" (54), describing Ramón as "too settled here": "he's the sort of man who'll go to the airport but won't be able to get on board" (54). Ana Iris's assessment of Ramón ironically describes the heft of the island's pull upon him, as she envisions him on the cusp of return before he affirms his loyalty to his "new life." Even Yasmin's description of her state of uncertainty reflects the vagaries of transnational settlement, as she employs an anecdote taken from Santo Domingo life: "Ana Iris once asked me if I loved him and I told her about the lights in my old home in the capital, how they flickered and you never knew if they would go out or not. You put down your things and you waited and couldn't do anything really until the lights decided. This, I told her, is how I feel" (66). Yasmin references the instability of the island, with its sudden interruptions of things like electricity, a luxury taken for granted in the States, because the uncertainty she feels for him is also tied to the island. Her imagery points to the very power of the island in memory that troubles her current situation. She sees the effects of these same damning island recollections upon her newly immigrated employees: "It is probably her son she misses, or her father. Or our whole country, which you never think of until it's gone, which you never love until it's no longer there" (60). Ana Iris advises Yasmin to forget: "Keep them out of your mind. You do not want to go crazy from them. This is how Ana Iris survives here, how she keeps from losing her mind over her children.

How in part we all survive here" (67). Yet the letters and photos from Ramón's Dominican wife leave Yasmin waiting for the lights to decide.

For all three immigrants, "to own a house in this country is to begin to live" (69); even marriage does not signify meaningful change as home ownership does, as Ramón and Yasmin's marital status remains undisclosed. The same paradigm of immigration, "a new place means a new life," bleeds into any important physical move, as only a new house, not securing a job, having an intimate relationship, or even building one's own business, indicates a "new life." When they find a house, Ana Iris tells Yasmin, "you are on your way to another life" (70), and Ramón asserts at the closing: "Now we can begin" (71). Their logic seems borne out, as an unspecified amount of time goes by where the new life sticks. Some nights Yasmin reads "the old letters" and thinks of "the one from the other life" (74), but she lives happily with Ramón and soon they are expecting a first child together. However, months or years into their new life, a new letter arrives from Virta.

Despite her fear of the new letter and her trip to visit Ana Iris and their old apartment to discuss what it might mean, Yasmin has finally become confident in her life with Ramón. Seeing the "new girls from the Island" now in transit in the house, she believes, as Ana Iris always had, they must forget the island: "I want to advise them: no promises can survive that sea" (74). Yet in an unexpected turn, it is Ana Iris's resolve that has softened. At the end of their long walk to discuss their futures, Ana Iris breaks into sobs, remarking on how much her sons' voices have changed on the phone. Yasmin sees Ana Iris, the most veteran of the group, the most dedicated to making a new life in the US, reach a breaking point. "She will bring them or she will go," Yasmin realizes: "That much has changed" (76). Ana Iris's reversal, after over eight years, shakes Yasmin's newfound certainty, and Virta's unopened letter questions Ramón's. The story ends in ambiguity: "That night I give Ramón the letter and I try to smile while he reads it" (74). However, an analysis of the actual neighborhood geography the two women traverse at the end of the narration resolves the uncertainty and indicates that none of these characters (Yasmin, Ana Iris, Ramón) will be able to fully sever ties and build wholly new lives in the US.

New Brunswick Barriography

St. Peter's University Hospital, where Ana Iris and Yasmin work, sits north of town. It lies on Easton Avenue, which grows steadily nicer as it gets farther from the city center. Easton, or route 527, is a main artery, and it boasts traffic lights such as the one Ana Iris and Yasmin wait at to cross the "highway" to the park (75). In a recent walk through the area, about fifteen years after the short story's fictional time frame, I find that the neighborhood seems mixed, though decidedly middle-class. On Huntington Street, the road perpendicular to the hospital, I see not one but two different college-aged men with fraternity stickers on their cars bringing out laundry to do. The large park directly across the street from St. Peter's and the laundry-doers, called Buccleuch Park, runs east to west for several blocks and a few blocks deep towards the river. On a Sunday, the only language I hear in the park is Spanish, as young kids play near the dugout of an empty baseball diamond, older kids and adults play soccer on a smaller makeshift field, and a few families are preparing to picnic. Runners use the path that runs parallel to Easton, and appear to be more diverse in composition, but in terms of those who are using the park facilities such as the fields and tables, everyone is Latinx.

According to the 2010 US Census, New Brunswick is majority Latinx/Hispanic, at 50 percent of the city. The Latinx percentage of the city, which includes Dominicans, Puerto Ricans, and Central Americans (Shaw 66), increased by 10 percent over a decade, since 2000—when a version of "Otravida, Otravez" was first published in the New Yorker. Over half the population speaks a language other than English at home, and two-fifths of the population is foreign-born (US Census). A striking 70 percent of residents live in shared, multi-unit structures, which, even allowing for the student population of Rutgers University, is high. The average per capita income is on a par with the average graduate student stipend, and as a result a third of the city lives below the poverty level (US Census).

The houses directly adjacent to the hospital are well-manicured and almost aggressive in projecting their Irish heritage, even though Irish immigration to New Brunswick effectively petered out over 150 years ago (Shaw 33).[10] Just a few blocks away, the houses start to falter in their pristine presentation, and several of the homes have clearly been split from single-family residences into two- or more family rentals, as evidenced by multiple mailboxes by the front door and the conversion of front yard space into expanded driveway space for more residents. One can imagine the scenes Yasmin describes, of sharing a room with Ana Iris in a house where new Dominican girls are always arriving and leaving and cohabitating, within one of these converted homes. One can also surmise, though not outright claim, that the more established residents of the neighborhood are wary of newer residents and seek to announce their identity as an older, probably sixth- or seventh-generation Irish American community, in the face of the post-1960s wave of more recent Caribbean and Central American immigrants to the area who frequent their closest park and work at the hospital next door (Shaw 58).

I retrace the steps Ana Iris and Yasmin take on their long walk at the close of "Otravida, Otravez." The women travel from Ana Iris's house, which I've determined lies two blocks northwest on Easton Avenue, across Easton, into Buccleuch Park, down its length and then back across and southeast on Easton toward downtown. I pass the baseball diamonds Yasmin passes with Ana Iris, as she remembers how Ramón and she used to sit in the park unconsciously plotting their affair (Díaz, *This Is How* 75). I walk past the hospital, and three female hospital workers in scrubs chatting in Spanish, and follow Ana Iris and Yasmin down toward Livingston Avenue and the municipal center of town, with its courthouse and small plaza. I pass several taverns that boast apartments on the second floor, possible inspirations for the site Yasmin recounts: "When I first reached the States I was like that, alone, living over a bar with nine other women. At night no one could go to bed because of the screams and the exploding bottles from downstairs" (61). Years after her arrival, when Ana Iris and Yasmin are walking home from the movie theater downtown, Yasmin cannot recall which window of the apartment she used to stare out of (71); already her social and economic trajectory has taken her far away from her first years in the United States (see fig. 25).

FIGURE 25. The tavern plus apartments of Easton Avenue, heading downtown, 2014

The apparent class status of the street decreases steadily as Easton crawls toward downtown, and the houses go from distinctly middle-class to more rundown, with trash-ridden, abbreviated front yards and more rickety wooden house frames that are peeling for want of paint and look in need of some structural renovations. Liquor stores begin cropping up, and more bars, as well as New Jersey's seemingly ubiquitous "pizza and grill" shops, which are intent for some reason on yoking these two types of cuisine. Yasmin's move from any apartment along this stretch of Easton to the home with Ana Iris further northwest is an obvious improvement. And her later move with Ramón to the more middle-class "quieter sections of Paterson" (57), with its "bird-filled hedges" (74), further north and west of New York City—fifty minutes away by car and an hour and a half by train and bus (Google Maps)—is another definitively positive socioeconomic transition. Yasmin notes that "Despite all the trees, the [Paterson] neighborhood is not easy" (72), but, compared to living in a rented apartment over a bar with nine other women in another neighborhood that is not safe (71), owning a home in Paterson marks an upward climb.

Yet Yasmin's walk with Ana Iris when she returns to New Brunswick reverses her social mobility. She travels back to the city from the suburban Paterson, over an hour away, and returns to the old house she lived in with Ana Iris, symbolically descending from homeowner to renter, seeing her former self in the young, transient, overworked dominicanas who now live there. Then she walks past her first American residence, the apartment she shared over the bar, in the less secure neighborhood that she lived in when her employment was also less secure, before her job at the hospital. As Ana Iris and Yasmin walk into the city, they physically mark the downward mobility of the neighborhoods as they travel. By the time they arrive at the courthouse, the city's municipal and figurative center, the reversal is complete, as they have moved from distant suburban enclaves into the city's downtown, where their lives in the US as immigrants began. It is when they are seated in front of the courthouse—a symbol of the tension between their unclear documentation status and their attempts to achieve stability as US citizens—that Ana Iris breaks down, dissolving her eight years of gritty determination to work alone in the US, separated from her young children. Yasmin realizes that Ana Iris will either return to the Dominican Republic or bring her sons over: if the former, her actions will create a perfect reversal, from immigration, to steady upward economic success, to return migration; if the latter, she will repeat the process, as her sons will arrive as new Dominican immigrants who need to make the social and cultural adjustments necessary to succeed.

Downtown New Brunswick figures as a beginning for both women. In Ana Iris's case, traveling into the city center sparks her nostalgia for her country of origin and reminds her of what she has left behind. The city also reminds Yasmin of what she has left behind, but in her case, it is the noisy bar apartment and uncertain social and economic status that she has consistently been moving away from since she arrived in the US. It's worth noting that this is not a short walk: from the house to the court-house is over a mile, and much further with a digression to "walk the length" of Buccleuch Park (75). These two characters are feeling physical distance keenly on this trajectory, allowing them to respectively see how far they've come, for Yasmin in terms of her achievements in the US, and for Ana Iris in terms of how far she's traveled from her family. This juxtaposition of the perspective each woman has on her progress as an immigrant is less polarized than it seems, however, as the unanswered question of Ramón's first wife and her persisting letter-writing hovers over the women's final scene and begs the reader to wonder how much distance Yasmin has really made between her origins and her new life. Paterson does not seem quite far enough to ensure her new or "other" life can be sustained, as a letter from the Dominican Republic literally brings her back, on foot, to one of her earlier selves.

The philosophy of all three immigrants, Ramón, Yasmin, and Ana Iris, that to move (up) is to start to live in this country, to get a better house further and further from the urban beginnings of one's migration, posits a linear, upward-traveling trajectory, which is impeded, taken off course, and essentially reversed by the circular motions of Dominican transmi-gration. The almost gravitational pull of the island, from those that have been left behind, takes the linear narrative of Ana Iris and evidently also Yasmin and curves it into the path of a boomerang. By plotting their movement, in the physical space of New Brunswick and its environs, we can see how the line they struggle so hard to build out of the city and into an established American life is being forced into a circle. This reading also forecloses the possibility, wished for by Yasmin, that Ramón's old life on the island will not impact their new life together. The symbolic import of her walk with Ana Iris indicates that the island's pull will inevitably affect immigrant trajectories in the US, no matter how far they have come.

The ending of "Otravida, Otravez" demonstrates that this Dominican American community is never fully free from the island, as the transna-tional strategies being used entail keeping close family members in two places. The fluid transmigratory character of the Dominican diasporic com-munity profoundly transforms how romantic and familial relationships function, regardless of whether one stays in the DR, is *left* in the DR, or is committed to a "new life" elsewhere. The projected permanent duration of a Dominican's stay in the United States allows him or her to find a new partner, have more children, and become a homeowner in two places, but the relative access of the Dominican Republic makes returning, and never coming back to the US, an ongoing option. The possibility of return, and the need to maintain two lives, affects everyone in the community, even if their own return is unlikely: Yasmin left the Dominican Republic and has no plans to repatriate, having built her life in the States, but she is still at the mercy of others in her community who have left someone behind. Ana Iris sacrifices being with her children in order to provide for them: in this radically transnational social field, abandonment is a mark of maternal love. And yet she has the power to almost instantly change the shape of her identity as mother at will, despite decades in a new country. This state of instability can take a character like Yasmin, described as a steady worker and a pragmatic, moral, rational person, and place her in the role of mistress and unwed mother. Despite Yasmin's hopes, many promises *do* survive that sea.

London Terrace Apartments Barriography

In "Otravida, Otravez," Díaz depicts first-generation immigrant women who must square diasporic uncertainty with their roles as mothers, wives, and breadwinners for families back home. Yet his use of setting detail to establish who the characters are is reflective of Díaz's own *second*-generation (or "generation 1.5") relationship to place. As recounted in "Invierno," Yunior moves from the Dominican Republic to the oft-mentioned, nonfictional London Terrace Apartments of Parlin, New Jersey, when he is nine years old. In the stories set in Díaz's own childhood neighborhood, we see how the instability of Dominican transnational strategies upon the family unit transforms gender expectations for men and women in the US, and when coupled with the shifting perspective on immigrants in the country of origin, leads to a culture of toxic machismo.

"Invierno" is told from Yunior's point of view as a young child who has just moved to New Jersey from the Dominican Republic with his brother and mother. His father's prior presence in the US leads to his policing of the boundary between his newly arrived family and their new country, enforcing a virtual imprisonment. Díaz utilizes the unifying metaphors of the glass window and the neighborhood's "ocean view" to encapsulate the split self and anxiety of belonging experienced by Yunior and his mother. The glass window—where Yunior, his brother Rafa, and his mother can see out to the United States that the man of the house forbids their entry into—portrays how the family's immigration pattern has fundamentally shifted the structure of their interpersonal relationships. The ocean view ironically symbolizes the foreclosure of possibilities for the recent Dominican immigrants, even as their father assimilates.

The story opens with their father driving them to their new home:

> From the top of Westminster, our main strip, you could see the thinnest sliver of ocean cresting the horizon to the east. My father had been shown the sight—the management showed everyone—but as he drives us in from JFK he didn't stop to point it out. The ocean might have made us feel better, considering what else there was to see. London Terrace itself was a mess; half the buildings still needed their wiring and in the evening light these structures sprawled about like ships of brick that had run aground. (121)

"Papi," who has already lived and worked in the US for five years, while his wife and children waited in Santo Domingo for him to bring them over, curates the US for his family.[11] The refusal to point out the view is the first of many ways that Papi prevents them from experiencing the outside, seeking to limit their assimilation, allowing him to remain the one in charge. The description of London Terrace as "a mess" and still being built reminds the reader that more established and thus more expensive New Jersey neighborhoods are outside the reach of this immigrant family aspiring to working class, but Papi is jealous even of their potential belonging to this neighborhood. The description of apartment buildings as "ships of brick that had run aground" echoes the earlier mention of the ocean (which "might have made us feel better") and symbolically links the three new Americans to unworthy sea vessels, "ships of brick" not built for the purpose. This cheap view from the unremarkable "main strip" becomes precious to the children and their mother because it signifies the freedom to look out as well as look back, to the ocean that holds their island, which they have crossed to be in the States.

The window glass figures throughout the story for the foreign world outside, as Papi, who works long hours and habitually returns home late, forbids both his children and his wife from going outside. Asserting that "you'll go out when I say you're ready" (123), Papi claims the family is not yet prepared to encounter or even host Americans. The kids want to touch the glass but are forbidden to; they wave to neighborhood kids through it;

when Rafa thinks they might leave the US, "he ran a finger glumly over our window; he didn't want to go" (131). When their mother can't sleep, she stares outside the glass, missing home and hoping for new neighbors from the island ("I'm going to pray for Dominicans, she had said, *her face against the glass*" [135; emphasis added]). Papi has told them that London Terrace is not "a slum," like what they are used to, and tells them they must learn to behave accordingly. Yet even *wanting* to go outside is grounds for punishment in the household. When the children are sent to their room for misbehaving, "if he burst in and caught us at the window, staring out at the beautiful snow, he would pull our ears and smack us . . . and we'd lay in bed, our knees burning with iodine, and wait for him to go to work so we could put our hands against the cold glass" (130). The peculiarities of London Terrace's architectural design further the family's experience of alienation.

London Terrace apartments spread out from Westminster Boulevard, a short road parallel to Route 9 whose main feature is this apartment complex, as well as Parkwood, the complex next door. The buildings are largely isolated from the other neighborhoods in the area. Even the apartments' numbering is indifferent to the other side streets the houses intersect, running north to south and left to right in a logic seemingly its own. Furthering this sense of the place as a world onto itself, in London Terrace, as in many "affordable housing projects" in the US, the units are extremely close to one another and the architecture is marked by common areas surrounded by apartments, which cordon off public spaces inside the boundaries of the constructed neighborhood. The apartment units' shared green spaces—perhaps too kind a description for a landscape of mowed browning lawn, cement sidewalks, and little else—are faced on multiple sides by the apartments' windows (see fig. 26).

As we will see in Angie Cruz's *Soledad*, the layout of affordable housing projects often helps craft and exaggerate a spirit of reputation-policing and neighborhood watchfulness within an urban transnational community. In London Terrace, the physical closeness of the buildings might confer a sense of potential community, but chiefly its message is that of surveillance. The proximity of the two complexes illuminates how Yunior always knows what the "Parkwood cats" are up to. It also explains how all the neighborhood kids know who Miss Lora is (in "Miss Lora") and where she lives—Unit 22, which sits at the edge of two parking lots in London Terrace. Such close quarters, and subsequent opportunities for illicit gathering, further justify what Yunior describes as immigrant parents' tight vigilance of their daughters: "we saw them on the bus and at school and maybe at the Pathmark, but . . . these girls weren't allowed to

FIGURE 26. London Terrace's closeness, 2014

hang out" (32). From an apartment window a resident can watch social dramas unfold with unencumbered sight lines. The absence of private spaces is vertical as well: Yunior remarks that "our upstairs neighbors, who themselves fought like trolls over everything, would stomp down on us" (129). The newcomers are thus conspicuous but not integrated: they become voyeurs barred from participating.

This closeness adds poignancy to Yunior and Rafa's jealously watching "the neighborhood children building snowmen and igloos," and intensifies the angst they feel seeing the brother and sister who "lived across in apartment four" playing in the snow, waving to Rafa and Yunior through the window to come join them (130). The structure of London Terrace means that Apartments 3 and 4 (another commonplace of affordable housing projects: the numbering of the apartments is hyper-visible and stenciled onto the brick itself) are less than 30 feet from one another, with only a sparse yard they share between them. The fair American children, symbolic representatives of a life in the US, are tantalizingly close yet inaccessible for the two new immigrant children. The unwelcome watchfulness of the neighborhood, and its inaccessibility, is lightheartedly depicted after Yunior very briefly ventures out to meet the two children, before being forced back inside: "two more snowballs exploded on the glass . . . We both stood behind the curtain and watched the brother throw fast and hard like a pitcher" (134).

The mother is also desperate to belong to the outside world. Mami, "who had been our authority on the Island, was dwindling" (131). As Mami was left behind on the island to run the household and raise the two children, she arrives to the US with no social network, no one to teach her English, and no one to talk to, finding herself cut off from both the US and her husband who is already embedded there. In the Dominican Republic, her role as matriarch was uncontested; her "dwindling" thus reflects a dramatic shift: "My mother was not a woman easily cowed, but in the States she let my father roll over her" (139). When the father found work in the US, Mami establishes her role on the island as head of the household; Papi thus must reassert his traditional male position now that the family is back together, demoting Mami's status after five years of relative personal autonomy and total parental authority.

Mami makes various attempts to remedy her isolation but is stymied by her husband. She desires to learn English, but Papi insists, "it's best if I take care of the English" since it's a "difficult language" that "the average woman can't learn" (124). The exchange reveals the tension Yunior's family is navigating between a "traditional" Dominican American home, where the father "takes care" of even the language, and the household created by transnational movements, where the father's migrancy left the mother as the household's authority. Papi's retrenchment in an outdated macho family structure reflects his unease with the shift in family dynamics his US job has caused. Papi's objections effectively silence Mami, who doesn't "say another word" (124), in English or in Spanish.

Faced by the likelihood of her husband's infidelity and insulted by the very helplessness that her husband has imposed upon her, Mami reaches a breaking point. Rebellion in this household means going outside the glass, and Mami finally revolts. When a blizzard comes and Papi is stranded at work, ordering them to "just keep indoors" (143) as they always do, she defiantly goes out alone for a walk. When they realize she's left, Rafa and Yunior go after her. They band together to keep from falling, unaccustomed to walking in snow. The story is written from Yunior's perspective, so Mami's interiority is unavailable in this final scene. She does regain control, however, deciding which direction they will walk: "Go straight, Mami said. That way we don't get lost" (145). At the top of Westminster, they finally see the ocean view their father chose not to show them, and Mami begins to cry. Considering the vista, these tears signify the identity Mami has lost, the authority she left behind in the Dominican Republic.

From this vantage, the ocean looks "like the blade of a long, curved knife" (145): not the symbol of freedom or of nostalgia from the opening but rather reflective of the painful rupture of their former lives and the difficulty of rebuilding in the US. Rafa, Yunior, and especially Mami ironically experienced a break from traditional family norms by *staying* on the island when the father of the household left: as in "Otravida, Otravez," narrow transnationalism affects everyone in the community, not just those who migrate. Yet now reunited, reverting to the expected, traditional roles of wife, mother, and son seems impossible, and their revolt suggests that Papi will not regain hold upon his family. Despite the ominous description of the sea, experiencing the view is a triumph. All three defy their Papi's will to keep them from settling on their own in the States, making their own connections to the neighborhood and beyond without him.

THE TOXIC INHERITANCE OF LONDON TERRACE'S LANDFILL

The sliver of ocean in the final scene is almost overshadowed by the landfill that sits in its foreground. The "misshapen, shadowy mound that abutted the Raritan," with "rubbish fires burned all over it like sores" (145), made its collection debut in "Nilda." Yet in the chronologically earlier "Invierno" the landfill already looms large: "each day the trucks would roll into our neighborhood with the garbage. . . . [T]he mechanics of the winter air conducted its sound and odors to us undiluted. When we opened a window we could hear and smell the bulldozers spreading the garbage out in thick, putrid layers" (134). This "undiluted" exposure will be literally connected to Rafa's sudden cancer and death, and figuratively connected to the social ills both Rafa and Yunior inherit from their father, as well as the neighborhood's norms of masculinity. Papi is gone by the time Yunior is a teenager, but his aggressive male dominance over the family, his unfaithfulness and eventual abandonment of Mami, live on in the roles his sons take on as they grow up. The landfill figures throughout the London Terrace sections of *This Is How You Lose Her;* Yunior's evolving narration of the neighborhood maps onto the real-life history of the Global Landfill next door.

The State of New Jersey's Department of Environmental Protection maintains a Division of Solid and Hazardous Waste (charming, no?), for keeping track of all dumps, landfills, and toxic waste sites; their database lists 96 different landfills and dumps in Middlesex County, where London Terrace is located, and five of those in the Old Bridge township specifically. Global Landfill's boundary lies directly next to the apartment complex, in an empty and fenced-off field that abruptly marks the eastern edge of London Terrace. The DEP's landfill fact sheet lists London Terrace and Parkwood Village as a mere "900 to 2400 feet from the Site," with single-family homes even closer, at 200 feet ("Global Landfill"). The privately owned, 58-acre site was operational from 1968 to 1984 and housed four types of solid waste, including industrial and manufacturing waste ("New Jersey Landfill Database"). The database lists the landfill's status as not "properly closed," indicating that the landfill was not shut down in accordance with the department's solid waste regulations and that "all known waste" may not have been removed.

Indeed, Global Landfill closed most improperly. In 1984, after a series of heavy rains, high tides, and too rapid filling of waste, the landfill had a "slope failure," creating a fissure on its southeastern side that was 60 feet wide, 600 feet long, and 40 feet deep ("Global Landfill"). The landfill collapsed into a large landslide, contaminating the nearby Cheesequake Creek Tidal Marsh. Despite being licensed only for nonhazardous waste, after the slope failure it was discovered that the landfill was in fact housing hazardous waste, when it leached toxic chemicals into the marsh and contaminated the groundwater. Global Landfill was promptly closed in light of these findings, though the thin soil covering left waste exposed in areas of the site ("Global Landfill"). Studies in the 1990s revealed that the groundwater underneath the landfill was completely contaminated, with pesticides, inorganic compounds, and metals. In 2010 the remediation process began of filling, venting, and capping the landfill to prevent further contamination of the soil, groundwater, and nearby wetlands ("Global Landfill").

In "Nilda," the landfill serves as a marker of both progress and deterioration, ever lurking in the background. The opening reads: "Nilda was my brother's girlfriend. This is how all these stories begin" (29). We learn from this introduction, and from the close of the story, that Yunior is looking back and speaking from the future. The habitual present tense refers to a repetitive action: Yunior seems to be remembering, as he often does, his failures with girls as an adolescent, and his time in the shadow of his older brother Rafa's numerous sexual exploits. Rafa, like Yunior's father, like Yunior himself, is depicted throughout *This Is How You Lose Her* as a compulsive, competitive womanizer. The London Terrace stories present the landfill as the symbol for this inherited, cultural, toxic masculinity, even as it indicates the literal toxicity of the neighborhood that eventually kills Rafa.

The first mention of the landfill in the story comes when Yunior and his friends, shunned by the girls in their grade at school, attempt to console themselves in the summer: "Me and my pathetic little crew hiked over to Morgan Creek and swam around in water stinking of leachate from the landfill" (35). Yunior swims in the contaminated waters of the Cheesequake watershed even though they are "stinking of leachate," a defeatist act indicating that while he knows his environment is toxic, he also knows he cannot escape it. The definition of "leachate" has metaphorical significance here: as water that has taken on the characteristics of its environment—usually negative ones—and in turn "leaks" those new elements into new waters, "leachate" serves as a descriptor for both Yunior and his brother Rafa, who take on the wholly unhealthy elements of their environment in different ways.

Rafa's contaminated inheritance appears to be physical: in the same paragraph, we have the first mention of his illness. Until now in the story he has been the over-muscled boxer full of energy and confidence: "Rafa was tired all the time and pale: this happened in a matter of days" (35). The coincidence of the first mention of both the landfill and Rafa's cancer ties them together, compelling the reader to connect the contaminated water and Rafa's sudden illness. The thematic correlation is explicit: the landfill for Yunior symbolizes his brother's sickness and death and, indirectly, Yunior's own "sickness." Both brothers feel the diasporic push to stitch themselves to a place now that they have moved to the US; unfortunately, this suturing is unfiltered and thus includes taking on all elements, contaminated and otherwise, of the new environment.

The next time the landfill is mentioned, it is again linked to Rafa. Yunior tells us: "My brother was gone by then, and I was on my way to becoming a nut. I was out of school most of the time and . . . walked down to the dump and smoked the mota I should have been selling until I couldn't see" (39). The open dump at the edge of the apartments becomes a site of mourning for Yunior, whose drug use here indicates his difficulty coping. In the span of two sentences, Yunior's mind travels from Rafa to the landfill at the edge of London Terrace. Here the landfill is also tied once more to Yunior's "sickness," or emotional instabilities, but the connection is different from Rafa's. Yunior deliberately chooses to expose himself more fully to the landfill, as with his swimming in leachate, and here his actions metaphorically match those of the landfill: he intakes so much marijuana, and so much landfill, that he makes himself ill, and he leaks his contamination unto others for years to come.

When the landfill is closed, it signifies an end of mourning for Yunior as well, though both the dump and Rafa persist in the present in toxic ways. Yunior, now twenty-three, still living in London Terrace with his mom and doing laundry up the street at the mini mall, tells himself repeatedly that it's okay to let Rafa go, in an attempt to convince himself (40). Yet Nilda walks into the laundromat and brings Rafa back into Yunior's mind, as they reminisce, confessing how they miss him. With Rafa conjured again, they return to the apartments: "We walk back through the old neighborhood, slowed down by the bulk of our clothes. London Terrace has changed now that the landfill has shut down. Kicked-up rents and mad South Asian people and whitefolks, *but it's our kids you see in the streets and hanging from the porches*" (42; emphasis added). Yunior's mind once again jumps from his brother's passing to the landfill. Just as his brother has been "gone, gone, gone" for years, so has the landfill, which shuts down before Yunior graduates high school. London Terrace management takes advantage of the closure and begins upselling their rentals, changing the composition of the apartments in terms of ethnicity and class. However, aspects of the old neighborhood remain, with "our kids" "hanging from the porches." The Dominican element is barely contained, "hanging" outside the houses and "in the streets," phrases associated with gang activity; "our kids" thus provide a conspicuous reminder of the apartments' economically and environmentally downtrodden past.

The known toxicity of the Global Landfill, which the DEP determined did not close properly and which continued to contaminate the surrounding areas, is crucial to this ending. The closure of the landfill ostensibly changes the landscape and improves the neighborhood, but, in reality, the Dominican community that was there first still loiters in the streets or, in Nilda's and Yunior's cases, lives in the same apartment units they grew up in. The landfill's closure also belies its ongoing presence, not just as a symbol for Yunior but as a real and continuing toxic threat. Its closure very clearly does not equal its erasure, though that is London Terrace management's goal—one it achieves in real life, as the current rental employees, lifelong residents of the apartments, were completely ignorant of the former landfill less than a mile away (see figs. 27 and 28).

Stunningly, nobody in the rental office knows what I'm talking about when I ask where the landfill was, which Díaz mentions multiple times in the collection, which was in operation less than thirty years ago, which you could see, and smell, from the apartments. The office's young employees Ashley and Aman (who did not want to give me their last names)

FIGURE 27. The edge of London Terrace, 2014

FIGURE 28. The backyard of the housing projects and former site of Global Landfill, 2014

seem genuinely surprised by the question. However, the empty land just east of the apartment complexes is the obvious candidate, though it is now a field with no visible signs of former toxicity. The apartment complexes here end abruptly with a parking lot periphery, then a chain link fence and "no trespassing" signs.

Analogously, Rafa's legacy, which has been tied to the landfill throughout, is also a real and continuing toxic threat to Yunior. This is evidenced by his opening line, "This is how all these stories begin," where Yunior indicates his obsession with narrating his brother's exploits. Yunior himself grapples with this psychological tic, questioning why he's even telling the story: "what's the point of all this?" (40). "Nilda" functions as a glimpse into Yunior's process of attributing the causes for his pathological cheating as it unfolds in the collection. Global Landfill, with its history of failure and continued threat to the present and future, as well as its role in the development of the London Terrace neighborhood, figures as an ideal real-world analog for Yunior's traumatic past and subsequent development into a manic philanderer.

Yunior consistently suffers from his need for approval from other male Dominican Americans in the work; he points to his upbringing as the source of this anxiety over his masculinity in "Miss Lora," when he pursues an older woman in his tenements, even though he has a "good" girlfriend: "Years later you would wonder if it hadn't been for your brother would you have done it? You remember how all the other guys had hated on her.... [B]ut your brother didn't care. I'd fuck her. You'd fuck anything, someone jeered. And he had given that someone the eye. You make that sound like it's a bad thing" (149). Yunior's own sexual interest in Miss Lora appears to be irrelevant, as Yunior's actions are motivated by the approval of the other Dominican American boys in his neighborhood. Rafa's proud assertion that wanting to "fuck anything" is a positive, not negative, characteristic, is in keeping with the sexual values expressed by the majority of Dominican and Dominican American male characters in the book. Rafa's toxic masculinity—itself an inheritance from his father— does not die with him but rather lives on in Yunior, just as leachate and chemicals live on in the contaminated London Terrace.

Santo Domingo: The Unwritable Island

In stark contrast to the excessively detailed and accurate representations of the New Jersey neighborhoods Junot Díaz knows from personal experience, descriptions of locales in the Dominican Republic in *This Is How You Lose Her* are far more poetic and far less anchored in specific place detail.[12] A brief look at the vastly differing treatment of settings on the island confirms Díaz's writing's intensified relationship to place identity. If the author's style in the New Jersey stories exhibits the stitching of self to place in the face of cultural dislocation attendant on binational social fields, the stories set in the Dominican Republic demonstrate the transnational subject's hesitance about claiming the country of origin for oneself and the subsequent avoidance of such place detail, in response perhaps to the island's deteriorated view of *Domincanyorks*.[13]

This Is How You Lose Her's opening story takes us to the Dominican Republic. Yet "The Sun, the Moon, the Stars" insists that the country defies written description. This ineffability points to Yunior's concern about his own uncertain status as "Dominican enough" to describe the island. Early on he offers a lengthy and telling aside:

> Let me confess: I love Santo Domingo. I love coming home to the guys in blazers trying to push little cups of Brugal into my hands. Love the plane landing, everybody clapping when the wheels kiss the runway. Love the fact that I'm the only nigger on board without a Cuban link or a flapjack of makeup on my face. . . . I love the bags my mother packs, shit for relatives and something for Magda, a gift. You give this to her no matter what happens. (9)

Yunior adopts the tenor of a love letter, opening with "let me confess." This introduction casts his love for Santo Domingo as if it were a secret. The string of anaphora following, each sentence beginning with "I love," continues the tone. The things he loves point to the ways he simultaneously is and is not part of the group of Dominicans onboard: he's the only one without ostentatious jewelry or overdone makeup; he's not reuniting with loved ones after many years, but his mother has enlisted him with bringing remittances to relatives on the island; and he takes pride in carrying the bags she has packed because it makes him belong more to the Santo Domingo he loves. The list of things he loves, incidentally, have nothing to do with the city of Santo Domingo, and most of the images he relates take place on the plane before landing. Yunior can speak to the experience of traveling to the Dominican Republic: his substitution of this for the experience of living in the DR is telling.

He goes on to address the capital and landscape directly:

> If this was another kind of story, . . . I'd tell you about the shanties and
> our no-running-water faucets and the sambos on the billboards and the
> fact that my family house comes with an ever-reliable latrine. I'd tell you
> about my abuelo and his campo hands, how unhappy he is that I'm not
> sticking around, and I'd tell you about the street where I was born, Calle
> XXI, and how it hasn't decided yet if it wants to be a slum or not and how
> it's been in this state of indecision for years.
>
> But that would make it another kind of story, and I'm having trouble
> enough with this one as it is. You'll have to take my word for it. Santo
> Domingo is Santo Domingo. Let's pretend we all know what goes on
> there. (10)

In this continued direct address to the reader, Yunior claims that his story
is not about Santo Domingo. He insists upon this with a series of conditional phrases: "*If* this was another kind of story," I *would* tell you. The
extended use of paralepsis, of course, does tell the reader about Santo
Domingo, as each conditional statement is followed by a description of
the very thing he claims he will not describe. This insistence on not narrating, but failure to refrain from it, demonstrates Yunior's need to relate
himself to the Island, which he doesn't want to acknowledge explicitly.
Hence his *inventio* "let me confess," which sounds like it will precede a
much darker monologue.

After an extended description of all the things he *would* tell us, Yunior
abandons description, stating finally, "Santo Domingo is Santo Domingo."
The use of a self-referential statement describes the place as sui generis,
impossible to explain except through self-identity. The paralepsis echoes
this, as the conditional phrases imply the narrator will not be fully capable
of defining the place. He insists on tying himself there with autobiographical detail, and with language, his street, his grandfather, his grandpa's hands,
all related in Spanish words. However, his mode is one of ambivalence
toward his success in proving himself as a spokesperson for the island.
The uncertainty of achieving a full definition is reflected in the follow-up
sentence, "let's pretend we all know what goes on there," a command given
to overlook the impossibility of knowing the city. Yunior's switch to the
first-person plural here, from "I" to "we," is telling: he admits that he is not
fully of the island either and thus equally unaware of "what goes on there."

The converse of the precariousness of Yunior's self-identification as
Dominican is his overstated confidence in narrating not just London Ter-
race but urban Dominican American neighborhoods throughout New
York and New Jersey. Díaz's unique position, as a Dominican immigrant

who comes to the US at a young age and subsequently self-identifies as a kind of qualified Dominican,[14] finds expression in the ways Yunior narrates or fails to narrate the places he encounters. The two strikingly contrasting modes of these place descriptions, on and off the island, point to the importance of place anchoring for the identity formation of transnational subjects in the US.

The focus on place detail betrays Yunior's need to project his identity outward; this same insecurity, born of the need to solidify his status as a straight Dominican man, compels both his cheating and his authorship. Paper trails from Yunior's conquests betray him throughout the collection. In "Alma," we see Yunior's twin insecurities play out, and the line between autobiography and fiction that Díaz later severs in his *New Yorker* article frays drastically. Alma is described in terms of her neighborhood and her ethnicity;[15] she's a Dominican American from the "burned out" Latinx community of Hoboken who is inspired to "reclaim her" Dominican heritage for Yunior, who she says is a "radical" and a "real Dominican" (46). Yunior focuses on her latinidad and recognizes that dating a Latina helps confirm his own Dominicanness: he jokes that on the "Plátano Index" he doesn't rank because she is only the third Latina he has ever dated (46), implying that his own ethnic identity is both a fixation and something he ties to sexuality. Given this anxiety, it makes sense that he dates the Latina officially and hides his affair with Laxmi, who is from Guyana. When Alma discovers Yunior has been cheating, her most damning insult is that he is a "fake-ass Dominican" (48) (though she also questions his macho status by calling him a "cocksucker," implying homosexuality): this epithet has nothing to do with infidelity but everything to do with how Yunior wishes to see himself. Alma exploits his uncertainty about his Dominican authenticity to pain him.

Yunior's relationship in Alma is undone, as are so many relationships in the collection, by written evidence of infidelity.[16] In this case, Alma reads about Yunior's affair in his own personal journal. When confronted, Yunior takes the tact of "prevaricating to the end" (48). The similes he uses to describe the journal brilliantly convey the particular incontrovertibility of the written: "you pick up the journal as one might hold a baby's beshatted diaper, as one might pinch a recently benutted condom" (48). The concreteness of the journal's words is doubly emphasized, as diapers and condoms already point to the substances they are built to contain, and Díaz's filling of each in his image insists on the unavoidable consequences of the written passages. If we follow the similes, a journal, like a condom or diaper, becomes an object that by its very nature implies the containment of something potentially incriminating, that already points to matter one wants to keep quarantined. Both images suggest the urgency of writing, equating it to bodily excretions that Yunior cannot fully control.

In response, Yunior deploys his role as author as a shield, glancing at the offending passages in his journal, smiling, and telling his girl-friend, "baby, this is part of my novel" (48). In his nonfictional essay "The Silence," Díaz claims that Yunior was "the perfect cover story," an alter ego that allowed the author to project a self that was more masculine and more Dominican. In this story, the narrator flips the categories, hiding behind the flimsy assertion of fiction to defend his real-life actions. That Díaz shows us how Yunior manipulates his position as author to protect himself at will adds a layer of metadiscourse: is *This Is How You Lose Her* Díaz applying the label of "fiction" to real-life pathology, or processing the urge to do so, using writing to reshape one's reality? The final story in the collection suggests that he is doing both: thinly veiling autobiography to solidify his identity on the page and using writing to work through his toxic inheritances. Unsurprisingly, given the unwholesome environment of London Terrace, Yunior's attempt at redemption must take place else-where: the story is set in the Boston area.

Greater Boston and "The Cheater's Guide"

"The Cheater's Guide to Love," the collection's final story, describes the gen-esis of *This Is How You Lose Her*, transforming the collection into the writ-ten evidence of a lifetime of infidelity: a literal and literary "cheater's guide" to love. The theme of destructive, compulsive male infidelity unifies the collection; *every* story presents men being unfaithful to their partners. This closing reframes *This Is How You Lose Her* as Yunior's slow process of disen-tangling the cultural pressures of hypermasculinity he believed expressed Dominican manhood from his own desires to identify more completely as a Dominican.[17] "The Cheater's Guide" delineates the psychological con-sequences of this kind of performance of masculine identity, ultimately suggesting that Díaz's writing must begin to serve his healing rather than announce his sexual exploits, if he is to escape the legacy of toxic machismo.

Yunior's acts of rampant unfaithfulness are marked by compulsion bordering on addiction. Yunior tells us his fiancée had warned him that cheating was the one thing she would never forgive and indicates his desire to comply: "and of course you swore you wouldn't do it. You swore you wouldn't. You swore you wouldn't. And you did" (177). Once she's gone, Yunior picks up his old habits, despite finding no comfort in them (178). His inability to stop from engaging in behavior that negatively affects him reinforces the idea that this is perhaps the sex addiction he claimed he suffered from in order to win his fiancée back. In the face of depression and suicidal thoughts, despite the "erratic" moods such acts bring on, Yunior continues "fucking everything that moves" (179).

As he enters "Year 2" of the breakup, Yunior stops pursuing "sucias," yet the fixation remains on his status as a macho. His friend Elvis, a Dominican American from Boston, insists that sex is the answer to Yunior's depression, advising him to attend yoga classes to meet women—"Mad fuckin' ho's in there" (188)—and then to "bone the shit out of" a "blanquita" he meets there (189). Meanwhile he tells Yunior stories of the women he's sleeping with. This same friend urges Yunior to "find yourself another girl," arguing that "clavo saca clavo" (nail removes nail), and a "good Dominican girl" (182) will resolve his heartache. Elvis's use of a common Spanish idiomatic expression implies he is speaking on behalf of typical male Dominican cultural norms. His own marriage to a Dominican American and his decision to stay in Boston's Jamaica Plain neighborhood, in the *banilejo* community where he grew up, further suggest that Elvis represents traditional dominicano values (Yunior, like Junot Díaz during much of his tenure at MIT, lives in Cambridge, in a fairly white, middle-class neighborhood outside Harvard Square).[18]

Reading Elvis as representative of a standard male Dominican American identity illuminates the pressures placed on Yunior to conform to these norms. Yunior follows Elvis's advice and finds Noemi, a "good Dominican girl" from the island. However, after the "first sleepover" Elvis asks Yunior "how sweet was that toto?" seemingly contradicting his earlier argument for dating a "good girl." Elvis's response points to his own unhealthy machismo: throughout the story he cheats on his wife with new women, including one in the Dominican Republic that he is convinced is the mother of his child. Immediately asking Yunior how the sex was introduces confusion over how to treat the "good Dominican girl" differently than the "sucias," behaving identically toward two supposedly antithetical groups. Noemi goes on to refuse sex for three more weeks. Yunior complains about it to Elvis—who is "shocked" there is still "no toto"—whining, "what am I, in sixth grade?" (184). Ultimately Yunior refuses to see her again unless she consents, telling her their next date is dependent on whether she is "planning to give me ass anytime soon" (185). She immediately ends the relationship. Yet Yunior's motivation to badger Noemi to submit sexually comes from having to admit his failure to have sex to Elvis, whose shock at the lack of intercourse, and insistence on knowing about Yunior's sexual prowess, encourage him to coerce a woman he wants to date seriously.

Yunior's insecurities about acting enough like a Dominican man fuel his writing: the author-protagonist is obsessed with detailing conquests and archiving his infidelities as proof of his virility. Ironically, his insecurity about belonging furthers his alienation: the urge to write down his sexual exploits becomes the way he differs from the other Latinos in the collection. Throughout *This Is How You Lose Her*, Yunior's cheating is on a par with the Latinx men around him, but his rate of being *caught* far exceeds them all: he is consistently found out because he commits his acts to paper. In "The Cheater's Guide to Love" this tendency ends his engagement: "She could have caught you with one sucia, she could have caught you with two, but as you're a totally batshit cuero who didn't ever empty his e-mail trash can, she caught you with fifty! Sure, over a six-year period, but still. Fifty fucking girls? God*damn*" (177). Keeping a record of six years of cheating is not a mere oversight: it reflects Yunior's insistence on documentation in the face of identity anxiety. When Yunior cautions Elvis to be careful about getting caught and being left by his wife, Elvis retorts, "Shit, no one could ever end up like you, Yunior. You're a DR original" (191). Considering the similarities in their sexual histories—both cheat on their long-term partners, both are told they are a baby's father when they aren't, both consider sex the cure for depression despite its low success rate—we must assume that what makes Yunior "a DR original" here is not being sexually promiscuous but rather keeping damning evidence and getting caught.

Indeed, Yunior's need to write himself and document his sexual exploits to mitigate his insecurity leads to his next work of fiction. Yunior's former fiancée collected all the emails and photos of his infidelities, collating them into what he calls "The Doomsday book": A bound collection—"(yes, she put covers on it)"—of every piece of evidence from his "cheating days" (212). When Yunior finally reads the book, which he keeps unread under his bed for five years, he is astounded by his own mendacity (212). The fiancée's inscription, "*Dear Yunior, for your next book*" (212), reiterates his compulsion to archive sex acts and also reproaches Yunior for using autobiographical details in his fiction. Yet even after admitting his faults (212), Yunior *still* wants to share this evidence of his sexual prowess with Elvis:

> She's right; this would make a killer book, Elvis says. . . . Hands you back the book. You really should write the cheater's guide to love.
> You think?
> I do. (212)

Eventually Yunior begins writing again, and we're left to assume that what he's writing is, in fact, *This Is How You Lose Her*. Elvis, whose advice he's followed throughout, and whose romantic trajectory mirrors his own, has suggested he write the eponymous story we currently read.

That the final directive to write the cheater's guide comes from Elvis is not arbitrary. Yunior's questioning response to him—"you do?"—reveals that he still seeks approval from his male Dominican American friend, despite the destructive results of following Elvis's advice and imitating his way of life. Yunior wants Elvis's approbation because Elvis represents a stereotypical Dominican male identity that Yunior aspires to but seems unable to fully commit to. In his chasing of sucias, his illegitimate child scare, his search for a "good Dominican girl" while not getting caught having affairs with "ho's," Yunior meets the norms for Dominican American maleness purported by Elvis (and by other Dominican and Dominican American males in the book such as Rafa, Yunior's father, and Ramón); but in his insistence on keeping evidence, collecting letters, and especially in narrating these exploits, Yunior is "a DR original."[19] It is the very uneasiness with the traditional model of Dominican masculinity that Yunior's "cheater's guide" exhibits.

As we've seen, Yunior's tries to self-fashion himself as an author, to write his way to belonging, as both a man and a Dominican. Yet this urge paradoxically reinforces how much he fails to be a Dominican *man*, because his archiving tendencies get him caught, and how much he fails to be a *Dominican*, because he cannot narrate the island with the same ease with which he narrates the US. The only identity he can securely claim is as a denizen of London Terrace, and even that self is under threat by the neighborhood's gentrification. As a "perfect cover story," Yunior fails: this protagonist cannot mask the insecurities of masculinity and ethnicity that plague him. However, by exposing this instability, this toxicity, and this fear of inauthenticity, and furthermore by linking such a protagonist to his own autobiography, Díaz crafts a quintessentially diasporic voice. Díaz, like Yunior, is trapped in toxic standards of heteronormativity, mired in a Dominican transnational social field, and torn between the inheritance of noxious outdated norms of masculinity and his own potential emotional growth. His writing shows us that to be a Dominican American *author* is to grapple with and process and put in the reader's hands the litany of uncertainties that a person caught between identities faces. Writing is not the source of Yunior's downfall, as a dominicano like Elvis insists: it is the key to his evolution as a man and as a Dominican American. Where the island is unwritable (for someone who will never be fully "from" there enough), and London Terrace is overwritten and overdetermined (the leachate has already seeped into the ground), the act of writing, or exposing, one's own flaws is generative: it calls into being the possibility of a new self. This self is neither Dominican nor American enough, it is neither masculine nor feminine enough, it is neither heterosexual nor homosexual enough, it is neither autobiographical nor fictional enough. It presents the process of becoming and the experience of being in between identities, and in so doing it makes a space for itself. *This Is How You Lose Her* presents the messy reality of the split diasporic subject, refusing to resolve its irrefutably dual nature.

6

"Washington Heights Is Like a Prison Sentence"

FEMALE SURVEILLANCE IN ANGIE CRUZ'S *SOLEDAD*

ANGIE CRUZ's debut 2001 novel *Soledad* offers us insight into the flipside of Dominican machismo Junot Díaz depicts, tracing how Dominican and Dominican American *women* endure the ubiquitous sexual attention of their male neighbors. The threat of sexual violence permeates the novel's narrative space, and the internalization of this fear by the women in the text results in women policing each other as a mode of self-preservation, which, combined with the ever-present male gaze, removes all individual privacy. The other potent menace in *This Is How You Lose Her*—fear for one's reputation—also finds voice in *Soledad*. Yet for women, good reputations mean purity, not conquest. In Cruz's text, the threat of blighting one's reputation, in such an intimate and omniscient immigrant community, profoundly and negatively affects the female characters: all female sexual experiences are silenced, left unsaid—or if said, unheard—by the family. Repressed sexual encounters manifest as hauntings, which force the women in the Sosa family to finally see the trauma in each other's lives. However, the spaces of the neighborhood do not allow the women to process these traumas, and only back on the island can mother and daughter be heard by one another. Thus Cruz, like Díaz, seems to suggest that the barrio helps craft unique Dominican American identities but also stymies attempts to transcend the inherited gender norms of the neighborhood community.

Today Washington Heights is home to the largest Dominican community in the United States (Hernández et al. 1). Yet the area has been a neighborhood of ethnic enclaves for various immigrant groups since the early twentieth century (Snyder 6). Drawn to its new-law tenements, which had running water, bathrooms, and exterior windows, and even elevators and courtyards, all missing from most crowded tenements of southern Manhattan, and aided in their work commutes by new subway lines connecting northern Manhattan to downtown jobs, German

Jewish refugees and Greek and Irish immigrants began settling in the area in large numbers in the 1930s (16). After World War II, Puerto Ricans began settling in the southeastern Heights, and African Americans, long restricted to Harlem by racist housing covenants, began pushing north (36). In Trujillo's wake, Dominicans began settling in the area in large numbers, just as the former ethnic strongholds of Jews, Greeks, and Irish were disappearing into the suburbs.

Historian Robert Snyder notes in *Crossing Broadway* that the nature of the Heights' ethnic enclaves was insular, and that identity was linked to the parish and even the street, rather than the entire neighborhood: "At its best, a local life . . . was intimate and nourishing . . . At their worst, enclaves bred exclusion and compounded the problems that in time tore the neighborhood apart. Living in almost self-contained two- or three-square-block cantons blinded residents to concerns they shared with people who lived ten blocks away" (6). Different immigrant groups were distinctly separated within the Heights, with Broadway splitting the Irish and Jewish communities, and less affluent groups taking up the southern and especially southeastern sections of the neighborhood. One's community was often demarcated not by the region or even the neighborhood but by the block. The street and its location—east or west of Broadway, north or south of the hospitals—served as a shorthand marker of a resident's identity. In *Soledad,* this narrow definition of self has profound effects upon the characters' ability to evolve.

Angie Cruz's negative depiction of her childhood street in northern Manhattan's Washington Heights neighborhood raises questions about how second-generation Dominican Americans—especially women—can forge new identities within the limiting confines of family and neighborhood expectations. *Soledad* explores the corrosive aspects of barrio community building, and the tension between self-expression and prescriptive social mores. The Dominican American section of Washington Heights is close-knit and family oriented, but it has also internalized a panoptic lens, as a result of external pressures upon the barrio as well as internal pressures to conform to traditional Dominican values. Cruz demonstrates at the formal level how the neighborhood disallows change, not only through her claustrophobia-inducing depictions of the spaces of West 164th Street, and the paradoxical combination of intense physical visibility and emotional *in*visibility experienced by the characters, but also in the very structure of the novel. The proliferation of the Sosa family's voices—interspersed, unlabeled, and crowding one another out in every chapter—mimics the proximity without genuine connection, or noise but not listening, that characterizes the neighborhood. The narrations, except for that of Soledad's mother, Olivia, remain in the present and are confined to Washington Heights. Cruz sets up the narrative so that emotional growth for the characters is tied to physical escape. This is despite the author's own well-documented positive experiences of West 164th Street.

Angie Cruz loves her barrio. She tells Silvio Torres-Saillant that she is "obsessed with the neighborhood" (121). After an entire childhood and adolescence in Washington Heights, and a mere four years away, she returned to her old street to live and relishes the closeness to her extended family and the streets of her childhood (Cruz, "Sublet"). The author sets *Soledad* on 164th and argues that in this novel "the street predominates" because of the "strong love" Cruz has for that street (Torres-Saillant 109). Cruz acknowledges the novel's tendency toward verisimilitude in its description of the setting as a way to preserve her own street memories: describing Washington Heights as feeling "like another world," she says she "wanted to document it in some way" (121). The author's impulse to "document," rather than imagine or invent, the details of the street and the "world" of this Dominican immigrant community, stems from pride in the uniqueness of her neighborhood but also an indebtedness to that community, "to give something back to the people there" (121).

The stark changes overtaking the neighborhood and changing its identity may also contribute to Cruz's consistent veracity in her setting description. Referencing Washington Heights' intense gentrification, she noted in 2003: "I almost feel like 20 years from now we're not going to be there anymore. Little by little Dominicans are being pushed out" (Torres-Saillant 121). Indeed, since 1999, the number of immigrant households in Washington Heights has declined dramatically, diminishing by 21 percent over fifteen years and rendering uncertain the future of Dominican immigrants in the area (Hernández et al.). As the poorest and largest ethnic immigrant group in the neighborhood, Dominicans in Washington Heights have been most affected by the sweeping gentrification that has taken place in New York City over the last two decades (1–2). The threat of the "pushing out" of this community—and now, eighteen years after the book has come out, the Dominican stronghold on the area has certainly waned[1]—only intensifies Cruz's mandate to capture, with as much real-life detail as possible, where she comes from.

Yet apart from the true-life nature of the setting, *Soledad* expands, reinvents, and breaks away from the autobiographical. Cruz is reflected in the main protagonist, Soledad, who leaves for school as Cruz does, who wants to become an artist as Cruz has, but the author also presents a twist: this character detests the neighborhood. This outsider perspective makes Soledad the ideal guide for the uninitiated reader. It also highlights the negative attributes of the barrio: the excessive surveillance of both strangers and family members, the dominance of the male gaze, the constant threat of violence, the claustrophobia and the inability to leave or to change, physically, economically, emotionally. While Cruz may not share her character's distaste for Washington Heights, Soledad and her mother, Olivia, find themselves trapped in the lives they've made in the neighborhood, forced into versions of themselves codified by the expectations of family and neighbors, and enforced by the threat of social shaming by the barrio. Like *This Is How You Lose Her, Soledad* refrains from idealizing the neighborhood, suggesting that what makes it inimitable—and thus impossible to capture except through precise realistic portrayal—is also what makes it difficult to escape, both physically and psychologically.

My reading establishes the particular form of surveillance propagated by the neighborhood, paying special attention to how the male gaze operates in the space and the subsequent formation of female defensive strategies against male attention and violence. I demonstrate how this family policing of the female body in *Soledad* silences the women of the barrio, causing their experiences to reemerge as hauntings so resolutely physical that they cannot be ignored. The resolution of all narrative tension is set in the Dominican Republic; no female character succeeds in expressing herself fully in the barrio.[2] Yet Cruz, like Díaz, cannot make the Dominican Republic home to her Dominican American protagonists' identity crises: the diaspora has distanced them too much from this nation of origin. Both *This Is How You Lose Her* and *Soledad* ultimately provide the possibility of a space for healing and self-expression for the second generation elsewhere: not in the concrete, and not on the island, but in the abstract through the pursuit of art; a pathway best exemplified in writing, by the novel itself.

Neighborhood Watch

The overwhelming majority of the story takes place on 164th Street in Washington Heights. The settings include the street, with its stoops, alleys, sidewalks, and rooftops, and the two apartments of Olivia and her mother, in facing apartment buildings. We take very brief trips to Soledad's life in the East Village, and to Olivia's past life in the DR, but until the final chapter, the reader feels as confined to the neighborhood as Soledad. Cruz characterizes the street as a space of intense surveillance upon female bodies, which manifests as both a familial watchfulness or policing of feminine virtue and as the ubiquitous threat of sexual, potentially violent, physical advances from men. The panoptic lens follows the neighbors from the streets into their apartments, as these cramped shared spaces ostensibly prevent the possibility of family members harboring secrets. The key narrative developments of the story—Soledad's escape and return, Olivia's condition, the hauntings of their apartment, Soledad's childhood molestation—all stem from the unique proximity without closeness fomented by 164th Street's production of space. By tracing the external surveillance of women in the text and in the present-day barrio, this chapter demonstrates the impossibility of privacy and of forms of individual self-expression that are not overdetermined by the eyes of the street.

Cruz develops the identity of Quisqueya Heights as closed off and close. Upon her return, Soledad remarks on the constant movement and contact of her family: "In the eighteen years I lived with my mother, my family moved in and out of each other's apartments, trading beds as if they were playing musical chairs. They ran across the street from my grandmother's apartment to my mother's apartment, back and forth, forth and back, front doors wide open, revolving, with neighbors and family coming through from D.R." (5). Soledad was constantly surrounded by her family, an exhausting experience echoed in the repetition of the passage, marked by activity without change or progress. The sharing of all private spaces as public family space, while partly fueled by economic necessity, was a sign of familial intimacy, to the point that refusing access is essentially an insult. Leaving the neighborhood is an even more serious offense: Soledad's move, despite only being from uptown to downtown, reads as the severing of family ties. The customs of the neighborhood dictate that one's individual space be wholly subsumed into communal spaces.

Everything is public: death, sickness, conflict, sex. The novel emphasizes the absence of privacy to show us the paths both Soledad and Olivia must travel to get beyond the confinement of the family and the barrio. All the formative moments of the narrative possess unintended audiences. Soledad recalls that the death of her father Manolo several years earlier— he is pushed out the apartment window by his abused wife, Olivia—was instantly a neighborhood spectacle: "He was lying on the street, a crowd surrounding him, as blood gushed out of his body" (30). We learn later that Soledad's father molested her, while "babysitting," in the same apartment, on the couch with her cousin Flaca there also (191). Public molestation and public spousal abuse are followed by public death. Olivia literally pushes her husband from the private sphere into the street.

Disease is also fair game for omniscient neighbors. Guilt and stress, combined with an island past she has failed to grapple with, lead Olivia into a strange sickness, which also becomes shockingly public. Unable to speak, and moving in a dreamlike state, Olivia is confined to her room, and her family takes on twenty-four-hour care. Twice, her illness transforms into a neighborhood event. When Soledad first arrives in the barrio, her family's plight is being aired: "Suddenly in front of my grandmother's building, the people multiply and my grandmother is parting the crowd, carrying my mother, Olivia . . . I shove past the vecinos and vecinas, tugging, pulling, dragging myself through the crowds" (5). "Crowd" is repeated three times, and conspicuously, Soledad observes them before she knows the impetus for their congregating. The crowd is closer to and knows more about Olivia's condition than her own daughter, and their implied hesitance to provide space suggests they feel entitled to this knowledge. Later on, when Olivia sleepwalks out on the fire escape naked, the seemingly always-present crowd returns:

> Olivia is standing by the window naked. Her nipples like chocolate kisses. Naked. . . .
> Victor climbs out to grab her. A group of people are already gathering around below her.
> Que viva la naturaleza! The frío-frío man yells, urging the crowd to say, Que viva!
> . . . . Get the fuck out of here, Flaca yells to all the people looking and standing. (45)

Olivia's illness again becomes a spectacle, complete with cheers from the crowd, a group call-and-response chant, and a mass of vecinos' stares.

Sex is equally public and available for an audience. The absence of individual space *within* the apartments results in the attempted privatization of the outside: Victor's mistresses yell up to him from the street, airing the intricacies of Victor's romantic life; the alley converts into a bedroom for Flaca and Pito; the front stoop for Soledad and Ritchie's "chance" encounters becomes the site for their flirtation. One "date" is a trip to the nearby playground, where Ritchie carries Soledad into a water feature, and they lay soaked on seesaws, seemingly indifferent to onlookers.[3] Even the roof, which could be a site for privacy, and for a potential reversal of the male gaze—for women to watch without being watched—twice becomes interpolated: Doña Sosa goes to the roof to be alone and finds herself in the midst of an unexpected flirtation with Ciego (71); Soledad and Ritchie go

to the roof to be alone and are caught having sex by Flaca, who is traveling across the block by rooftop with Cady to avoid being seen by the rival
girls from 163rd Street. In fact, none of these spaces succeeds in being private: Soledad sees Flaca and Pito leave the alley, with "a grin that screams
success" on Pito's face (124).

At the opening of the novel, Soledad is returning home to the neighborhood after leaving two years ago to pursue art school in the East Village.
Upon arriving on the street she grew up on, she is immediately menaced
by the space:

> As soon as I arrive at 164th Street I'm attacked. I trip on the uneven side-
> walk. The air-conditioners spit at me. The smell of onion and cilantro
> sting my eyes. I start to sneeze, the humidity is thick, sweat beads drip
> on the small of my back. Hydrants erupt, splashing cold water over the
> pavement. I know I should turn back while I still can, before anyone in
> my family sees me, but when potbellied, sockless men and pubescent
> homeboys call me mami, as if I'll give them the time of day if they stare
> at me long enough, I know I must keep moving forward. The last thing
> I want to do is look lost or confused about where I'm going. There are
> more cops on the streets than fire hydrants. Merengue blares out of car
> speakers, the Dominican flag drapes in place of curtains on apartment
> windows, sneakers hang from lampposts, Presidente bottles, pizza boxes
> and old issues of *El Diario* burst out of the trash cans on the corner, a side
> of pernil grills by a building's basement.
>
> The way I'm figuring it, my time in Washington Heights is like a prison
> sentence. (3)

"Attacked" is a strong verb that of course connotes physical violence, which
makes the passage's linking of the verb to the inanimate objects of the street
(the sidewalk, air-conditioners, smells, hydrants) even more intensely
threatening. The street has agency and exercises malevolence against Soledad that is expressly physical, including her feet, head, eyes, nose, back,
and ears. The personified aspects of the street also demonstrate how the
neighborhood makes her fundamentally aware of her body in the space.
This bodily awareness takes two forms as the passage progresses, introducing the two key ways the neighborhood confines its female members in
the text. The first is the fear of a tarnished reputation or of being judged ("I
should turn back while I still can, before anyone in my family sees me"),
and the second is the fear of the male gaze and its implied threat of sexual
violence ("sockless men and pubescent homeboys call me mami, as if I'll

give them the time of day if they stare at me long enough"). Both fears prevent her from reversing direction and make her perform confidence ("the last thing I want to do is look lost or confused"), to prevent being accosted by the men on the street or shamed by her own family. Time on this street, with its attacking elements, both animate and inanimate, and its constant threat upon the body, seems to compare easily to "a prison sentence."

The more explicit of the two fears operating upon Soledad and the other female characters in the neighborhood is that of potentially violent male sexual intent. The novel gives us several disturbing scenes set in the tucked-away spaces of 164th. Flaca initially feigns interest in Pito, Ritchie's friend, to try and make Ritchie jealous, but Pito converts her play-act into action, in the alley near Flaca's apartment building. By manipulating the space around her, he forces her into an initial intimate encounter, which, while consensual, is still threatening in nature. First, he stalks and then restrains her: "he stops her by catching her hand in the air, pulling her close to him" (94). Then he literally corners her:

> Pito leads the way, walking Flaca past the garbage piles in the basement, through the skinny passageways out to the back of the building, where the alley exposes itself to hot sun. The concrete shimmers in the sunlight. The smell of old garbage blends with the smell of sweat and marijuana. Pito picks up his cap hanging off a pipe and then pushes Flaca softly against the wall. (95)

As with Soledad's opening passage, the setting is vividly cast as a bystander or even abettor: the alley "exposes itself," the concrete shimmers, the smells of the garbage blend in; Pito even uses this alley as an extension of his home, hanging his cap routinely on the pipe. The agency of the various alley elements is contrasted with Flaca's lack of agency: while the inanimate objects are subjects, "Flaca" is a grammatical object, who is "walked past" the setting. She is pushed against the wall, subject to the alley's strength. When Flaca tells Pito that she may not be ready, she is met with more, less subtle, violence: "Pito punches the wall and scrapes skin off his knuckles. You see what you made me do, Pito says, blowing on his scraped fingers" (95). After punching the wall and blaming his action on Flaca, she assents, only to find that his feigned anger was a ploy.

Makeout Alley

On West 164th Street, there's still a mounted basketball hoop (far from regulation height, I suspect) at the end of an alley on the south side of the

FIGURE 29. The alley and basketball hoop behind 610 West
164th Street, 2018

street, where Ritchie comes to play with Pito. The entrance to the alley
is visible from the stoop across the street, and while it has a door and a
fence, it's unlocked and ajar. The hoop is surrounded by buildings on all
sides (see fig. 29). This alley is tucked next to 610 West 164th, the building
directly across from apartment 615, where Cruz lived while writing *Soledad*. The alleys on the south side are long but not as narrow as the north
side and don't require going underneath the buildings. Based on description, then, what I call Pito and Flaca's "makeout alley" is on the north side
of the street. There's massive construction going on (not to mention the
alleyways are fenced and often locked for tenant-only access), so this alley
that "exposes itself to hot sun" (95) behind the 615 building is off-limits.
These northside alleys sport extremely narrow passageways that descend
under the buildings to then emerge to street level and sun behind them.
However even back here the alley is exposed to potential onlookers from
the apartments on both sides (see fig. 30).

FIGURE 30. "Makeout Alley," behind 625 West 164th Street, 2018

Pito and Flaca's next encounter heightens the threat of physical violence. She has decided "she isn't going to walk down the block anymore," but by tracking her whereabouts, Pito corners her again (123). When "they go to the alley behind the abandoned refrigerator," the verbs suggest a less than pleasurable experience: he "covers" and "clumsily grabs" her breasts, hushes her, is "pushing" his body against hers, "pressing his tongue" down her throat, and even "hurting" her "at times" (124). In response, she "moves" his hands away and "pushes" his body off her, but her hesitance is indifferently overridden. Flaca ultimately "lets" Pito do things to her body, after twice trying to get him to stop. Flaca describes the negative shift in the encounter in relation to the environment, as "all of a sudden the garbage near them starts to stink" (157).

The male menacing of Flaca's body reaches a climax midway through the novel, when she and Caty "bounce quick" to the Wendy's (103). The Wendy's on 165th and Broadway has a large dining area with floor-to-ceiling windows, so people inside can be seen from both 165th and Broadway. Flaca is sitting at a table waiting as one, two, three, and eventually *seven* male strangers surround her. They stand while she remains seated. Several of them confirm to each other that she is "from 164" while "leaning over her." They close in so tightly that "she can no longer see Caty unless she stands up on one of the chairs" (104), which is what she does. This Wendy's back door is usually locked, leaving only one entry and exit point; that nonfunctioning door means one is cornered in the back dining area. Yet there is nowhere you could sit to eat where you would not be seen. For Flaca to be surrounded in this space means she would be physically trapped, while still being wholly visible from the street: another moment where a female character is seen but not heard.

Flaca *is* seen through the window by her mother, and Flaca knows "she's in mad trouble" (104). Despite being accosted by over half a dozen adult men, Flaca is the one blamed for the street-level male attention. Immediately afterwards, for fear of and for Flaca's body, her mother, Gorda, beats her first with a belt and then with her fist (106). By virtue of being a resident of the street, Flaca is condemned to constant male attention, and that attention is inevitably threatening in nature. Whether in a pseudoconsensual sexual encounter or just leaving her apartment building, her body is watched, and violence against it—from a manipulative love interest like Pito, or a crowd of leering young men, or her own mother's fearful fists—is imminent.

Lest Flaca's experiences read as the exception, or the result of a precocious teen courting the male gaze, Soledad's street encounters are similarly fraught. Soledad makes reference throughout to all the "guys around the neighborhood" who catcall and leer at her in the street (97). Yet even her love interest Ritchie behaves towards her in a subtly threatening manner. When Soledad attempts to enjoy the peace of a Saturday morning when "people sleep in," she is surprised by Ritchie: "I'm glad to see no one is out yet as I sit in front of my grandmother's building. For once I have the block to myself. Except for the early birds at the luncheonette on the corner it's pretty much just me, the mailbox, parked cars and the old lady walking the poodle" (74). When she says that she possesses the space, even though she mentions early bird diners nearby and a woman walking a poodle, what she is actually referring to is the absence of leering men on the street. When present, *they* own the block.

Of course, Ritchie spoils her brief moment of ownership and immediately interpolates her as an object of sexual interest:

I'm surprised you're out with all the shit that's been going down around here, Ritchie says. . . .

Where else am I gonna go? I live here.

So you're telling me you're not just fine, you're brave too.

I'm telling you it's my first Saturday off in a long time and I came out for a breath of fresh air. (74)

Ritchie alludes to the recent shootings in the neighborhood. He also couches his compliment of Soledad as brave with another of her as attractive, which places her back in the context of the street-level male gaze. He continues to flirt but also menace her, by chastising her for being too uptight: "Why are you so stiff, Soledad? You act like I want to bite you" (74). Like the other male neighbors, Ritchie criticizes Soledad's standoffishness, and essentially gaslights her for being on her guard in the midst of persistent unwanted male attention, claiming her reserve is unwarranted. Ritchie invalidates Soledad's behavior as excessively "stiff," while the number of coerced sexual encounters in the text—Pito and Flaca, Olivia's rape by a taxi driver as payment for her fare, Gorda's nonconsensual penetration by the ghost of Manolo—piles up, suggesting such wariness is prudent rather than prudish.

Despite his characterization as a sensitive, caring man, Ritchie's romantic scenes with Soledad are deliberately similar in tone to the lurid alley makeouts of Flaca and Pito. In every interaction, Ritchie grabs and pulls Soledad: "Ritchie grabs me before I can escape into the building" (96); "C'mon, he says . . . He takes my wrist and pulls me through" (158). While flirting on the stoop, he occupies Soledad's space like the men in the Wendy's occupied Flaca's, touching her hair and "leaning over" her. When she tries to "push him away," "he's a rock" that won't budge (127). Their climactic love scene, while wholly consensual, betrays Soledad's continued focus on being watched and being bodily threatened:[4] "On the rooftop nothing seems to matter. No one can touch me . . . I want to forget my mother, forget myself, forget we are on a roof and down the block my grandmother is already making dinner. I want him to roll me under, twist me open like a bottle cap, kiss my spine gutter deep" (159). The rooftop being the only place she can't be touched points to her intense awareness of her body's vulnerability in the neighborhood. The ostensible openness of the roof space is belied by the paralepsis of her thoughts, which even in the midst of a sex act return to her mother and grandmother, and specifically to locations: to the roof, to the block, to the apartment. The phrase "gutter deep" demonstrates her inability to forget where she is, even on the roof: this space, and this encounter, are not separate from the "snake sounds" and catcalls and leers she experiences in the rest of the barrio. The final line is disturbing in its imagery. The stream of figurative language is marked by either danger (being rolled over by a wave) or by heightened objectification (Soledad as a bottle cap being twisted). Altogether, the scene forecloses the possibility of Soledad escaping the frightening male dominance of the neighborhood.

BROADWAY AND 164TH

This male dominance of public spaces is apparent when I walk the neighborhood. Washington Heights' main drag, Broadway, has tree-lined islands that form part of the Broadway Malls, a 150-year-old Upper West Side parks project that runs from 169th to 135th Street, with benches, a pedestrian path, and numerous chess tables along its length ("Broadway Malls"). Small and large groups of Latino men gather, either to play dominoes on concrete chess tables scattered throughout the malls, or to sit on the wooden benches and foldout chairs, and watch the traffic go by. The benches face cross traffic on the north and south sides of the malls, and these men, even when they have brought their own chairs, elect to sit side by side, facing outwards toward pedestrians. I missed the opportunity to interview one group I saw of perhaps ten men, walkers and wheelchairs nearby, who were chatting in Spanish as I passed by (when I returned to the spot the next day, they weren't there; their schedule surely has a logic I was ignorant of). Walking past almost a dozen men, all facing you, is not *necessarily* threatening, but it is disconcerting.

Off the main road and on side streets, men are to be found against building walls and at corners, in twos and threes, talking together. Usually they refrain from intercepting passersby, though there are some catcalls aimed at me and other women. I see no women doing this, standing and watching the street, only men. There are both women and men who set up sidewalk sales of clothing or produce along Broadway, but only men appear to be standing without a visible purpose. Their ages range from young to old. Even when they don't verbally harass passersby, their presence suggests that ownership of the sidewalk is theirs. On a weekday morning in Wahi Diner, the twenty-four-hour unnamed "luncheonette" of the book, at the corner of 164th and Broadway, there are a number of Dominican men in uniforms having breakfast together at the counter before heading to work. Besides the waitresses, I am the only woman in the restaurant.

The ubiquitous male gaze and the threat it implies result in an intense policing of female bodies in the barrio by their families, especially by female relatives. Rather than curbing male street attention, mothers, aunts, and grandmothers tighten their grip on their daughters, nieces, and granddaughters.[5] Gorda constantly watches Flaca from the apartment window, telling her, "if I can't see you from the window you've gone too far" (17). If Flaca is out too early, she is chastised: "you better not be out here when I return" (84), If Flaca is out too late, she is chastised. Flaca complains that her mom yells out the window at her to not "let me catch you in the calle when it's dark," "so loud like she doesn't care that the whole neighborhood could hear" (43). The teenager believes her mother "has spies everywhere" (84).

Soledad's actions are similarly monitored, to the point of hilarity: she feels as "if I'm being watched and laughed at" by the neighborhood women for not knowing how to pick out produce properly at the grocery store: "I can almost hear the other women in the store thinking to themselves, How is she ever getting married, she still doesn't know how to pick fruit" (52). This combination of male sexual attention and female watchfulness result in a total absence of privacy in the neighborhood, which generates the intergenerational conflict of the narrative and forces Soledad and Olivia to leave the barrio in order to heal. In a sense, the positive value of family concern turns negative as fear fueled by the neighborhood's closeness and latent violence transforms protecting into policing.

The novel's closed and resolutely public setting is matched by the claustrophobia of *Soledad*'s cluttered character perspectives. Dialogue in the text is interspersed throughout without quotation marks so that external voices intrude into the interior narrations of any given character, eliminating the sharp distinction between the personal and public. There are very few attributions to dialogue, so that a character's words often appear anonymous. These words without owners make it more difficult to ascribe personal thoughts or values to certain characters through speech. In this crafted cacophony of voices, individuality is lost to the noise of the neighborhood. Furthermore, the chapters present multiple unlabeled narrative perspectives, divided only by a line of space, so that each character's voice appears and disappears within an always-changing cycle of voices, with no consistent logic for transitioning from voice to voice. The characters' personal experiences are constantly interrupted by other characters, and the characters' private selves are rendered nonexistent through the frequent mixing of spoken conversations, other perspectives, and other times and places. In short, Cruz makes the space of the novel itself bereft of privacy.

A History of Violence and Loving Voyeurism

THE CRACK YEARS

The fear and watchfulness of the block emerges from the neighborhood's harrowed history, as its community was besieged by economic and social turmoil throughout the second half of the twentieth century. In a story played out all over America's cities, the composition of the Heights changed drastically in the 1960s and 1970s. Aided by tax breaks, Robert Moses's extensive new highway infrastructure, unionized jobs, and their relatively recent status as ethnically "white," Jewish, Greek, and Irish residents moved to the suburbs in large numbers. Newcomers to the city found the downtown manufacturing jobs that new immigrants depended on disappearing, as the push for cheaper labor, and the new highway grid, moved factory and manufacturing jobs out of Manhattan (Snyder 116). The thriving hospitals in the region also closed and moved out: of the six in northern Manhattan, by 1983 only Columbia Presbyterian remained (138). Yet, as those who could started moving out, the Dominicans were moving in.

Dominicans began arriving in Washington Heights as part of the first waves of post-Trujillo immigration and continued to immigrate throughout the twentieth and twenty-first centuries. The composition of the Southern (and Eastern) Heights was already majority Black and Puerto Rican (100). In 1970, northern Manhattan was 78 percent white and only 2 percent Hispanic. By 1980, it was 19 percent Black and 38 percent Hispanic (with Latino/as likely being undercounted) (138). This Hispanic majority was largely Dominican. An informal economy arose, in the Southeastern Heights especially, revolving around home labor (childcare, sewing), street peddling, and sweatshops, which attracted undocumented Dominicans who could still earn a better wage than back home (140). As elsewhere in the Dominican diaspora, the majority of Dominican immigrants to the neighborhood were women (144). By the 1980s, Dominican "migrants were ever more likely to be working-class people whose skills were poorly suited for the new economic order of New York, with its emphasis on finance, media, and real estate" (142). Given this difficult economic climate, when the crack epidemic hit in the 1980s, it decimated the Heights.

"When crack dealers took over blocks" in Washington Heights, Robert Snyder explains, "one of the first things to go was places for kids to play": "Dealers set up shop in apartments, seized upper floors for their lookouts, and made sure no street games interfered with the customers who drove into the neighborhood. Sidewalks became dangerous. Parents kept their children indoors. The drug trade cast a shadow over the entire neighborhood" (1). Public and private space was taken from neighborhood residents. In the Heights, where the murder rate peaked at 119 murders in 1991 (Bernstein), well-meaning residents who were seen talking with police became targets of violence by drug gangs. The competition for drug-dealing was so intense that rival gangs played out turf wars at the level of the block. Parks, playgrounds, and green spaces became popular sites for drug use. While some residents of the Heights were crack users, much of the trafficking was with commuters from the suburbs, aided by the new highway infrastructure, who came into the neighborhood to buy drugs (double-parked cars up and down the block became the symbol of the drug trade in the Heights) (Snyder 168).

Heights residents survived the crack years by turning to self-policing of their blocks and apartment buildings. Police helped to curb the drug trade, with more patrols and eventually with the redistricting of precincts in 1994, which gave the Southern Heights its own police force (189). The drug trade changed too, becoming less territorial and moving operations more indoors in the early 1990s (190). However, the role of the neighborhood in protecting itself cannot be overstated. The formation of community organizations, campaigns to reclaim parks and public spaces and to look after one's own neighbors, slowly helped change the face of the neighborhood. The Dominican community, which now had elected officials to represent them (192), was still largely suspicious of police, a result of both the Dominican Republic's own troubled authoritative past and the at times tense and racially charged relations between cops and immigrants in the area. Neighbors recognized that "building strong communities was a big part of fighting crime": several blocks came together *as* blocks to "run their own safety patrols, register voters, and pressure landlords to improve their buildings" (193). By the late 1990s, murder rates had declined, and the slow rescue of the streets was well under way (189–90).

By 1997, when Angie Cruz moved back to 164th Street to work on what would become *Soledad,* the neighborhood was just emerging from the ravages of the drug trade, unemployment, and political powerlessness that gripped the region in the 1970s, 1980s, and 1990s. That history brought residents together to form a safer and more unified, but also a hypervigilant, community. The crack epidemic had passed, but the culture of self-surveillance and the fear of public spaces remained. "What did remain in the Heights from the crack years," Snyder notes, "was a deep strain of fear" (195). Cruz acknowledges the profound effect the neighborhood's culture of fear had on her relationship with her mother, noting in her interview with fellow Dominican Silvio Torres-Saillant that her growing up in the barrio was shadowed by "all the things that worry overprotective Dominican parents" (111). Her mother's concerns, in particular, "were so much informed by the thought of losing me to men" (111).

This history helps explains why Gorda and others in the text view the heavy surveillance by and of family members (and by extension neighbors) as a positive characteristic of 164th Street. Both Soledad and Olivia ultimately find the public nature of the neighborhood too overwhelming and either turn inward or move out. However, Gorda seems to voice the opinion of the barrio when she describes such intense closeness as a virtue. Cruz also celebrates the positive aspect of this inward-looking neighborhood mentality: "I feel that *Soledad* was created by a community of people, not just me, and also all my mother's sacrifices and my grandmother's stories and all their love. I have an intense supportive family" (Torres-Saillant 117).

BARRIOLOGY AND BARRIOIZATION
Gorda's philosophical discussion of neighborhood surveillance points to its emerging not just out of internal crime and violence, but also from sieges by the outside by what she views as white outsiders. She describes an immigrant barrio closing its ranks as insulation from the non-Dominican world that does not let them in. Convinced a white obstetrician might steal a poor Dominican baby to give to a rich white family, Gorda views the walls of the doctor's office as furtive (108), explaining aloud that she had a home birth to not "take the chance" (108). As her tirade accelerates, Gorda assigns positive attributes to the watchfulness of her own community: "Imagine if all these walls were transparent like a fishbowl, she says, and think how much goes on inside of walls. All these walls. We live behind walls, even our bodies are walls" (108). A "fishbowl" usually connotes a cramped space with a painful absence of privacy; Gorda however finds this arrangement ideal. She wants to see (and arguably be seen) through walls. Privacy is a tool of the white world, while Gorda's world values shared experiences and intense intimacy.

Raúl Homero Villa offers a schematic for interpreting the relationship between the external and internal forces that create a barrio that can illuminate Washington Heights' mix of care and self-surveillance. *Barrio-Logos* focuses on Chicanx urban practice in California, but arguably its model can be applied to any ethnic neighborhood that has been historically shaped by what he calls "barrioization": a combination of "dominating social processes originating *outside* the barrios" (4), including the physical, legal, and ideological control of the space and of its residents. Barrioization alone does not make a barrio. Villa demonstrates that the response and resistance on the part of the community against barrioization *also* shapes the space, transforming space into place: these internal forces, which Villa (borrowing from the 1960s East L.A. underground magazine *Con Safos*) calls "barriology," operate in a dialectic with barrioization; together barriology and barrioization build and develop the unique cultural practices of a barrio, or the neighborhood's "geographical identity."

A recent study of Washington Heights by CUNY's Dominican Studies Initiative reflects both barriology and barrioization. Dominicans in the county who identified as black, indigenous, or mestizo felt less access and support from city services in their neighborhoods than Dominicans who identified as white. Race and ethnicity was the single most important factor in determining perception of access to social services (Hernández and Ortega 6). This perception of inequity and restricted access is compounded when language serves as a barrier, and many Spanish-speaking residents remain isolated from the English-speaking city. When asked a series of questions related to comfort interacting in English and Spanish, as well as the frequency of interaction with non-Dominicans, Manhattan Dominicans reported that a staggering 90 percent of their friendships were with other Dominicans, 86 percent of their household and neighbors were Dominican, and 63 percent of their coworkers were Dominican or Dominican American. Only in schools was there an opportunity to forge relationships with non-Dominicans (at 49 percent of fellow Dominicans and Dominican Americans). This tendency to seek out other Dominicans is directly correlated to the residents' facility with English and Spanish: participants who were eighteen and older living in Washington Heights said they felt much more comfortable speaking in Spanish to people they don't know (88 percent) than speaking to strangers in English (54 percent). The study runners concluded that the level of internal interaction and the seeking of relationships within the Dominican community of northern Manhattan is particularly high (Hernández and Ortega 10).[6]

While it is inaccurate to say that barrios are formed wholly from negative external spatial practices, it is also imprecise to claim that the internal spatial practices of the community developed in response are wholly positive. Barrio culture tends "towards positive articulations of community consciousness," yet the neighborhood can also be home to poverty, crime, illness, and despair (Villa 5). In response to the barrioization of Washington Heights in the second half of the twentieth century—effected through the architectural isolation of "new-law tenements," the political isolation of the newly arrived Dominican community, the geographical isolation of northern Manhattan, and the economic isolation brought by New York City's shift to finance and the disappearance of manufacturing jobs (making the area vulnerable to rising drug dealing and crime rates), compounded by the excessive policing of poor ethnic neighborhoods and the ideological "othering" of working-class Latinx immigrants in the US social and racial ordering—the transnational Dominican community has developed a series of cultural practices to defend itself. *Soledad* suggests that self-surveillance and hyperwatchfulness are the tools the neighborhood uses to protect against violence and to support one another in the face of social ostracism.

WASHINGTON HEIGHTS BARRIOGRAPHY

Based on *Soledad*'s depiction of barrio space, one expects to find the streets of Washington Heights besieged by crime, noise, watchful eyes, and the public airing of family dramas. Yet the area has transformed in many ways since the novel was written. Today, eighteen years after the publication of *Soledad*, the neighborhood feels safe, and crime rates have dropped precipitously since the 1990s. Newer immigrant groups from Latin America and Asia have joined the Dominican demographic majority. However, the neighborhood remains profoundly marked by its history and by the dominance of Dominican culture; the distinct sense of each street as an insulated community, and the vigilance of the residents, remains. Washington Heights retains the image of itself as an explicitly Dominican immigrant community, despite the increasing forces of gentrification. The male gaze that follows Soledad and Flaca—spurred on by an urban culture of men performing command of outdoor spaces and many neighbors' inheritance of traditional Dominican gender roles—persists. The vigilance of both men and women, born of decades of violence and drug trafficking, reinforced by the Dominican community's positive outlook on knowing one's neighbors, results in streets that are still intensely watchful.

I take the subway from downtown to echo Soledad's hesitant return to the neighborhood in the opening of the novel. As the A train climbs north in Manhattan, there's a bellwether moment when the crowds disappear at Fifty-Ninth Street: "the tourists, the white folks, the kind of people who are too scared to go uptown, get off the train" (2). Indeed, even now, when northern Manhattan has largely recovered from the crack epidemic, there is a massive exodus of subway riders. The only stops after this are Harlem, the Heights, and Inwood. The white families with strollers, which had cluttered the train, clear out, and the composition of the traingoers becomes more homogenous, as mainly Latino/as and African Americans are left.

168th Street Station, one of these last stops on the A Train line, places you in the heart of Washington Heights. The station is surrounded by the Columbia Presbyterian Hospital Complex and full of bustle. But just a few blocks south, the traffic is sparse enough for you to fearlessly jaywalk across major intersections. Broadway is the exception, full of cars and pedestrians, but St. Nicholas and Fort Washington (the other north-south streets in the neighborhood) are surprisingly calm. Riverside Drive is even bucolic, lined by greenery and "the wall," which divides the neighborhood from the edge of Manhattan Island that falls below it. I'm staying in an Airbnb on St. Nick and 165th Streets. Initially I assumed foolishly that my host, who was blonde (dyed, I learned) and pearl-necklace-laden in the photo, with an Anglo first name, and an interior decorating style that favors those wall hangings that are phrases—"What I Love Most About Home Is Who I Live With," "Be Yourself, It Suits You"—which I associate with upper-middle-class white "beach chic," was a sign of the inevitable gentrification of the area. But when I arrive to the apartment building and find myself sharing the entryway with an energetic middle-aged black man, who proceeds to sit down and excitedly light up his crack pipe in front of me at 4 p.m. on a weekday (and then just as jauntily walk back out to the street), I suspect I misjudged the character of the block. When I make my way up to the apartment and learn that my host's surname is Piedra and see the railroad-style apartment full of family portraits, Latin American tchotchkes, and a homemade painting of a Caribbean beach in my room, I joke to myself that I have a Dominican home stay. The family of five is incredibly welcoming; the parents are native Spanish speakers, the young children breezily bilingual. They moved from Brooklyn five years ago and love the neighborhood for its relative safety and community (Piedra).

Despite the passage of time, several of the landmarks from the book remain and indeed appear to be neighborhood institutions. The apartment on 615 West 164th is the same one that Cruz grew up in and returned to write *Soledad*: this real building shares all the characteristics of the apartment building in the novel. It boasts brick construction and a U-shape or horseshoe design so that the outer edges look out onto the narrow gap between buildings, the back of the building faces a large alley, and all the apartment windows face inward toward the other apartments and a courtyard (see fig. 31). The design is literally panoptic, with the courtyard figuring in for the watchtower. The courtyard has a pine tree (no longer dead as in the book) and a garden, but no seating area,

FIGURE 31. The view from the street at 615 West 164th Street,
2018; notice the conspicuous fire escapes

and a walkway surrounding it with four doors at the corners for access
to the different sections of the building. The courtyard sits up from the
street somewhat, as the building has two stoops of a few steps each,
the first on the sidewalk, and the second at the end of a short corridor.
This feature creates some privacy along the corridor, though really all
can be seen from the interior windows or the street. The fire escapes
are placed on the windows that look out into the courtyard, because of
the very small space between buildings. The front-facing windows of the
horseshoe also have fire escapes facing the street. These fire escapes, and
Soledad's description of a kind of tucked-away entryway where she and
Ritchie could not be seen, suggest that Olivia's and Ritchie's apartments
are in 615 (or the identical building next to it) and that Gorda's is across
the street. A public display of nudity on the fire escape, such as Olivia's,
regardless of which apartment she lived in, would be seen clearly from
multiple vantage points on the street. The courtyard garden itself is not

large, maybe fifteen feet across. It would be easy to know who is home and who comes and goes. In a nonfiction essay for the *New York Times* about her childhood apartment building, Cruz mentions how her family could always see when her light was on and would frequently stop by unannounced.

That Flaca and Caty would take the roofs to a gang meeting with girls from 163rd also confirms her building is on the south side of 164. The fronts and backs of the complexes touch, so going from roof to roof is less superheroic than it sounds. There is a distinct difference between the south side and the north side of 164th that is visible in the level of upkeep of the buildings—615 and 625 are owned by Columbian Presbyterian Hospital and are under private management. The apartments across the street are public, several residents (of 615 and 625) tell me, and are thus less well maintained and have less illustrious residents than the doctors and hospital employees housed on the north side (Raju, personal interview; Levi, personal interview).

164th is a short block, and most traffic is from people who live on the block, rather than people passing through. West of the street there isn't much: Fort Washington Street, and then Riverside Drive, which becomes a busy roadway, and then the Hudson River Greenway. This geographic position somewhat insulates this block and the blocks directly south of it. Less foot traffic means that unfamiliar faces are often met with stares. It also feeds into the block's awareness of itself and its residents. On the block I pass a troop of very young girls in matching shirts who are in a summer day camp. One girl says "Hola" to an older woman who passes by, proudly telling her friends, "She's my grandma's friend." The woman exchanges greetings with the camp counselor in Spanish, as they know each other as well. I get looks from a neighbor who is standing in the alley with the basketball hoop (but why is *he* in the alley?), along with the occasional, but lackluster, catcall on the block. While Broadway is full of people, walking on 164th, even though it's adjacent, seems to breed suspicion. With only apartment buildings on the block, the travelers on it are mainly neighbors.

Given our contemporary moment of Trump terrorizing migrant communities, it's unsurprising that many neighbors don't want to talk to me. Several older Spanish-speaking women refuse to answer questions; one woman told me I couldn't walk with her to her apartment on nearby Fort Washington Street because she was in a big hurry ("tengo prisa"), which was hilarious considering she was using a walker and going a pace approximately a quarter of my natural gait. However, the residents of 615 and 625 164th Street were generally amenable to being interviewed as they entered the complex.

One pair of immigrants willing to talk were Juan and Matilde Sedano, a well-heeled married couple in their sixties who live in 625 West 164th Street. They tell me the neighborhood has changed very much for the better since they moved here forty years ago. It was very bad at first. Lots of drugs and drug dealing on the street. They credit Mayor Giuliani (as do most of those I interviewed) with cleaning up the streets. The hospital too has done a lot to change the character of the neighborhood, as Columbia Presbyterian owns several buildings in the blocks surrounding the medical center, which lies north of 164th. Matilde gestured to the manicured garden in the quiet courtyard and said it's like this, "tranquilo," all day and night now. Juan pointed out the cameras mounted along the street and explained the heightened police surveillance of the neighborhood as another positive change. Mohammed Raju, originally from Bangladesh, who has lived in 615 164th street for nineteen years, also describes the street as "better than it was before": "it was rough. But the government and the community came together to clean it up."

Many of the residents of the two buildings on the north side of 164 (numbers 615 and 625) are hospital employees. All the residents tell me that the composition of the buildings is cosmopolitan and diverse. Yahoshua Levi (another long-term resident) and Raju both highlight that the buildings across the street are public and thus under different management. The "curb appeal," or lack thereof, of the apartments on the south side suggests this economic distinction. And just a few blocks south and east from the hospital, apartment buildings begin sporting seven-foot black fencing around the entirety of the front entrances, complete with a sort of locked cage around the front door between residents and the street. This fencing lines entire blocks, running along various apartment complexes. At my own apartment entryway on St. Nicholas, a few blocks east, which like the apartments on 164th is U-shaped with a narrow walkway into the building, I am joined not once but twice in two days by two different men who each walked into the entrance from the street in order to sit quietly by the door and smoke crack. Both times at mid-afternoon. In contrast, the apartments on the northern side of 164th Street have well-kept gardens at a recess from the street and litter-free stoops (my entryway has dirt, trash, and the occasional sign of late-night whippet usage).

The Sedanos tell me that initially (in the late 1970s and 1980s) there were more Dominicans in the neighborhood, but now the building and the surrounding area are very mixed: whites, Africans, Latino/as, and some

Chinese. Yet Spanish is everywhere. Interviewees tell me that there are many different groups of Latinx immigrants in the area, from Mexico and Central America in particular. On Broadway, Spanish is more common to hear than English, and most signage is in Spanish as well as or often instead of English. Many stores cater to Hispanic immigrants, such as calling centers, Latin American women's fashion stores, restaurants with names like "La Tropical," "El Bar Latino," and "El Nuevo Jobo," *pastelerías* (bakeries), and grocers with catchy Spanish taglines ("Su Nombre José Liberato; Su Destino Vender Barato" ["his name is Liberato, his destiny is offering a bargain"]) who display produce with Spanish labels. Hispanic Caribbean culture dominates. Street vendors and grocers offer a number of staples of the Caribbean diet: *ñames, yautía,* coconut, and yucca. At the Wahi diner, they have a "Dominican Breakfast" on the menu (two eggs, "sacchichón" [*sic*], fried tropical cheese and *tostones* in addition to home fries and toast).

Broadway's hustle initially feels like the opposite of 164th Street's insularity: there is constant pedestrian traffic, and a mix of neighbors and hospital employees who commute in. Black, white, Asian, and Latinx blend in on the street. Yet inside the Dominican and Latinx neighborhood haunts, the foot traffic generally ceases to be diverse, and a sense of community—with its concomitant notion of outsiders—creeps in. Liberato Grocery for instance, called Liberty Butcher in the book (the *carnicería* in the back is the store's focal point), has a steady stream of Latinx customers exiting with heavy plastic bags in hand; laden with produce and freshly butchered meat on a hot summer day, they are clearly neighbors. I draw eyes in Liberato as I scan the aisles. The local nature of the store makes any outsider instantly noticeable. Soledad is afraid the older Dominican women are judging her produce selections (52), and I know exactly how she feels. Inside Tu Sabor Latino Bar and Grill, another Dominican establishment, the TV is set to news on the Spanish channel, Latinx immigrant families sit to eat in, the feisty jukebox is steadily streaming Latin American music, and most customers appear to be Spanish-speaking regulars who live nearby. The two subway lines and the economic pull of the hospital somewhat evaporate the intense feel of surveillance that hangs over 164th, yet these pockets of the neighborhood frequented by the Latinx community maintain a knowledge of who belongs, who lives here, and who is just passing through.

Washington Heights, and more specifically 164th Street, demonstrates the positive values of a close-knit Dominican immigrant community as well as its unintended negative consequences. Each block truly functions as a neighborhood: families know each other, recognize each other, support the same local businesses, and keep an eye out for strangers or threats to the block's relatively newfound and hard-won safety. This necessary watchfulness, however, can become stifling, especially to women who must still navigate streets dominated by men. External pressures on the enclave as an immigrant community in the US, facing discrimination, difficulties finding political representation, and the issues of assimilation and belonging that face any ethnic group, are countered by internal pressures from within the community to protect their own sons and daughters (especially daughters) and to maintain their own traditions.

Neighborhood Deafness

This climate of closeness could suggest that neighbors would be hyper-communicative with each other, but the watchfulness in *Soledad* is strictly visual. Olivia and Soledad are seen without being heard, as their past traumas are considered inappropriate for discussion. In one of Olivia's dream monologues—she no longer speaks aloud at the time of the narrative—she describes her mother's stark denial of her abusive marriage: "*I ask her if she desired my father, or did he just take her when he pleased? Did she ever say no to him? And if she did, did he hit her, like Manolo hit me? And when we talk she's not looking away from my bruises*" *(120)*. Olivia's stack of questions points to the lack of genuine conversation between them in terms of the responsibilities of being a wife. Doña Sosa *looks away* from Olivia's bruises, seeing but not acknowledging the abuse. This glaring lacunae in an otherwise intensely sharing family eventually results in Olivia's psychological breakdown, as for decades she is compelled to keep her emotions secret, prevented from processing past traumatic experiences.[7] As Donette Francis explains, "Her [Olivia's] story . . . is not one of immigrant success in coming to America but rather one of entrapment in the immigrant space of Washington Heights as well as an entrapment in identities of wife and mother" (122). The novel shows us how first Olivia and then Soledad grapple with the silence of the family and their social "entrapment" and then how hauntings emerge in their lives as the unintended consequences of their suffocating of the past.

Olivia inherits her mother's inability to speak about trauma, and Soledad in turn inherits Olivia's learned reserve. When Soledad tries to talk about her father's abuse or his death she is literally silenced by her aunt's hands: "Gorda covers my mouth with her hands and pretends the words were never spoken. She waves her arms in the air as if she can make the words evaporate somehow" (Cruz, *Soledad* 134). Soledad in turn turns inward, like her mother. Soledad shares a room with her cousin Flaca, separated by an unlockable door to her mother's apartment which she now shares with her aunt, but with all this closeness she still feels obligated to "push every painful feeling deep inside" herself. Her memories, uncontainable, transform into apparitions that fill the room. Soledad tries to hide under the sheets but knows that "there's no safe place" (191).

The hidden and silenced memories of Olivia and Soledad reappear as hauntings, which ultimately become embodied when Soledad discovers Olivia's written list of clients from her short time as a sex worker at a DR island resort as a teenager. When Soledad reads aloud the entries, these hidden memories become visible:[8] "they sit down on the sofa, on the windowsill, on the floor, all naked, penises exposed con mucha confianza. They drape themselves on top of the dining room table, lean against the wall, lie on one another as they wait" (195). The haunting is resolutely physical and overwhelms the confined space, literally filling the apartment with trauma. Their aggressive relationship to the space—"penises exposed" arrogantly, draped, sitting, leaning, laying—echoes the male relationship to space experienced outside the apartment. Domestic space, supposedly the domain of women and a respite from the surveillance and bodily threat of the outside, is also dominated by male aggression and the claustrophobic intimation of violence against female bodies.

Only in a space free from the barrio's claustrophobic watchfulness can these hauntings be fully exposed and confronted. The characters must return to the Dominican Republic not just to recognize that their pasts selves are inseparable from their present selves but because their new "home" in the US prevents them utterly from voicing their pasts. As visible but mute neighbors in Washington Heights, the family fears scandal too much to talk about who they were, fears violence too much to leave, and fears public opinion too much to break away from abusive or destructive relationships. Thus, the return to the DR is inevitable from a narrative standpoint and arrives in the last twenty pages. The uncharacteristically short closing chapter departs from the structure of the rest of the novel: here we only have two voices, Soledad and Olivia, both in first person, the only chapter that is entirely from the characters' perspectives. In the end, Olivia finally speaks aloud and begins to tell Soledad all the "things [she] want[s] to hear." Yet while Olivia is able to return to the source and find redemption, Soledad's experience of the island is not one of homecoming. Unmoored from the neighborhood she knows so well, and not a part of the island her parents call home, the novel closes with Soledad adrift between worlds.

Island Escape (But for Whom?)

Like many transnational neighborhoods, the Dominican community in northern Manhattan remains very connected to most residents' country of origin. The majority of residents interviewed in 2010 said they had traveled to the island in the last year and a full third of those who hadn't returned in the last year planned to do so soon, leaving only 15 percent of Dominicans in the county who had no plans to visit. Over 60 percent of Dominicans in these communities send remittances regularly (Hernández and Ortega 20). This sustained relationship to the Dominican Republic, reinforced by the cultural and linguistic insularity of the neighborhood, affirms the first generation's identities as Dominicans rather than Dominican Americans. Indeed, when I asked how Juan and Matilde Sedano identify—after forty years living in Washington Heights and becoming US citizens—they responded instantly that they were Dominicans (personal interview). Such loyalty to the Dominican Republic is further reflected in the results of the study: Almost 38 percent of New York City Dominicans said they planned to return to the island permanently (21). Whether or not these plans manifest, the data suggests that many in the first generation consider the DR their home. In *Soledad,* the island becomes the site of healing for those immigrants who left it behind, though not for their children, whose home is Washington Heights. The Sedanos emphasized this shift when they jokingly told me the term "Dominican Yorks" refers to kids born in the US—like their own—but not to themselves.

In the wake of "the list," Gorda has Olivia return to a "special place" in the DR to "erase her past step by step. She will start again" (206). Olivia echoes this language as she reflects: "*I want to erase all those years I lived with Manolo . . . I can cleanse my spirit and start again*" (219). While their language reflects the belief, deluded at best, that Olivia can "erase" her past and start over—this is the exact logic that fueled Olivia's move to the United States in the first place—both Gorda and Olivia feel that the island provides the *in*visibility and openness, contrary to the surveillance of the neighborhood, needed to confront one's former self to become a new self. Identities in Quisqueya Heights are fixed and anchored in public opinion; the island allows those who call it home to unfix who they are and forge new selves.

Olivia in particular reinforces the distinction between the two islands (Manhattan and Hispaniola). Despite the violence she's experienced on the island, it is New York she fears: "*I'm tired of being afraid, of hiding inside an apartment with gates so the burglars won't come in. I'm tired of running,*

I'm tired of letting what other people think of me, or will discover about me, control my life" (221). Washington Heights is where she lives behind gates and in fear for her reputation. She can only imagine securing renewal and freedom in the DR, and in fact the family's ritual at the "special" pools accomplishes this feat: Olivia finds her voice again. The role of place in Olivia's transformation cannot be overstated, as she imagines a new life that requires a "land" she calls "mine," "made especially for me," with beaches where her dancing feet can leave impressions on the sand (226).

In his chapter on *Soledad,* Irizarry points out that Cruz fictionalizes the site of Olivia's healing, turning the actual Tres Ojos, three connected pools of cave water outside Santo Domingo, to Tres Bocas, which she places further in the countryside (107).[9] Irizarry smartly argues that the change from "eyes" to "mouths" carries symbolic weight, implying "that Dominican women's silence began on the island and can be ruptured only by a return to it" (109). Given how surveillance—the work of the eyes—has haunted both Olivia and Soledad, the name change also removes any trace of watching that might follow the women to the island. This end to voicelessness is Olivia's however, not Soledad's.

Soledad's experience of going "back" to her parents' country of origin is very different, and forecloses the possibility for a new self that it promises her mother:

> Home. República Dominicana home. Every time my mother says home she means San Pedro de Macorís, and my grandmother means Juan Dolio . . . It is clear that my grandmother's house in Washington Heights is temporary, until they make enough money to return home . . . In the end they are born and want to die on the island they think of as home . . . In New York, they don't live, they work, until we go home. My mother always told me that home is a place of rest, a place to live. (Cruz, *Soledad* 219)

"Home" has never been the United States for any of Soledad's family. The repetition of "home" anchors it as the permanent place, "a place to live," in constant contrast to the impermanent place of *work:* New York. This stark opposition transforms even thirty years living in Washington Heights into a temporary stay. Such a perspective on work and living abroad clearly informs the family's inability to establish themselves as new people or to grow out of their pasts: if this "new life" is temporary (and no life at all, just work), important life changes must happen back "home."

Like her mother, when back in the DR, Soledad remembers her past there, yet her reminiscences are tellingly marked by her disconnection from the place. Symbolically, the daughter does not want to ground herself to the island: as a child she hates the way the rocks and sand get in her sandals (219–20), and when playing in the waves she cries, "I don't want to touch the bottom with my feet" (223). Her island reveries contrast starkly to her narration of her own neighborhood, which is always in the present tense and always full of sensory detail. While this visit "back" has opened up her mother, it remains unclear how Soledad can resolve the tensions *she* feels between being seen and not being heard.

Cruz leaves us questioning how, and *where*, Soledad can heal. The narrative ends in the Dominican Republic, not the barrio: this striking narrative choice gestures toward the impossibility of making Washington Heights an open space. Many critics read the ending as positive, arguing that with the rupture of Olivia's silence the narrative has resolved. Cristina Herrera claims that motherhood is ultimately what saves Olivia from madness in the end;[10] Ylce Irizarry, while acknowledging that this ending leaves readers "to wonder how this healing will manifest itself in the United States," still asserts that the mother and daughter are embarked on a path of understanding (110). By escaping to the island, Cruz defers the completion of Soledad's development, situating the protagonist's full arc of growth outside the scope of the story. The novel, which so vividly describes the neighborhood, often in first-person detail, fails to imagine, or more precisely, is *unable* to imagine, how Soledad might transform *her* home into a stable and nourishing site for cultivating her own identity. For an answer, perhaps we must look to the author herself.

A Third Place

In an autobiographical essay for the *New York Times,* "A Sublet in Washington Heights," Cruz describes returning to her childhood neighborhood in 1997 to attend an MFA program at NYU and eventually work on her first novel, which will become *Soledad.* She rents an apartment on West 164th Street, in the same building complex that houses her "sassy grandmother" and her aunt and teenaged nephew. As all the apartments face the derelict courtyard, Cruz has a front-row seat to the neighborhood drama: "as if watching a stage from a production booth, I saw my relatives and longtime neighbors across the way from my second-floor window" ("Sublet"). The short piece begins with her family's curiosity and endless questioning about her activities and whereabouts. They ask why she doesn't answer the door or pick up the phone, even when they can see her light is on; they see male visitors and ask why they are there; they come by with Tupperware containers of dinner and see writing groups inside and ask what Cruz is doing. They know when Cruz is home, when she has visitors, when she has "locked [her]self up." Cruz repeats to them that she is "estudiando" (studying), which satisfies their questions but not their prying inquisitiveness. Initially it seems this lack of privacy grates on the burgeoning author.

However, later in the piece Cruz describes her own enjoyment engaging in the private-as-public spirit that dominates the block: she faces her writing desk to the courtyard, yells greetings from her own second-floor window, looks to see if the lights are on, indicating her grandmother is home from her *fábrica* job, and watches as her aunt publicly chastises her unruly teenaged nephew. Adopting the culture of the neighborhood, she welcomes writers into her home for short- and long-term stays, saying her rooms "swelled in size" when needed: "and so my apartment was often full of people coming and going" ("Sublet"). She recognizes the busyness of the apartment and the housing complex but offers her revelation when the draft of her first novel was complete that "if I had waited to tell my story until I had a room of my own, as opposed to a place that always brimmed with people, I would never have finished that novel." The closeness and crowdedness of the barrio actually inspires the work because Cruz learns how to "tell her story" in the midst of "a place that always brimmed with people" rather than seeking to escape the din.

Angie Cruz is hyperconscious of her barrio's distinct notions of privacy, yet she recognizes the positive as well as negative aspects of neighborhood surveillance. In fact, she closes the piece not in criticism of the lack of space and absence of privacy of the street but with gratitude for it: "It was the spirit of all that collective activity inside that apartment with elastic walls that gave birth to my first novel" ("Sublet"). The metaphor of an apartment with "elastic walls" aptly describes both the claustrophobia of the neighborhood, which pushes the walls inward, and the valuing of togetherness, which expands the walls outward. She finds her voice in this space by embracing the noise, yet also by not fighting to be *heard*: her words are "birthed" (telling metaphor) on the *page*, to be read silently, even if they are written in a collective. Through art, Cruz—and arguably Soledad—will be *seen* rather than watched.

Cruz says she chose the title "Soledad" to "bring together the plights of all these women" who, though they "share the same location," are each "very much alone" (Torres-Saillant 123). For Cruz, Soledad's character encapsulated "the lack of communication among these women," which "creates a common isolation" (123). When asked whether this reflected the isolation of the human condition, Cruz countered that the referent was much closer to home (literally), positing that "the women in my community, even going back to the old country in the Dominican Republic . . . simply don't want to talk about anything that has to do with their sexuality," and telling her interviewer that, growing up, she felt unable to communicate with the women in her life, especially her mother: "I remember . . . feeling there was so much I couldn't tell my mother. I feared that if I told her she would hate me or not accept me" (123). Despite Cruz's positive associations with the neighborhood, she had to evolve out of a culture of silence around the struggles of Dominican women, even within a family unit.

Yet, like Soledad, Cruz cannot travel to the Dominican Republic to find her voice, as an older generation might, and she also cannot fully identify with the neighborhood. Cruz's few years living outside Washington Heights are held against her by the family, who say she "doesn't know" the "Dominican community" because she "left" (121). The Dominican Republic is not wholly home either: "It is very easy to romanticize that place that's home especially if we don't feel completely accepted where we live. I was never American enough in this country or I was never Dominican enough over there. *So where do you go?*" (126; emphasis added). Not American enough and not Dominican enough, Cruz balances out the emotional instability or anxiety by partially claiming both, a common response for someone with a transnational identity. Yet the question, "So where do you go?" looms large, not just for Cruz but for a generation of Dominican American women.

Soledad is itself the way the author breaks the female inheritance of silence and unspoken experience. Soledad's own way out is implied, though not shown, by her status as an artist: as she learns to love the Heights, and to listen to her mother, she gains the power to express her own emotions—but through her painting, not on the street. Cruz embraces the responsibility she feels to her own Dominican community: "writing . . . has to in some ways give back an idea or suggestion, something, for change" (10). By narrating the lives of strong yet unheard women, and showing their transformations, Cruz "gives back" the idea that women's stories deserve to be heard and that there are spaces for these stories that can't be seen on the block or the busy street corner or the crowded apartment. Her act of artistic expression, in light of the street she calls home, is a radically political act.

PART IV

SOUTH

Cuban Miami

"BROWN SUGAR HISTORIES": CUBA AND THE
UNITED STATES IN THE TWENTIETH CENTURY

CUBA'S EXCEPTIONAL relationship with the United States does not begin with Fidel Castro's rise to power. Indeed, what historian Louis Pérez Jr. calls the "ties of singular intimacy" between North America and Cuba, mutually entrenched in the slave trade and plantation economies, form in the eighteenth century. North Americans, including many Northerners, ran sugar plantations on the north coast of the island; North Americans built the railroads, ran the new machines for sugar mills, bought up huge swaths of land, and supplied Cuban slaveholders with both the ships and the African slaves needed to continue the transatlantic slave trade after the US abolished the importation of African slaves in 1808 (over 90 percent of the ships used to illegally carry slaves as cargo to Cuba were built in Baltimore). Annexation to the US had supporters on both sides throughout the nineteenth century, though for Cuban separatists the goal was statehood, rather than the transfer of colonial rule the US envisioned, which would make Cuba a territory at best. Fearful of an independent Cuba and reluctant to integrate into its body politic a black-majority population, when Cuba fought the Ten Years' War for its independence from Spain, North America quietly backed the peninsula. Yet with the Spanish-American War in 1898 and the subsequent four-year US occupation of Cuba, *cuba libre* sentiment only strengthened, and with it a growing discontent with US political meddling. After leaving ample loopholes for itself in the Platt Amendment to the new Cuban Constitution, the United States settled for financial colonization, continuing to penetrate deeper into the Cuban economy.

Although Cuban creole families had long sent their children to be educated in the United States, with the Ten Years' War (1868–78) came the first large-scale emigration from the island. Nearly 10 percent of the Cuban population resettled in the US (Pérez 253). Cuba's entire tobacco production infrastructure, from executives to skilled cigar rollers, fled social unrest for Key West (and later Tampa in the 1920s), establishing a robust industry and the first Cuban colonia in the US. In the late nine-teenth century, Cubans emigrated in large numbers, predominantly to South Florida, as well as eastern cities, including New York, Boston, and Philadelphia (Duany 65). Many Cubans, both on and off the island, attained US citizenship as a means of protection during and after the war.

During the depression era on the island and through World War II, Cubans flocked to the US, joining colonias in the Northeast and South Florida. Despite ongoing threats from the Ku Klux Klan in South Flor-ida, the stifling prejudice against Afro-Cubans, and violence motivated both by racism and by antiunion and antilabor groups (Pérez 215), Cuban immigrants overall flourished economically. Yet such racialized, nativist treatment added to the growing anti-US sentiment on the island, which gained traction in the 1930s–1950s. Civil unrest, economic disparity and poverty, and political malfeasance (tainted with US interventionism) led to the overthrow of Batista and the revolution of 1959. Cuba expropriated and nationalized the substantial US holdings in property, mills, utilities, sugar estates, banks, cattle ranches, and petroleum assets (242–43). The Soviet Union took over as Cuba's chief export market for sugar and as their importer for crude oil. The United States' centuries-old and extensive hold on the Cuban economy was finally severed in 1961 when the two countries ceased diplomatic relations.

The Cuban Revolution is "the most significant event in Miami's demo-graphic history" ("Tropical Dreams"). Half a million Cubans come to Miami between 1959 and 1980. This immigration has several phases, each marked by distinct socioeconomic realities (Pérez 253). First up are the "Golden Exiles," the nearly 250,000 who fled the revolution from 1959 to 1961, so-called because they largely consisted of well-heeled political and business elites opposed to the revolutionary government. Whiter, more educated, more urban, and richer than the average Cuban (Duany 43), these immigrants also benefited from their unique status as anticom-munist symbols: the US government encouraged their defection, imple-mented public assistance and social programs to aid in their integration, and eased their legal path to citizenship, all in the name of promoting the "American way of life" (Pérez 254). The second phase, during the "Freedom Flights" from 1965 to 1973, began with a similar demographic, though restrictions eventually imposed by the Cuban government meant that, overall, there were more women, more skilled and semiskilled work-ers and small farmers: by 1973 the flights were more representative of the island's population (Duany 44).

The last two waves of immigration pulled from a different sector of the Cuban social strata. The Mariel Boatlift of 1980 brought another 124,000 Cubans, more Black (20 percent identified as Black or mixed race), less educated, from the working and peasant classes, and more aligned with the economic immigrants from the rest of Latin America than with the Golden Exiles (Duany 45). These *"marielitos"* clash not only with the "old" Cubans in Miami, some of whom clutched their pearls and feared for their reputation (almost a quarter of the boatlift had been imprisoned in Cuba, after all! [45]),[1] but also with US policy: the social services that met the first Cuban arrivals evaporated by 1980. In the wake of US sanctions in the early 1990s, the fall of the Soviet Union, and Cuba's increasing economic hardship, Cuban refugees began streaming into the US both legally and illegally. During the *balsero* (rafter) crisis from 1990 to 1994, over 60,000 Cubans arrived to the US by boat or raft (Duany 47).

Cubans have maintained political advantages in the US throughout the twentieth century. The Cuban Adjustment Act of 1966 made provisions for Cubans, as political refugees, to obtain permanent legal status—a path to citizenship (or at least legal residency) denied economic refugees such as Haitians fleeing Papa Doc Duvalier. President Kennedy's Cuban Refugee Assistance Program provided health care, educational services, and employment to new Cuban immigrants until 1974. In 1984, under a revision to the 1966 act, the *marielitos* were awarded permanent legal status, and Cubans found in US waters qualified for expedited legal status ("Mariel Boatlift of 1980"). In 1995, in the midst of the Cuban rafter crisis, President Clinton inaugurated the famous "wet foot, dry foot" policy, a revision to the 1966 Cuban Adjustment Act, which granted automatic visas and expedited legal permanent resident status for any Cuban who set foot on US soil (while returning to Cuba those found at sea). President Obama rescinded the "wet foot, dry foot" policy in 2017 (Labott et al.), but the Cuban Adjustment Act still allows Cubans in the US to apply for lawful residency, or green cards, if they enter the country legally, and remain in the US for one year plus one day (Wile). One profound effect of their preferred immigration status is that the Cuban community generally has higher levels of documentation than other Latin American groups, who might be politically or socially inconspicuous in order to be prudent.

Today, Cubans account for more than half of Miami's Latinx population and over a third of its total population ("Tropical Dreams"). However, this population is not homogenous: geographically, politically, and economically diverse, the Cuban diaspora in Miami consists of several subsets, and there is ongoing tension between the first- and second-generation Golden Exiles and the continuing stream of Cuban economic refugees. What unites Cubans in Miami is sometimes only their Cubanness, in the face of newer waves of Central American and Haitian immigration to the city.

In the 1960s, the Golden Exiles set up shop in what was a decaying section of Miami near the central business district, building what will become Little Havana or Calle Ocho (Duany 43). In the 1980s and 1990s, as middle-class Cubans began moving out of Little Havana and into the suburbs (Sweetwater, Kendall, Coral Gables, Westchester), working-class immigrants and newer Cuban refugees established the nearby city of Hialeah as "Little Marianao" (43). Hialeah is Little Havana's hip, spunky, streetwise kid sister. If Little Havana is the barrio of the Golden Exiles and "Freedom Flyers" (despite their residences further afield), Hialeah belongs to the marielitos and the balseros: the small city is home to more recent Cuban immigrants and more reflective of the Cuban American working class.

Little Havana and Calle Ocho thus reflect the history of a profoundly unique diaspora: many of the Cubans who arrived at the end of the 1950s, even into the 1980s, saw their time in the US as temporary, a rare condition for an immigrant group seeking political asylum (rather than transnational economic gains). As they slowly settled in and built lives, they shared the trauma of lost country, lost status, and lost wealth with one another. They maintained a demographic majority that allowed them to remain turned inward and worked for economic stability that allowed them to build and preserve spaces where they could maintain Cuban cultural traditions, from the Cuban market on Eighth Street to the Cuban-owned farms on the outskirts in Homestead, to the Cuban restaurants, bodegas, and businesses that are run by and cater to a generation of exiles.

"Between Two Really Imaginary Worlds": Richard Blanco's Miami

On a Boston Book Fair panel titled "Country of Immigrants," Richard Blanco quipped to the audience, "we like to say in Miami that we love living there because it is so close to the United States. You don't need a passport." Blanco went on to tell the standing-room-only crowd that he grew up "between two really imaginary worlds." One world was "the

1950s Cuba of my parents," "this place we were supposedly going back to," a Miami that was full of Cubans waiting to return; the other was America as an idea and an icon, which didn't seem to match the country he now lived in: "nobody in the neighborhood looked like what I saw on TV." As a result of growing up a denizen of two "imaginary worlds," Blanco became interested in questions of belonging and identity, "all that revolves around this sense of place." He describes his own upbringing as marked by what he calls an "inherited exile" ("Country of Immigrants").

Before traveling to Miami, I assumed that that joke about not needing a passport was just that, a humorous commentary on the large Latinx population and the predominance of Cuban language and culture. Considering the first big wave of migration to Miami from Cuba was over fifty years ago, I figured the community would be modest and fairly culturally assimilated. I was so wrong. The Cuban neighborhoods of Miami (which is to say, much of Miami) are still *very* Cuban. Fresh influxes of Cuban immigrants (along with Central and South Americans) has guaranteed that barrios like Little Havana and Hialeah maintain their ethnic identity *as* barrios. Aside from the tourists in Little Havana and Wynwood, I did not hear a word of English on my visit. In the old locales built by "Golden Exiles," older Cubans congregate and often know one another, sharing traditional Cuban baked goods and *cafés con leche.* The Cuban community's insularity, and the simultaneous self-aware commodification of that insularity, calls to mind New York's Little Italy (once upon a time) or San Francisco's Chinatown. It is authentic and on display all at once.

Richard Blanco subtitles *The Prince of Los Cocuyos,* his 2014 memoir, "A Miami Childhood": this tagline is neither insignificant nor arbitrary. Indeed, his first poetry collection, *City of a Hundred Fires,* already belies the poet's fascination with the Cuban exile culture of Miami that surrounds him. The son of Cubans who flee Castro but who has never set foot in Cuba himself, as a child the poet's hometown and home *nation* is everyone else's elsewhere. The peculiarities of South Florida's Cuban colonia permeates the poet's writing, and his own development as American, Cuban, male, gay, and a poet, is inextricably woven into his experiences growing up between two worlds.

7

"Why Don't I Got a Street?"

LITTLE HAVANA IN RICHARD BLANCO'S QUEER CUBAN AMERICAN BILDUNGSROMAN

BLACK FEMINIST thought and critical race theory, from voices as distinct as Kimberlé Crenshaw, Audre Lorde, and bell hooks,[1] have taught us the importance of intersectionality: to consider how, for each of us, our various social identities impact one another in a confluence that is more than the sum of its parts.[2] According to the theory, a Latinx gay man has three legible social locations—ethnicity, sexuality, and gender—that will interact with one another in unique ways. In his 2014 memoir, Richard Blanco deploys generic conventions to present the development of his own intersectional understanding of identity: *The Prince of Los Cocuyos* takes the form of a traditional bildungsroman—a literary formula that follows a protagonist from birth to social assimilation, as he/she learns to become a functioning member of civil society—only to reject the neat narrative resolution of the genre. Blanco stacks multiple bildungsromane, ultimately crossing their narrative arcs, to show us how the author (as protagonist) cannot fit within a tidy binary. By presenting multiple social positions, each of which subverts full assimilation, Blanco queers the bildungsroman:[3] the formulaic conclusion of the protagonist's journey becomes an embrace of multiple identities, which together defy easy categorization or simple absorption into the body politic. In effect, *The Prince of Los Cocuyos* offers us an intersectional bildungsroman, which contests the form while adapting it to its subject.

How do you stitch your identity to a place that everyone around you is convinced is temporary? A place that, given the chance, everyone around you will leave? A place that, in every detail, will never compare to what was left behind? Blanco's poetry and nonfiction both demonstrate the epistemological tightrope of building one's world within a space no one else wants to claim for their own. The memoir presents a sustained first-person narrative that complicates Blanco's notion of identity: while his semiautobiographical poetry collection *City of a Hundred Fires* emulates the binary identity Blanco feels as a Cuban

American, with its sharp formal division between the US and the island, in the memoir we learn that "Cuban" is only one of the many selves that Blanco must learn to navigate, in addition to "American," "gay," and "male." Crucially, *The Prince of Los Cocuyos* stays in Miami. It is here in his neighborhood—and only here—that Blanco can integrate the many identities he feels swarming within. Considering the memoir as the conclusion of the narrative arc of the poetry collection completes the cycle of growth, voyage, and return, taking us from the US to Cuba and finally back to Blanco's hometown.

Miami: Everyone Else's Elsewhere

In a trend common to contemporary transnational literature, Blanco splits *City of a Hundred Fires* into two parts, the first in his hometown in the US and the second in the country of his family's origin. Part 1 is full of snapshots of Blanco's Miami. The places of Blanco's childhood— the neighborhood stores, the main drags, the restaurants, the market, the backyard—are permeated with the places left behind by those who surround him. Blanco's Miami is heavy with memories that are not his, so that ironically his memories are full of the memories of others that he cannot access.

Nearly every poem in part 1 presents a Cuban remembering, regardless of the American location. In "Teatro Martí," patrons have "so much to remember in 1972" as the cars outside on Eighth Street "wake us from the slow annihilation we pretended to ignore each Saturday and each day since la Revolución" (7). In "La Revolución at Antonio's Mercado," all the bodega customers are haunted by Cuba as they shop, dissatisfied with the products of their new life. Everyone around Blanco is lost in Cuban reverie: Blanco's grandfather takes him to the Eighth Street market for the mango shake of *his* childhood ("Mango, Number 61," 10), the fisherman's pier filled with voices "with the wind from a distant 1940s Cuba" ("Islamorada," 12), his mother's skill selecting fruits in the produce aisle reveals her rural Cuban upbringing ("Mother Picking Produce," 16), his father teaches him to skin a rabbit in the backyard, remembering "mountain trails, barefoot country" ("The Lesson," 17), relatives complain about how the seafront is so much uglier than the beaches of Cuba ("The Silver Sands," 30), and patrons at the neighborhood restaurants and cafés of Miami, permeated with Cuban foods, recollect Cuba and their meals there ("What Las Palmas Mean:"; "Contemplations at the Virgen de la Caridad Cafetería, Inc.").

Miami is treated as a way station for most of these characters. In "Mail for Mamá," Blanco recounts his mother's relationship to the mail from Cuba, "Always waiting for your letters, your face worn," "your eyes forever fixed / by a sentence of time, in a garden of never" (14). Described as a stone statue who is a prisoner to her sentence, and a prisoner to *the* sentence—from relatives writing from home—his mother "parcels" her "desperation" into "discrete brown packages" she sends home, standing sentinel for news from the only place that actually matters to her. Blanco is left trying to belong, scouring the faces of his Cuban relatives in the photos his aunt sends, "looking for resemblances in the foreign / image of an ear, an eyebrow, or a nose" (14). *Blanco's* home in these poems appears to be his alone.

The final poem in part 1 of *City of a Hundred Fires* addresses this tension between two homes directly. In "Contemplations at the Virgen de la Caridad Cafetería, Inc.," the speaker sits in an eatery full of Cuban exiles: he tries to join in their communing with the spirits of the past but ultimately remains on the outside of their reveries. The title's "Inc." riffs on the café's jarring name, playing on the idea of "incorporated" as incarnate rather than secular, describing it as a "holy" place (33). The ballad form contributes to this confusion of purpose: is it a love poem detailing the beauty of Our Lady of Cuba, or a story of exilic woe? The "worshippers" revere— what else?—Cuba, and assemble as congregants for "a standing breakfast of nostalgia." In their forty-cent cups of cafés con leche the parishioners taste their pasts. As someone who does not share their memories, he has to ask, "what have they seen that they cannot forget—," *guessing* that they see "the broad-leaf waves of *tabaco* and plantains / the clay dust of red and nameless mountains" or hear the "guitar of a tropical morning," "speaking Spanish" through "cane oceans," accompanied by the "drums" of "the African gods" (33): stereotypical images of a Caribbean island.

From the outside you'd be hard pressed to know what's inside the actual La Virgen de la Caridad Supermarket: the storefront along South West Seventeenth Street has no windows, just the hours and the words "todos los días." However, the store's one outward sign offers a clue. The entrance on the corner has a rectangular marquee with the iconic devotional image, rendered in a neoclassical painting style, of the Virgin Mary in her "Caridad del Cobre" aspect: awash in pastels, framed by cherubs, she hovers over three men, one black, two indigenous, struggling in a wooden rowboat on the open sea (see fig. 32). While Marian devotion is shared by much of Latin America,[4] "La Virgen de la Caridad del Cobre" means "Cuba": it is believed that in this aspect she appeared to three men, a slave and two Taínos, in Cuba in the early seventeenth century.[5] Many

FIGURE 32. Our Virgin of Charity Cafeteria, 2019

depictions have moved the vision to stormy seas, with "los tres juanes" ("the three Johns") as fishermen or, in this case, rafters. This classic depiction makes Mary the protector of those who cross "stormy seas," a fitting emblem for Miami's Cuban diaspora. The image, mounted high atop the roof of the store, is a shibboleth in a part of Little Havana that is becoming increasingly diverse in its Latin American population.

Like many of the Cuban bodegas in Miami, this one is a coffee shop, cafeteria, butcher, liquor store, and grocery all in one. Upon entering, the register is on the right against the outer wall, and on the left and in front is the L-shaped counter, lined with backless stools. The produce section in front has avocados and other tropical fruits and vegetables. The aisles have all the Caribbean staples: Goya products, Café Bustelo, even citrus juicers, *mofongo* molds, and a collection of Santería prayer candles. On one aisle's corner there is a large poster labeled "Dolor Cubano" (Cuban suffering), proclaiming, "todo por una causa" in English and Spanish, with the Virgin Mary in the middle and an American and Cuban flag on either side.

The cafeteria takes up about a third of the store but seems to account for the majority of its business. Despite this hefty output, the operation is modest. I never see more than two women working, one as the waitress and the other as the cook and dishwasher. To make her job easier (I imagine) the dishware is all Styrofoam, and the placemats, which depict a map of Florida with a large Cuban flag floating nearby, are paper. Teresa, one of the waitresses, calls everyone "niño" or "hijo" regardless of their age or literal familial relation. She doesn't like me very much at first and seems wary that I have found the place, which is clearly packed with regulars and appears to rarely have a non-Cuban customer, let alone a tourist. She does warm up to me when I confess that my café con leche is the most delicious I've ever had (which was true, for the record, may my Puerto Rican relatives forgive me); she cracks half a smile and tells me that the secret to it is the "punto cubano."

No English is being spoken. In fact, there is very little noise altogether: there is no ambient music, and while those at the counter exchange some words with each other and the waitress, there is a fair amount of staring into space from all of us. On a weekday morning it is mainly workers here before work, men in matching landscaping shirts with business logos, women in nursing uniforms, a few well-dressed women and casually dressed older men. On the weekend there are still workers, a few older Cuban couples who amble in, and a flank of men around the same age who sit on the short side—closest to the espresso maker—and all know each other. In three mornings, I only see one customer looking at his phone (and one woman who was using the phone to *talk* to someone, old-school style, while she ate her eggs). It's slightly more festive on the weekend, though still somewhat solemn. It feels true that everyone sitting here is somewhere else, that "this holy, incorporated place" transports the patrons to a different time.

The cafeteria allows customers to return to the Cuba of their past unhindered. The long side of the food counter faces a giant whiteboard filled with menu items written in Spanish only (and Cuban Spanish at that: I have to look up "Quimbombó" and "Sopón"), on the partial wall which blocks the view of the small kitchen where the waitress and cook banter. The short side of the counter faces a wall decorated with black and white family photos, a large picture of men on a boat at sea, a few framed color drawings of Cuban mountains and fields, a somewhat whimsical painting of Cuban instruments (a *djembe* drum dominates the foreground, surreal piano keys lace the backdrop), and a map of Cuba.

As he begins to imagine the "delicacy of memories" that "swirl" like "brown sugar histories" in their coffees (33), Blanco literally draws from his surroundings. The Cuban staples mentioned—the tobacco leaves, red mountains, cane fields, and African musical instruments (33)—purport to be "what they have seen that they can't forget," but sitting at this counter, the inspiration of the lines is clear: The wall I face actually *has* pictures of Cuban mountains, cane and tobacco fields, Cuban music, and Cubans at sea. Blanco's references are not Cuban, or, at least, not directly Cuban: the poem filters the images that are proudly displayed in this exile space, as a way to try to access those real memories of these other customers. The poet does not share their histories; he only shares the counter. The atmosphere generated by a clientele remembering is so thick it envelops him, but his own past prevents him from joining the revelry. He recognizes both the power of this mass displacement and his own distance from it. This disconnect is highlighted by the poet's grasping for insight into these exilic reveries, as the words scan the store, pulling details he can use to fill in the aspects of this unknown longing.

Blanco makes the distance between himself and the other patrons explicit as he inserts himself at the end of the third stanza as a first-person speaker, claiming "I too am a speck," and begins to envision himself where all the other cafetería Cubans assembled are. "I am the brilliant guitar," he asserts, though the quick shift from "speck" to "brilliant" indicates the uncertainty of the speaker. Indeed, the following two stanzas overcompensate, and smack of exaggeration, with its "green cane oceans" and "waist-high steam," the sound of drums and the presence of "African gods that" "cast spells" amidst the "tropical dance" ("tropical" is repeated twice in two stanzas). The speaker, in his fervor to belong, has sped past the Catholic ritual under way in the café and into the rites of Voodoo. His imagined Cuba has tinges of a tourist's version of Cuba, placing him further on the outside, despite being inside one of its places of worship.

In the last stanza the speaker recognizes his failure to belong to the Cuban faithful. The phrase "*que será*"—which can function either as a question ("what will be?") or a statement, as in the saying, "*que será, será,*" ("what will be, will be")—haunts the poem, appearing in a different position in each stanza, sometimes as a question and sometimes as a statement. In the last stanza, for the first time, the phrase appears twice. The questioning is directed at the speaker, whose palms (signifying both his own hands and the trees of Cubans' memories) are marked by "exotic confusion" concerning the legacy of his "wild birthright." The Cubans in the café have wondered *que será* of their island, of their lives *there*, of their future *there*; but for Blanco his actual identity is the question: how does his own past constitute his present self? If he can't remember what those surrounding him remember, how does he know who he is?

The ballad form breaks down at the end, sharpening the divide between the speaker and the exile congregation, and bringing about the resolution of the poem. The regular *abba* switches to two rhyming couplets in this stanza, and further, the final couplet is marked by a significant wrenched rhyme, which pointedly struggles to harmonize "know" and "home." The couplets separate him stylistically from those he is among: they get the first two lines, as he wonders about his relationship to their island, and he gets the second two, as he asserts an identity that is distinct from theirs. Despite this introduced separation between the Cubans and the speaker, and despite their very different pasts, they are still linked by their uncertain futures, by the anaphoric "*que será*"— demonstrating that his connection is maddeningly tenuous.

In response to his question, sparked by those who remember around him, "what have *I* seen?" "what do *I* know?" the speaker ultimately affirms that he too is anchored in a place and its memories: "culture of *café* and loss, this place I call home." *His* Cuba is Miami. *His* culture is one of exile, loss, and nostalgia. *His* home is not their home, and so he will not find the answers to who he is by figuring out who they are. The speaker locates his identity and differentiates himself from the Cuba worshippers in the coffee shop, but the wrenched rhyme and the repetition of the question ("*¿que será?*") reflect the destabilizing force of having a home marked by a displaced population, who constantly remind you that "real" home lies elsewhere.

LITTLE HAVANA BARRIOGRAPHY: CALLE OCHO

Eighth Street ("Calle Ocho") has bottled the essence of this nostalgia worship. The street runs, with a few name changes, from the water's edge of downtown Miami westward all the way to Everglades National Park. From about Twelfth to Nineteenth Street, Calle Ocho is filled with tourists, whose buses pull up by Domino Park (at Eighth and Fifteenth), a half block from the Little Havana Visitor Center. It is jarring to see the large batches of white American and European tourists arrive by charter to watch the older men play dominoes: they congregate in large groups near the domino tables to take pictures, and many even walk up to the edges of the game tables, literally standing over the men (mostly men) to catch a shot (see fig. 33). The scene to me was zoolike and rude; I felt like Máximo, Ana Menéndez's older Cuban widower, who comes to Domino Park to reminisce with old friends and is tortured by the droves of tourists

FIGURE 33. Domino Park and its tourists, 2019

who come to gawk: "'Tell them to go away,' Máximo said. 'Tell them, no pictures.'" ("In Cuba I Was a German Shepherd," 29). However today I don't see anyone complain. In fact, one table is even allowing a female tourist (a blonde) to sit next to them and watch.

Old Cuba is on display throughout this strip of Eighth Street, from the formidable Bay of Pigs Statue (complete with actual burning flame) next to Domino Park on one end down to the famous fruit stand Los Piñeros at the other. Along the way there is a "Cuban Walk of Fame," like Hollywood's Walk of Fame but with all Cuban stars. The Cuban restaurants in this "official" Calle Ocho section are the kind of establishments that have bilingual menus and pictures of the food: they are inundated with tourists. Gift shops, most with "Havana" in the name, litter the street (see fig. 34). Some small places along the strip advertise "Cuban coffee" (in English), but I don't see any Cubans drinking coffee at them. At Los Piñeros Frutería, tourists snap shots of the produce aisle, as the decor looks stereotypically Caribbean. When I order a *mamey* shake, inspired by characters in Blanco's and Cristina García's writing who taste their childhood in a Calle Ocho *batido*, the Cuban gentleman manning the stand asks a number of qualifying follow-up questions: do I know it is cash only (the sign already indicates as much), do I know that the shake has milk in

FIGURE 34. Cuban Miami on display, 2019

it, do I want juice instead? At first, I'm puzzled, and then I hear the British woman next to me ask, in English, for a number of healthy substitutions: tourists approach the *frutería* like a Jamba Juice. It is their loss: the shake was otherworldly good.

Further west, Calle Ocho still advertises its Cubanness, but the crowds have many more Cubans, and certainly more of the older generation. Versailles Bakery for example (on Eighth Street at Thirty-Sixth) has every table full at 9 p.m. on a weeknight, and the crowd is much older, entirely white, and entirely Cuban. Customers amble from table to table to greet old friends and sit in groups of four and five over paper cups of *café cortado* or café con leche and pastries. A few tourists make their way in too, but they don't seem to linger. I go to this bakery a few times over the weekend, and it always has a healthy number of exiles in the eatery. The adjacent Versailles Restaurant[6] has a line (well more like a mob) out the door on a weekend night, of both tourists and locals.

Across the street, La Carreta Restaurant is exemplary in this confusing dual appeal to older Cubans and curious visitors. In his memoir, Blanco mentions the locale as a favorite among Golden Exiles, describing "cigar-smoking men gathered for coffee at La Carreta, debating how Cuba was lost, again" (227). The restaurant has all the aspects of a tourist trap: an over-the-top exterior (the giant, two-story cart wheel out front for starters), uniformed servers (women in white frilly tops and red kerchiefs evoking "traditional" Cuban garb), paper place-settings selling the restaurant's branded coffee, in English, with mention of its Instagram, Facebook, and Twitter handles. The menu pushes *mojitos* and *ropa vieja*, quintessentially stereotypical Cuban food. And yet, while half the clientele are tourists, the other half are Spanish speakers, and the entire staff, including the cooks, are Cubans. Furthermore, at the "little window" directly behind the restaurant, with a counter and standing-room tables looking on the parking lot, the crowd is all Cubans, and the scene is much busier than the one indoors. The younger Cubans frequenting these Cuban exile spots don't mind that they have become tourist destinations. Like good capitalists, and proud immigrants perhaps, this community is ready to share its locales with tourists.

This is my first time in a Latinx barrio that brands itself so explicitly as a barrio. Of course, East L.A. and Washington Heights have pride, but no one is taking a tour bus to those communities, and their businesses are not marketing to outsiders. Insularity is not enough of an answer: while Washington Heights is a mixed neighborhood, El Monte and East L.A. are majority Mexican and Chicanx but still don't court visitors. Little Havana has added something to its insularity: marketability. Calle Ocho is branded to cater to a tourism industry. This commodification of Cuban exile culture has ironically remained although most of the original Cuban families have moved to the suburbs. Like Ana Menéndez's *Máximo*, the 1960s immigrant generation may take the bus or drive back to the old neighborhood to play dominoes, but the actual population of the tourist section of Little Havana now has more Central and South Americans than "Golden Exiles," along with newer Cuban immigrants, who are divorced from the grandeur of Old Cuba. José Gutierrez, whose father fought in the Bay of Pigs invasion, grew up in Westchester (like Blanco, and many second-generation Cubans I met): he said that when he went to Calle Ocho's main drag he "felt like a tourist in Miami."

An unlikely interviewee put his finger on the unique status of this Cuban political refugee population for the US and for Miami in particular. As I'm walking down Calle Ocho toward downtown, where the tourist section turns to more typical postindustrial cityscape (as in, no more tourists), a very tan, possibly inebriated, definitely vocal, man is loudly engaging passersby—mostly women. As I pass, he asks if he can marry me, then gets annoyed as I pause to take a picture of the Cuban grocery store in front of me (it has a sign saying it accepts food stamps, indication we are in the part of town for newer, economic refugees rather than the older political set). He yells, "Don't you have that kind of store where you come from?" He starts to walk with me, occasionally sipping on his second beer (in a Dunkin Donuts iced coffee cup for discretion). It's 10 a.m. He introduces himself as David Pierre Cortez, a Puerto Rican from Camden, New Jersey. He launches into a litany of complaints about Calle Ocho's tourism, mentioning Domino Park and the Bay of Pigs statue. He is frustrated with the special status the city of Miami confers on the Cuban community, especially since they are immigrants and there is no equivalent commemoration of the natives. He says, "I've been here 57 years—where's my strip?" He keeps repeating, "I'm an American. Why don't I got a street?"

After Cortez left me to re-up his beer levels at a 7–Eleven, I was left pondering the question. Why *do* these Cubans get a street? The tourist aspect of Little Havana is unlike most other barrios. The prominent statue memorializing an all-Cuban military operation, the reverence for Cuban culture evident in the protection (and city subsidizing) of the domino games, the construction of a walk of fame, the promotion of the neighborhood to tourist companies and the establishment of a visitor's center, all point to a vested interest in this diaspora. I realized that the success of Cuban immigrants in particular is ideologically useful for the United States. Unlike barrios founded by economic migrants from other capitalist countries, fleeing postcolonial states or the adverse effects of postindustrial globalization,[7] the Golden Exiles were fleeing communism. As political or even *ideological* refugees, their success as immigrants is a valuable demonstration of the evils of communism and the superiority of capitalism. The Calle Ocho strip says to tourists, "Look at how these Cuban exiles became good capitalists." In essence, this barrio serves as a symbolic rejection of communism and an endorsement of the American Dream.

But how do the recent Cuban refugees, from the Mariel Boatlift of the 1980s to the balseros of the 1990s to the twenty-first-century waves, many of whom are economic rather than political defectors, fit into this paradigm? And how does the nostalgia sit with the new immigrants—from Cuba but also elsewhere, like Central America and Haiti—who keep coming? For the old guard, both the Cubans who arrived in the early 1960s and their children, the "Golden Exile" reputation is at stake. I heard often the notion that those early immigrants were very different from those who come now, from Cuba or elsewhere. These interviewees echo Blanco: "Cubans who had been in Miami since the sixties didn't typically socialize with refugees from El Mariel. Miami Cubans had adopted a 'we were here first' attitude toward the Marielitos, whom they generally regarded as bumpkins and riffraff tainted by exposure to Castro's socialist regime" (*Prince of Los Cocuyos* 220). There was pride (or annoyance, depending on the speaker) about the unique insularity and determination of those fleeing the Cuban revolution to build a community in Miami. While that Cuban insularity somewhat remains, everyone laments the work ethic of the newest immigrant waves, and some even question their loyalty to capitalism (gasp!).

I found the most strident denouncers of Communism to be the Cuban veterans of the Bay of Pigs invasion. Just off Calle Ocho there is a modest Bay of Pigs Museum, manned entirely by veterans of that military conflict, all of whom are Cuban-born, most of whom fought in their early twenties. Humberto Lopez Saldaña is the director of the Asociación de Veteranos for the Bahia de Cochinos Brigada de Asalto 2506, which manages the museum. The Brigade achieved some recent fame by publicly backing Donald Trump in his 2016 run for president (Anderson). Originally from outside Veradero, Cuba, Saldaña comes to the US in 1960 at eighteen years old and signs up for the invasion almost immediately. Afterwards, Sandaña returned to Miami: Going back to Cuba was not an option while it remained under communist rule. When I asked the three veterans there if they ever wanted to go back, in unison they said "*nunca*" (never), "as long as Castro is in power."

Speaking of the changes to Little Havana and Cubans, Saldaña says, "éramos la mayoría, y ahora no" ("we used to be the majority, but no longer"), mentioning how Central Americans and Haitians have displaced the Cuban majority. He's right and wrong: in 1970 Cubans made up about 90 percent of all Hispanics in Miami-Dade County, whereas now other Latin Americans make up more of the pie, but Cuban-born immigrants are still the single largest group of foreign-born Hispanics, at 48.5 percent of the county's total foreign-born population (Wile). He says the Cubans in Miami back then wanted to make a better life for themselves, work hard, and open businesses and that, when they succeeded, they moved out to the suburbs. Saldaña and his son tell me that later waves of Cubans were less inclined to work hard and more apt to try to game the system (Gutierrez; Saldaña).

This idea that "these newer immigrants aren't ready to work hard" was repeated to me many times. I heard it from my Colombian immigrant hosts, particularly in terms of the young Cubans coming to Miami. I also heard it from Bibi and Anna, two thirty-something Cuban Americans, children of Golden Exiles, who were equally disappointed in the Cubans and the Central Americans now coming to Miami in large numbers. José

Gutierrez and Juan (my host, who did not authorize me to use his surname) both noted that these economic refugees are products of a system: Communism under Castro makes stealing or cheating imperative for getting by. Yet while that might mitigate the behavior, the prejudice against contemporary Cuban migration remains, both within and without the Cuban community. Everyone appears to agree that the new wave threatens the good name and reputation of Cuban Miami.

What differed, depending on whether one was Cuban or not, was the perspective on the Golden Exiles themselves. Bibi expressed pride in Calle Ocho and the way the first large wave of Cubans managed to make it by banding together in the US. Despite Little Havana's hyperactive tourism and commodification of nostalgia, Bibi felt there was an authentic community there and that those businesses represented a pride that was well earned and worth celebrating (and even making money off of). Yet for my Colombian hosts Juan and Anita, who have lived in Little Havana for over twenty years, Cuban pride reads as unwarranted Cuban exceptionalism. Juan remarked that Cubans seem to think they have the monopoly on suffering, though all of Latin America has experienced dictatorship and violence, and in Cuba alone of those countries citizens never die of hunger (Juan and Anita, personal interview).

To Juan and Anita, the first wave is living in the past. Juan joked about this tendency in older Cubans: "you can mention your Volkswagen, and they'll say, 'oh, that car is nothing compared to the Volkswagen I had back in Cuba.'" With that comment Juan echoes almost verbatim a scene from "In Cuba I Was a German Shepherd," where the Dominicans push back on the Cuban urge to remember: "Oh Jesus, you people" Antonio says as Raúl mentions a woman he remembers in Cuba: "I think that *americana* there looked better than anything you remember," he retorts, which draws a long laugh from his fellow Dominican. At Máximo's restaurant in that story, "Havana's old lawyers and bankers and dreamers would sit around . . . and . . . late in the night . . . someone would start the stories that began with 'In Cuba I remember'" (Menéndez 7). My own Puerto Rican grandfather used to jokingly call Cubans "*los tuvé*" ("the 'I hads'") because he said they were always talking about what "I had" back in Cuba. This resentment of a perceived haughtiness is compounded by the differing treatment of immigrants by the US government: Cuban refugees or immigrants have a much easier path to securing visas and to getting papers than other groups, and many feel new immigrants take advantage of this (José Gutierrez, himself Cuban-American, shared this sentiment, as well as Juan, Anita, and David Cortez).[8]

The political favoritism conferred on Cuban immigrants seems to be internalized by the Cubans themselves. The Golden Exiles are perceived by the United States *and* by themselves as ideological refugees whose immigration story is different from any other Latin American group—*even* later waves of Cubans. They want their particular history of great financial loss, communist takeover, and ultimately capitalist triumph to remain distinct from Miami's other Latin American migration streams. Theirs is a tale of achieving the American Dream, and although they were bolstered politically, economically, and culturally in that endeavor by a city and a government vested in demonstrating the superiority of capitalism, they believe newcomers are simply failing to do what is necessary to succeed.

Blanco's Cuban Miami is indeed a world of its own, permeated by nostalgia and marked by a longing to be elsewhere. Yet that "elsewhere" is a different world the poet has never known, while the city of his childhood is where he wants, or is trying to want, to be.

Cuba: Everyone Else's Home

Given Blanco's "exotic confusion" over his "wild birthright" in part 1 of *City of a Hundred Fires,* part 2's journey to Cuba makes narrative sense; yet what Blanco needs to find will not be in the Cuba of his parents' past. Part 2 of the collection opens with an epigram, which establishes the new location. In a classic Cuban American author move, Blanco quotes José Martí: "in the mountains, I am a mountain" (35). Coming fresh out of Little Havana's Virgin de la Caridad Supermarket just a page earlier, this title page's triumphant first-person speaker declaring he is one with his Cuba reads as a reach for our own speaker. When asked about the effects of the permanent displacement of his family from their country of origin, Blanco says that "the inability to return increased my desire to know the 'homeland,'" that not being able to go back made the displacement more pronounced and the desire to establish connection more intense ("Country of Immigrants"). This ardent desire to belong to Cuba saturates the rest of the collection.

When Blanco tries to fit in to the Cuban locales he describes in part 2, the poems tend to fall into somewhat clichéd tourist language, further demonstrating his alienation from the space.[9] Several of the poems in the Cuba section have the speaker positioning himself as a native islander witness to Cuban tourism, a rhetorical strategy that feels aspirational rather than actual. The poet seems conscious of the pitfalls of speaking as an unqualified Cuban, and the poems are most effective when the speaker acknowledges his status as not belonging, announcing this disconnect rather than attempting to hide it. When the poems recognize where the speaker does not have a home, they achieve transcendence, and it is this hard-won recognition that will lead us back to Miami in Blanco's memoir.

When Blanco speaks in the voice of his family, especially his mother and grandfather, he is able to powerfully inhabit their experiences. The collection highlights this strength by using the actual histories of his mother, father, and grandparents as the basis for poetic personae ("Found Letters," "The Reservoir," "Abuelo Valdéz," "Décima Guajira"). One of the most successful poems of the collection, "Décima Guajira," relies on this trope. The *décima* is a common verse structure throughout Latin America, a forty-four-line poem consisting of an introductory stanza followed by four ten-line stanzas, with a rhyme scheme *abbaaccddc*. In Cuba the form is often set to music as a *guajira*, a folkloric song hailing from the countryside. The poem both *is* and is *about* the décima: consisting of two parts, each ten lines, and each following the conventional rhyme scheme and structure. Yet Blanco introduces a crucial variation: his ten-line stanza is split into a set of five Spanish lines and a set of five English ones. The rhyme scheme presents in effect one décima verse in Spanish, and one in English, where each language's verse alternates (so that the structure is *abbaa* [Spanish], *abbaa* [English], then *ccddc* [Spanish] and *cddcc* [English, with a rhyme anomaly we'll discuss shortly]).

Elsewhere in part 2, the occasional Spanish lines at times feel forced: they are usually translated in English verse within the same poem, either as a concession to monolingual readers or as a vaguely ersatz performance of Spanish language mastery. Here though, even despite the alternating structure, the Spanish and the English need each other and do not repeat sentiments. Given that the topic of the poem is the speaker's inheritance of his Cuban grandfather's "gift" of crafting the décima, choosing to write the verses in both Spanish and English honors the legacy, demonstrating the speaker's inborn skill in fashioning poetry (in English) as well as acknowledging its source (in Spanish). That both languages are needed to complete the form signifies what the poet owes to his grandfather, and asserts proudly (rather than sheepishly, as in other poems) that his own native language differs from his ancestors. The Spanish, like the décima, is an inheritance, but to make it authentically his own the poet must use English to complete the verse.

The first verse introduces the first-person speaker, who "sees the loved earth" ("*Veo la tierra amada*") and the steps of his parents (66). He claims that "inside these dead eyes / now dance and sing / the sugar, the *décima*" ("*dentro estos muertos ojos / ahora baila y canta / el azucár, la décima*" [66]). "Dead eyes" is deliberately ambiguous, but the passive voice of "loved earth" suggests that it is *the speaker's* eyes that are being awakened, that he was "dead" to the sights and sounds of his ancestors prior to this moment. This admission of a disconnect is rare in the collection and makes the verses to follow more compelling.

The next stanza offers five lilting, enjambed lines that follow the sounds of the guajiro's arias over "the meter, the rhyme, the ten-line craft / of my grandfather's melancholy gift" (66). The poet plays with the rhythm, slipping in and out of iambic pentameter—the décima is loosely octosyllabic, translated to a tetrameter or pentameter in English—breaking up five lines without break with a fourth line rife with caesuras, which self-consciously mentions the rhythm. This is Blanco being playfully erudite, as in his poems about Wallace Stevens or William Carlos Williams, but here the meta aspect has a function: he is demonstrating his own "melancholy gift" of craft. The Spanish lines hinted at the landscape belonging to someone else; these English lines capture the same scene, but with no hesitancy or uncertainty.

In section 2, the speaker in the Spanish stanza says that in the dust he finds and protects a piece of himself ("*aquí encuentro y guardo / mi alma tallada*" [66]), introducing a metaphor for the Cuban dust as marble encasing the speaker's soul. As in the first Spanish stanza, Blanco does not balk from the tenuous connection to the land but rather highlights its preciousness and precariousness—dust and talismans, and the repetition of "guardo" ("I guard" or "I keep"), point to the fragile nature of the link. The English stanza leans on this discovery of the soul encased in marble, as the language becomes far more abstract: both "deep" and fragile, marble and drifting sand, the grandfather's song is tied to the land but also carried by the speaker (66).

The closing verse enacts the inheritance and the loss at once, as the final stanza diverges from the traditional décima rhyme scheme. Blanco writes a final couplet instead, creating a significant allusion to the canonical English poetic tradition, from Shakespeare through Pope. Not strictly tied to his past, and not limited to his ancestors' Spanish, the poet creates himself in English, demonstrating that not just the décima but also the heroic couplet and iambic pentameter are his as a student of poetry in two languages. The "loss" of the décima form is simultaneously the inauguration of something new and unique to the speaker. The author uses poetic language to write across the divide, without denying his own "home" in English. Ironically, in order to authentically tie himself to the island, Blanco must honor his linguistic separation from his ancestors.

Back in Miami: Everyone Else's Elsewhere Is Home

A decade and a half later, Blanco confronts directly his dual inheritances, this time in prose. The quest for wholeness will lead him not to Cuba but to Miami. The power of place is signposted in the very first pages of *The Prince of Los Cocuyos*. The memoir's subtitle "A Miami Childhood" uses "Miami" as an adjective for a kind of childhood, implying that the locale has impacted the author so strongly that it can serve as the single descriptor for his development. The epigraph, a quote from Cesare Pavese, is also expressly about place identity: "You need a village, if only for the pleasure of leaving it. *Your own village* means that you're not alone, that you know there's something of you in the people and the plants and the soil" (emphasis added).

The memoir follows and complicates the narrative arc of a bildungsroman, with a subtle Künstelrroman woven in. As the author works to resolve his binary Cuban/American selfhood, the plot takes on and incorporates additional social identities that Blanco initially sees as mutually exclusive: to be a Cuban *man* or an American *man,* to be a *Cuban* man or a *gay* man. In *City of a Hundred Fires* (that title, incidentally, is a reference to the city of Havana), Blanco had traveled to Cuba to attempt to find out who he is; yet the only place to reconcile these seemingly incongruent selves is *his* village. By becoming a *Miami* man, Richard[10] learns he can be both Cuban and American, both a man and an artist, and, perhaps most important, both gay and Cuban.

SQUARING CUBAN AND AMERICAN IDENTITY

As in *City of a Hundred Fires,* in the memoir, young Richard grows up surrounded by Cubans. His Miami suburb, named Westchester, or "Güescheste" as his family calls it, is populated by "working-class exiles like us who had begun to settle there once they got on their feet" (*Prince of Los Cocuyos* 4). Richard lives with his mother, father, brother, and *abuelos,* all of whom were born in Cuba (they flee in 1959), most never forgetting that fact. While his mother usually references Cuba as a rhetorical technique—periodically lamenting, "Is this what I left *mi madre* and sisters in Cuba for?" (41), Richard's grandparents persist in living as Cuban a lifestyle as possible. Abuela only frequents Cuban groceries and businesses and takes pride in her traditional Cuban cooking; Abuelo plants the same trees and acquires the same animals he had in Cuba, from chickens to a German Shepherd just like "the dog he'd left behind" (52). There are only "a handful of gringos" in Richard's classes (8). The grocery stores, the neighbors, the family's friends, his schoolmates and schoolteachers, are all Cuban.

Despite the Cubanness of everyone around him, in school Richard learns about being American and yearns for the customs of *that* culture, so foreign to his own neighborhood's way of life. Blanco recounts a series of anecdotes demonstrating his binary sense of identity, as well as his growing desire to be one or the other. America is symbolized for Blanco by the Winn-Dixie, the only non-Cuban grocery store in the neighborhood, "where a still plentiful but shrinking number of *americanos* shopped": the only place in "Güescheste" where you could get "treats" like Pop-Tarts, Ritz Crackers, and Cool Whip (8). Through the cunning use of coupons, he gets his Abuela to take him to the megastore, after her usual tour of local Cuban bodegas where she barters shared feelings of *la patria* for discounts (8). He describes in detail his elation inside the Winn-Dixie, with its bright lighting, wide aisles, and overpackaged products: "this is the way it should be" (16), he remarks to himself, clean and neat and quiet and organized.

Richard does not approve of the mixing of Cuban and American foods that Abuela insists upon once he starts introducing his favorite American dishes: to Richard, "the combinations just didn't belong together—they were from two different worlds" (18). "You had to be either Cuban or American; you couldn't be both," Richard thinks as he watches his family scarf down adulterated "American" food (20). The foods represent two distinct and exclusive identities to the child, and they cannot, or should not, be combined; the prospect of Richard's "wish for something *really* American for dinner, just once" disappears as quickly as Abuela's "Cubar-oni" (20–21).

Blanco's Güescheste

Richard Blanco was kind enough to give me his street address, and perhaps he even warned his mother in advance that a nosy journalist might be skulking around the property. Blanco moved back with his aging mother and lives part-time in his childhood home (he splits time between Maine and Florida). Unfortunately, he was out of town during my visit, as he says he often conducts informal house tours for his own students, to show them the physical spaces he describes in the book that have inspired his own work with space. A former urban planner, as well as an architect and civil engineer, Blanco remarked to me how important space is in crafting identity and how the ways we shape space can in turn shape us. I nodded vigorously, as the poet laid out the thesis of my book, although his perspective was as a person who *makes* space, first with blueprints and maps and building, then with words.

My impression of Blanco's childhood street matched my impression of Miami: much more Cuban than I expected. I hear only Spanish, see a few saint statues on lawns (La Virgen de la Caridad del Cobre among them), and note several signs of Cuban pride (a mailbox with the shape of the island, flags in cars). Four blocks over from Blanco's house, the bustling four-lane Fortieth Street dons pawn shops, auto shops, loan stores, and big storefronts all with Spanish-language advertising. I pass a front yard avocado stand where a father with a thick Cuban accent takes a break from playing with his kids to sell two to me from the unpriced display. Some of the mailboxes are elaborate, and there are a lot of animal gargoyles (lions are a favorite). The houses are ranch style, one story, most with Spanish tiled roofs, many in the brightly colored pastel palette of Caribbean architecture. Many have columns, several have fountains and animal statues atop fences. The styles suggest a not wholly successful attempt to demonstrate wealth; I might call it "faux opulence."

Westchester was also more modest than I pictured. The houses are very close together, and the small backyards touch. There are usually low, metal chain-link fences between properties, but despite the proximity there is a notable absence of fencing in the front of the homes: the fronts of the houses are undivided. In many cases the front yard has been shortened to make room for parking spaces, to allow more cars to fit. The grassy shoulder of the street has been transformed into part of house driveways, or if the shoulder remains, stones are placed along it to deter traditional street parking. There are multiple cars in front of most houses. There aren't a lot of bars or windows on Blanco's street, though elsewhere in the neighborhood it depends on the street. Many homes have a few chairs outside the front door facing out toward the street. My parking on the street is noted by several suspicious neighbors—the innovative configuration of front yards-as-driveways makes any uninvited visitor conspicuous. The proximity of the houses to one another, the absence of all but the most minimal fencing, the extensive visibility, and the pastime of sitting outside the house to watch the street, all make the street feel intimate, bordering on claustrophobic (to me).

Next, I head to Blanco's primary and secondary schools, St. Brendan's and Christopher Columbus High. St. Brendan's parking lot happens to be filling: I hear "¿a que hora es la misa?" "a las seis" as I'm parking. Apparently, there's a Friday night mass. I hear the priest addressed in both English and Spanish as he prepares for the service. The mass appears well attended. Christopher Columbus High School's athletes, incidentally, are

the "Explorers," and the logo is of a fifteenth-century Spaniard with hel-
met and mustache. I'm slightly shocked that a school would pick a conquistador as their mascot, but then, Christopher Columbus as a namesake
is also problematic. Here, as elsewhere in Westchester, the ties to Cuba are
clearer than I anticipated.

I go to the Winn-Dixie supermarket on Coral Way, Richard's respite
from what he feels is the relentless Cubanness of his upbringing. Yet,
although the supermarket is more Anglo than the bodegas and storefronts surrounding it, even it is not the haven for americanos it might
have been (nowhere is safe!). There are a few families and individuals
speaking English here, but every cashier is speaking Spanish and has a
Spanish name on their nametag, and it is Spanish that is carried on the
loudspeaker. The aisles are well lit and proffer the usual supermarket fare
but also have imported items from Spain or the Caribbean, and the produce reflects a Caribbean diet. The store has a perfume and jewelry counter by the exit, staffed by an older Spanish-speaking gentleman who is
arguing confidently in Spanish with a not-so-potential customer.[11]

Blanco's line about how Miami natives say what they love about Miami
is how you don't even need a passport to visit the US resonates. The barrio
is so overwhelmingly Spanish-speaking that "*los americanos*" enter these
spaces at their own peril. Richard, who grows up with a Cuban farm in his
backyard, with all his neighbors from his Abuelo's campo or from Havana
or Veradero, patronizing all the bodegas his Abuela favors because they
have all the Cuban staples and allow haggling, attending a school proud
of its conquistador heritage and boasting students whose parents still go
to Spanish-language mass, hearing his mother's oft-repeated retort, "Is
this what I left Cuba for?" would naturally feel very much a part of an
imaginary world, a part of America he never saw on TV or read about in
his textbook.

Diasporic Miami Beach

Recognizing that he is a part of these two worlds, and not quite belonging
to either, Richard learns to recognize that ethnic identity is not necessarily fixed or unitary, which allows his to be both Cuban and American
as he develops. This lesson, part of the first arc of the bildungsroman,
in turn will inform the second narrative arc, as he grapples with what
he perceives as his dual sexual identity—being Cuban and being gay—as
a young adult. His path to an intersectional ethnic selfhood is literally
inscribed in a physical journey, and the unique space of Miami Beach
provides the ground for his transformation.

On a summer vacation to old South Beach, Richard meets Yetta, the "Queen of the Copa," an elderly widow. Yetta is part of a longstanding Jewish community in Miami's South Beach, which like Little Havana had been insulated and somewhat self-contained. Since the late 1800s Jews have emigrated to South Florida, mostly Ashkenazim from other parts of the US who first immigrated to escape persecution in Eastern Europe. Restrictive housing covenants limited where Jews could live or buy property: until the 1930s they could only move in south of Fifth Street, at the tip of the island. During the Great Depression and after, with such barriers to house ownership lifted, the Jewish community in Miami Beach grew and was instrumental in building up the tourism industry of the area, including its Art Deco hotel district. The peak of Jewish settlement in Miami Beach was 1980: in the 1970s (approximately when this portion of Blanco's memoir takes place) Jews made up 80 percent of the Miami Beach population (Greater Miami Jewish Federation). The home of the Jewish community was Miami Beach.[12]

Never having met a Jew, and flummoxed by her Yiddish-strewn vocabulary, Richard asks where she's from. She replies that she is a "little from everywhere" (*Prince of Los Cocuyos* 126). When he is asked where he is from, he first replies with his neighborhood—Westchester (125). Yet later he offers that he is "from Cuba" (127). When pressed, he admits he was born in Spain, and then moved here. Then Yetta asks the question that haunts him for the rest of his trip: "So what does that make you?" (127). It is a question he has never been asked before. It turns out "Where are you from?" is something none of Blanco's family can help him answer. When he asks the question of his cousins and brothers, they each respond immediately with a US city (128), but Richard claims they misunderstand his question. When he asks his mom "what he is," the answer further unsettles him: "*bueno*, yes, you're *cubano*, but you are also a little *americano*; and *un galleguito* from Spain, where you were born" (133).

Like Blanco's Abuela, Yetta speaks her native language still, and visits ethnic sites that allow her to reconnect with her past. However, as a Polish Holocaust survivor Yetta does not tend towards rosy recollections of her childhood home; she has assimilated into Miami Beach culture and allowed herself to be changed by her adopted town. Unlike Blanco's family and Cuba, Yetta has seen her home deteriorate: "the place to see and be seen" when she was young is now "a real dump," "concrete walks crumbling like chalk," "grimy" store windows, "faded and tattered" awnings and "out-of-date" wares; "there was an eerie sensation of emptiness" all through the main drag of the once fashionable Art Deco district. Also unlike Richard's grandparents, parents, and most of the Cubans he meets, Yetta fills the space with her memories, but her memories are *from and of these very same spaces*—a completely different mode of remembering than what Blanco is used to. As they walk Lincoln Road, Yetta "filled in the blanks with her memories," remaking the street as they pass: "I caught glimpses of just how glamorous it must have been back in her time" (137). Yetta reflects nostalgia for the place she is in: she is the first person Richard meets who cherishes her Miami past. She will become a model for Richard for how to identify with his own home rather than the homes of others.

When Yetta asks Richard if he feels Cuban, he rambles in response: "Sometimes I do, but sometimes I hate being Cuban . . . Sometimes I feel very American . . . but sometimes I don't feel American. Then I feel like nothing" (145). Yetta consoles him that she feels her different identities—Polish, American, even *cubana*—at different times too: "So what? So we're a little from everywhere—not so bad I think. Not so bad" (145). Yetta's lesson is that "change can't be changed" and that to "look at the world not like it is, but like it was" becomes inevitable with age (139). The richness of this lesson is evident in the story itself, as the memoir looks at Blanco's Miami "like it was." Accepting change, for a transnational subject like Blanco, will entail accepting ambiguity in how he answers the question, "where are you from?"

Squaring Cuban and Gay Identity

The second question Yetta asks, "What does that make you?" shapes Richard as well, and his other internalized binary—gay or Cuban—will need to dissolve for the young man to achieve a healthy adulthood. Indivisible with being Cuban for Richard growing up is being a Cuban *man,* and the rules for being *un cubano* are many. Abuela suspects that Richard is gay, and admonishes him often, "it's better to be *it* and not look like *it,* than to look like *it* even if you are not *it*" (72). From a young age, Richard understands without understanding: "*it* meant watching telenovelas; *it* was my paint-by-number sets; *it* was my cousin's Easy-Bake Oven I wanted for my own—all the things I enjoyed for which she constantly humiliated me" (72). When Richard is a teenager, Abuela starts a campaign to make Richard "*un macho,*" in the aptly titled chapter "It takes *un pueblo.*" He begins working at El Cocuyito, the grocery store owned and run by his uncle Pipo's father-in-law Don Gustavo. Don Gustavo gives him lessons in being a man—don't use straws, don't wear shorts, don't be afraid of getting dirty (157), and of course, the unspoken commandment, don't be gay. Yet, much like his binary sense of Cuban versus American identities,

Richard will learn to weave together his various selves, becoming a Cuban man and a gay man at once.

El Cocuyito

El Cocuyito is an aggressively Cuban space. Don Gustavo, who comes to Miami in 1965, when there was "nada, not even a place to get un cafecito" (158), forges a grocery store that can transport exiles back to their lost homeland: "El Cocuyito was more than his livelihood, it was a substitute for the life he had left behind in Cuba" (158). Visitors to the space inhabit their Cubanness, and Richard learns lessons about not only becoming a man but becoming a *Cuban* man: Nuñez, a regular customer and lecherous old man, teaches him how to speak *Cubichi,* a language of Cuban idiomatic expressions and "hablando mierda" (talking shit) (163). Richard develops the art of nicknaming, builds a vocabulary of *dichos,* and of course learns how to blurt *piropos* or come-on lines to women (163). "In *Cubichi* I could think like a Cuban, be a *cubano* without translating words or myself into English" (166).

Richard learns enough in the Cuba-by-proxy space of El Cocuyito to be able to riff on the references. Richard achieves belonging to this "pueblo," but only by imitating the exiles around him, by pretending, with them, that "they were still in Cuba" (181). Further, acceptance into this village is predicated on a version of Cuban masculinity that does not match Blanco's personality or his nascent sexuality. Don Gustavo and his Abuela are thus teaching him how to play the part of the *macho* Cuban rather than become it. The space of El Cocuyito makes such identity policing easy.

El Cocuyito is actually Galiano market (Blanco changed the name for copyright purposes since his uncle sold it), which is in Coral Gables, a more affluent section of Miami, southwest of Little Havana, where more established Golden Exiles have settled. If you can divide the Cuban spaces I encounter in Miami into those that are built for the Anglo visitor and those that are not, El Galiano would be in the latter category. It is not advertising itself unduly to the street; like La Virgen de la Caridad del Cobre Cafetería, you need to know it's there to go there. Only Spanish is spoken. An older gentleman leans against the café counter; the female cashier exchanges pleasantries with customers she appears to know. As in Blanco's description, there are the same green stencils on the glass front door, the same mint green shelves, the same wine aisle, butcher shop in the back, and small cafeteria. "Cafeteria" is a bit of an exaggeration: really it is just a counter and a few stools, with a handwritten menu of a handful of bread-based dishes and, of course, Cuban coffee on offer. The store is smaller than I expected, though comparable in stature to most of the bodegas I visit. Perhaps due to its outsize influence on Blanco I expected it to be larger. The aisles are quite narrow, and the cafeteria section is highly visible, with clear sight lines to the cashiers (set very close to the entrance) and to the back door of the store. As on Blanco's neighborhood street, there is not much space to hide in. There is storage space behind the wall of the butcher shop, where Blanco will spend time helping roast a pig or baking bread (there is a sign for "pan cubano" in that doorway with an arrow pointing to the back), but inside the store itself everything is out in the open. El Cocuyito is a little Cuban Panopticon.

Under the tutelage of the Cuban bodega, Blanco learns how to be a Cuban man: how to roast whole pigs, drink beers, play dominoes, talk shit, and eventually, how to get married, or more specifically, how to have sex with a woman. As Deycita's date to her "*quince*," Richard completes his macho training. Much like he learns to approximate knowledge of the Cuba he doesn't know, Richard learns to perform the existence of heterosexual urges he does not feel. Learning to dance and pretending to flirt, he plays the role of "Prince of the fireflies" for Deycita and his com-munity—the nickname is one he gives himself, aware of the duplicity of the act, and the fragility of his kingdom. Not just Deycita, but all of his "village" congratulate him on his performance: the El Cocuyito regulars sign a card telling him how much they appreciate him, how proud they are of him (188). The entire pueblo affirms Richard as a Cuban (straight) man, yet both his Cubanness and his manliness are performances he has been taught, not innate identities.[13] The sources of both these identities—the loss of physical Cuba, the desire for women—are unknown to Rich-ard, but they are also the glue that connects the community. Yet a series of encounters as a young man will show him how he might square his outer cubano and his inner yearnings, to figure out how to belong as both Cuban and gay.

A key moment in this development comes when Victor begins work-ing at El Cocuyito. Victor is a "dissident" who was jailed in Cuba for being homosexual, which Richard learns only after establishing a relationship with him, where they share coffee in the morning and set about work together, exchanging life stories. Richard recognizes that Victor grows up after the revolution, in "the Cuba I would have grown up in had my par-ents decided to stay" (209)—the halcyon Cuba of the Golden Exiles are unknown to both of them. Victor's Cuba is "*muy diferente* than the Cuba all these people talk about here" (208); or as he puts it succinctly, "Cuba was hell anyway—it was *de pinga*" (205). Victor thus takes the shine off of the Cuba endlessly recounted inside El Cocuyito, allowing Richard to see the positive aspect of his own country in *comparison* to this mythical place. In fact, Victor explains he *prefers* "Miami, where I can do what I want, love who I want, and no one put me in jail for it" (208). Miami, a place that is still so restrictive for Richard, is a place of freedom for Victor. As this binary of America versus Cuba becomes further destabilized, the other dichotomies within Richard also loosen.

Victor provides a guide for Richard as a burgeoning artist as well. As an immigrant and refugee, Victor's status as Cuban is unquestioned, and as an "inmate," with his "scruffy beard," "thick, hairy forearms," and "brawny chest," Victor is accepted as a macho; but he is also painter, who stocks the aisles listening to opera music on his Walkman. Thus, Richard is shown how one can be both artistic and manly. Spurred by Victor's example, Richard reads Victor his favorite poem from school, and even stands up to his Abuela: when she questions the art supplies he buys for Victor's birthday, "*Pero,* those aren't gifts for *un hombre* like him" since "only *un maricón* would. . . ." Richard retorts, "he's my friend, Abuela—he's an artist. So what? Just leave me alone!" (213–14).

Victor also awakens Richard's sexual desires. When Richard touches Victor's bare back, he "knew without knowing" (212), comparing the sensation to kissing Anita, his supposed girlfriend. They have a tense pseudodate at Victor's apartment, where Richard finally admits he has feelings for him. They remain chaste, but as a much older man, Victor counsels the still teenaged Richard in navigating his sense of self: "You know who you are, Papo—that's never going to change—*nunca.* I know it isn't easy, but one day you'll know when the time is right" (217). Subject to the same regulations concerning Cuban manhood and yet unabashed about who he is, Victor's words and his example encourage Richard to "be yourself as much as you can" until he loses his fear of dropping his outward-facing persona (217).

BILL BAGGS STATE PARK

All Richard's binaries—to be Cuban or American, to be gay or straight, to be "un macho" or not—are finally dissolved when he meets Ariel. Ariel is a Marielito, a few years older than Richard, who comes to the US when he is twelve. He defies Richard's black-and-white ideas about Cuban identity. He mixes Spanish and English but is "*very* Cuban"—showing the old-timers how to roast a *lechón* in a *caja china* (a technology they had forgotten) and making a *mojo* with Richard's mom. During a beach picnic, as the older men turn to "their usual conversation" about how wonderful Cuba was and about how terrible the revolution is, Ariel surprises the older generation by adding, "Cuba will always be Cuba, and Cubans will always be Cuban" (235). Finally realizing that Ariel had actually been *living* in Cuba, "one by one, the men asked Ariel what he knew of their homes and the places they had left behind" (236). Ariel can not only remember the island (a feat to someone like Richard)—he can even update the exiles about their former houses, friends and family. Both Victor and Ariel have seen what Cuba has become, and what it is now. It is not coincidental that they help open Richard's eyes to his sexual identity, since they destabilize the Golden Exile myth of Cuba that is tied so tightly to his own myth of Cuban masculinity.

Yet Ariel is *also* American, listening to New Wave, attending Hialeah High School, and enjoying American culture, asserting "I like what I like" (231). Richard is incredulous that Ariel loves his high school, because it is full of Marielito refugees, unlike his own Catholic school in Westchester: "'But Hialeah High is *so* Cuban. How could you like it there?'" (231). However, its Cuban character is precisely what appeals to Ariel—"'Yeah, *primo*, that's why I love it—feels like I never left Cuba. You know it's not easy fitting in when you come over like I did, *broder*'" (231). Richard also reads signs of Ariel as either un-*cubanaso* (the term for a super Cuban man) or homosexual: perfectly manicured fingernails, his love affair with his pug Yakson, his masterful way around the kitchen, his pukka shell bracelet. The identities of Cuban male and gay male are presented to Richard as two mutually exclusive modes of being: but the figure of Ariel offers a glimpse of a "*very* Cuban" and *macho* man, accepted and even admired by the older Cuban *exilio* men who look to him as the standard of Cubanness, that might also perhaps be gay.

Richard argues with Ariel that he likes American stuff, which to his logic disqualifies or cancels out his Cubanness. Ariel's response, "I like what I like," cracks open the bind Richard feels, the rigid dichotomy between who he is and who he feels he is supposed to be. Suddenly (but also after many years of searching) he sees that one can occupy the space between identities, and that a person can choose to select aspects of different cultures or ways of living based on one's own preference or personality. "I like what I like" becomes a mantra for Richard, a way to give himself agency.

Richard grapples with who Ariel is, as well as who *he* is in relation to Ariel—whether the desire is there, and whether it is mutual. Amidst his confusion over his feelings for Ariel, and about Ariel—how could someone be so American and so Cuban? How could someone be such a Cuban man but also, possibly, gay?—it is instructive that Blanco turns the focus of attention to a known quantity: Miami. As the family drives to the beach for their usual Sunday picnic, with their marinated raw *lechón* swaddled in the backseat like a baby, notice how detailed Blanco's description of the urban landscape becomes:

> The morning air rushing in was still relatively cool and crisp for a Miami August. The city felt strangely peaceful at that early hour, empty without peddlers trolling the intersections selling one-dollar bags of peeled oranges; without its senate of cigar-smoking men gathered for coffee at La Carreta, debating how Cuba was lost, again; and without its ladies in curlers and old men in straw hats leaning on canes at the lonely bus stops. This empty Miami felt like an unfinished canvas. There was no honking as we sped down U.S. 1. No line at the Rickenbacker tollbooth. No windsurfers gliding on the bay. No cyclists pedaling through the thicket of sea grape trees lining the causeway. No traffic through the business district of Key Biscayne ending at the beach park entrance. (227)

The passage is saturated with intimate knowledge of the place. Opening with a statement about the weather, which tells us the narrator knows what is normal for this time of year, Blanco goes on to show us an intricate Miami *that is not there* at the time he is describing it. At *this* hour, he is struck by absences—indicating to the reader that he knows the city so well that he can notice the shifts in its life. He begins to populate the empty Miami before his eyes with the Miami he is familiar with, through a series of "withouts" and "nos" insistently stacked with anaphora. He knows which characters are missing. He knows that there are usually windsurfers and cyclists and traffic on this particular stretch of road. What better way to show one's belonging, one's accumulated place memory, than to describe the sleeping city with details of that city when it is awake? To know the city so well that you can, from memory, narrate it as though it were in front of you in its usual vividness? Compare this intimacy and the reflection of self-knowledge created by the landscape to any Cuban beach scene in *City of a Hundred Fires*, and the contrast is stark: Blanco knows his village, and its inhabitants, better than any stretch of Cuban shoreline.

Richard's confidence as a Miami narrator falters briefly when they reach the park entrance, but the resolution is monumental (that's a pun! You'll see). When he sees the signs for Bill Baggs State Park, he wonders "the way he often wondered," about who Bill Baggs, and for that matter José Martí and Máximo Gómez, actually were; was Baggs a general, a

president? Richard knows his relationship to American history, and even
to this state park sign, is different from his parents': "To them Bill Baggs
was just something else in *Inglish* that had nothing to do with them, two
words they could at best only mispronounce" (227–28). To illustrate the
distance between his Cuban family and the namesake, Richard tells us
how Abuelo amuses the family every Sunday by attempting to recite the
name: "*Bil-Bá, Bil-Bá, Bil-Bá*" (228). As Richard feels a pang of guilt for
not knowing who Bill Baggs is, and curiosity about who he was, the rest
of his family performs their happy lack of connection to the name: just
another nonsense word in "*Inglish.*"

Richard underestimates his family's desire to belong to the place as
much as he does, and he also underestimates how much he really is a
part of this Miami (despite not knowing who Bill Baggs was). Abuelo
ultimately coins the term "El Farito" (the Little Lighthouse) to refer to this
beach, based on the lighthouse, which is *not* small, as the name would
suggest, making "*farito*" both a term of endearment and an in-joke for
the family. With this christening comes a new sense of ownership for
the Blancos: "El Farito became *our* family's park. The beach became *our*
beach, and the sun, *our* sun, . . . as we drove into *our* lot, and parked in
our usual spot by the rusty bicycle rack" (228). It is especially noteworthy
that Blanco does not italicize "El Farito," as he assiduously italicizes Spanish words throughout the memoir. By leaving it un-italicized, the name
enters English, and thus becomes his as much as his parents' and grandparents'. Blanco codifies the possession by titling the chapter "El Farito."

Richard jokes to Ariel that "with so many Cubans here they should
just call this place Cubanoso Park" (247). Indeed, Bill Baggs State Park
belongs to Latino/as on a weekend. The stretch of sand and pines at the
edge of Key Biscayne feels like the end of the world, or at the very least,
the end of Miami, and it is ground zero for barbecuing on a Saturday
afternoon. Raccoons come in droves to be fed (yes, people were feeding
the raccoons) and to help themselves to the table scraps of a dozen families. Every occupied picnic table had Caribbean music emanating from
portable speakers. A few blast Cuban songs from boom boxes. Several
families make use of the grills provided at each site, which are scattered
throughout the grassy area adjacent to the parking lot, separated from
the beach by a narrow but dense crop of trees. The pines, the surprisingly
forested greenery, are all as depicted in *The Prince of Los Cocuyos*. From
some of these tables you can't see the Cape Florida lighthouse, despite
its proximity, because of the thickness of the foliage. While you can walk
to the lighthouse from the beach, you can't access it beachside (without

squeezing through an iron fence): you must walk along a trail through the trees to get to its entrance. On the beach, the majority are still Spanish-speaking families that I assume are Cuban (I don't feel like interrupting their beach days to ask them, but they don't look Central American, and my Puerto Rican relatives tell me 85 degrees Fahrenheit is winter weather, so I'm guessing they aren't Puerto Rican). The family groups are multigenerational.

While "El Farito" belongs to the whole family, and maybe to "The Cuban Family" in abstract, the beach belongs to Richard in a more personal way. When the family first arrives to set up, he escapes through the "labyrinth of sea grapes" (clearly a route he knows well) to walk the beach alone. He links his own being and becoming to the sea: "I became conscious of my feet stamping the sand—step, step, step—as I walked around the big bend where the lighthouse came into view—step, step—each step a question: . . . Who was Ricardo Blanco? Would I be an architect? Would I be a husband and father, or would I grow up to love men as Abuela feared?" (229). The familiar lighthouse and the sand and the sea conspire to bring to the surface the questions Richard has about who he is. The questions reflect the pressure Richard feels from his family—he uses "Ricardo," what they call him at home, he mentions his parents' dream of him being an architect, and he asserts that it is Abuela who fears that he might love men.

Richard's location offers a space for questioning but also provides a space for resolution. Faced with swirling queries about his identity, he takes action: "I dove into the ocean, swam eyes-open underwater, fast and hard until I had to come up for air. Heart thumping, I floated on my back and stared straight up at the clouds" (229). His relationship to his surroundings is marked by force and agency; diving "fast" and "hard," swimming "eyes-open" into the ocean, he stares "straight up" at the clouds above. The writing inflects Richard's surety within the space. This self-knowledge, born of intimate knowledge of a place, allows him to weather (pun intended) existential uncertainty and change: unflinchingly he watches the clouds as they are "continuously becoming something new." He experiences a complete habitation of this beach he knows so well, that answers for him the question of who he will be (or rather, teaches him that questions are constant and selves will always change).

In one of several turning points in this concluding story, Richard loses his fear of being perceived as not manly enough, emboldened by the setting and by Ariel's example. Surrounded by the family and the old cubanos on the beach, Richard "lunges" into the dance circle: "I . . . cut in on him and Danita, taking her into my arms as if I knew exactly what to do" (239). Danita takes the male lead, since Blanco doesn't know how to salsa. The crowd delights in the spectacle. Then, Ariel cuts back in, to dance with *Richard,* not Danita: "'*Así mismo,* Ariel. Show Riqui how it's done. You make a beautiful couple,' Danita said, and the crowd roared, so amused by his antics that I had to play along . . . 'Look, I've turned *el gringo* into *un cubanaso!*' Ariel shouted" (239). The whole community, the very men and women Richard became the "Prince of los Cocuyos" for by being the perfect manly *quinces* date for Deycita, approves of his dancing with a man. In fact, his very act of dancing with a man confirms his Cubanness, as Ariel exclaims he has turned him into a "*cubanaso.*" The scene suggests that as long as he is adequately Cuban (like Ariel), there is space for Richard's nonheteronormative sexual desires.

The climax of the memoir comes when Ariel and Richard set off on a walk alone. Ariel offhandedly asks why the Blancos call the beach "El Farito" (as I mentioned, it is not visible from the picnic area), and Richard explains that there is a lighthouse: "*De verdad?* A lighthouse? Where? Let's go, take me!" (241). Richard is thus able to perform his knowledge of the location, giving him confidence in at least *one* of his identities—as a Miami native—even while Ariel teaches him how to become comfortable with his *other* identities (as gay and Cuban American). The Cape Florida lighthouse stands at the very edge of the Southeastern edge of Florida. It looks out on ocean on three sides, and if you drew a straight line south from its top you would hit Cuba. An obviously phallic landmark that is staunchly American, or even more accurately, staunchly south Floridian, while at the same time looking out upon and harkening back to Cuba and its influence, the lighthouse operates cleanly as a symbol of both Cuban American and male homosexual identity (see fig. 35).

Both men recognize its symbolism. For Ariel, the expanse of ocean between the shore and his country of origin recalls for him his traumatic experience in the Mariel boatlift: "some days, *como que,* I'm nowhere . . . It's like I'm still somewhere in the middle of that ocean, *primo,* on that boat with all those people" (242). Ariel is also trapped between identities, but his uncertainty is geographical: being "not really here or there," he feels that he is neither Cuban nor American (242). While Richard knows intimately the struggle of managing disparate selves, he has always had his anchor in Miami: the one identity he has never questioned. Showing Ariel the lighthouse, a commonplace of Richard's own local childhood, confirms his regional expertise and contrasts the different character of the two men's internal conflicts.

FIGURE 35. Cape Florida Lighthouse, in all its phallic glory, 2019

They make it to the lighthouse, whose phallic aspect is, again, unde-niable. When they arrive, Ariel declares it "beautiful," while Richard had "never thought of the old lighthouse as *beautiful,* exactly" (242). After being denied entrance into it, Ariel *teaches Richard how to handle the lighthouse:* "'*Primo,* check this out—do this,' he said when we reached the base of the lighthouse. Following his instructions, I stood beside him, leaned my body face-first against the lighthouse, and hugged it, my fingertips almost touch-ing his. 'Now look straight up,' he said. I tilted my head back. The lighthouse seemed a hundred times taller and more massive than it ever had before, and yet it also felt small and vulnerable in my arms, as if *I* were mightier than it. '*Coolísimo,* no?' he said" (243). Close reading this passage to point out the sexual overtones is so easy it isn't really close reading at all, but here goes: Ariel shows Richard how to touch the lighthouse, as an older, more experienced lighthouse-toucher; as Ariel guides him to engage with the monument (there!), Richard experiences the size and stature of the light-house more intensely, while also recognizing his own power and potential to make the lighthouse "small and vulnerable in my arms." As Richard is having this experience, Ariel is close by having a similar experience, and their fingertips almost touch as they share the moment.

That Ariel and Richard "discover" the lighthouse together, and hug the lighthouse together, and that it is here, in the shadow of a metaphor for male sexuality, that Richard finally decides to act upon his homosexual desire, makes neat narrative sense. The tangling of two signifieds (to be gay and to be a Cuban Floridian) in one signifier (the lighthouse) reflects how these identities are indelibly linked for Richard and how their development has been coextensive. In other words, "coming out" and "coming to" America are linked for Blanco's dual bildungsroman: by crossing their narrative resolutions, queering the coming-of-age story with an immigrant story and vice versa, he offers a literary space to recognize and explore his intersectional identity.

Bolstered by his successful dance stunt earlier, encouraged by the sexy lighthouse hug, and buoyed by his familiar surroundings, Richard takes the lead. He has Ariel close his eyes, locks arms with him, and then throws them both into the water, shouting, "¡*Vámanos pa' Cuba!*" ("Let's go to Cuba!"). Richard proceeds to chase him in the water, pretending to be a shark, finally catching him, finally "ready to take his face in my hands and bring him to my lips" (245). Richard is on the cusp of putting into action the feelings that have haunted him throughout the narrative. Yet the moment is intruded upon, not arbitrarily, by Ariel's sudden reliving of his traumatic boat voyage to the US: triggered by the shouts of "*tiburón*," he pulls himself out of the water. Thus, Ariel's pure Cubanness involuntarily gets in the way of Richard's impulse to act upon his own homosexual desire. But despite his spurred advance, by the close of the memoir Richard has achieved what Victor promised, that he would know and that he would lose his fear of being himself.

This sense of inhabiting multiple identities, of being able to "like what I like," to be Cuban and male and gay and American, *has* to happen in Miami. Amidst his evolving conceptions of manhood, latinidad, and sexual orientation, Richard's barrio and his identity as a resident of that barrio is his one identity beyond question: the certainty of his belonging to Little Havana gives him the core sense of self requisite to discover his other, less fixed, selves. Cuba does not provide the space for Blanco's many selves to coexist: *City of a Hundred Fires* only explores two of Blanco's selves—the Cuban and the American. To portray the full range of Blanco's experience and his identity, his narrative must return to his village. The final line of the memoir, "time to go, indeed, time to go" (249), while it of course gestures to the genre of memoir as a history of a piece of the past and functions as Blanco poetically nudging his reader that the extended reverie of *The Prince of Los Cocuyos* is now over, also demonstrates that the crucial dimension of the story is not time but *space*. It is the "to go," not the "time," that is operative in this last sentence: the verb indicates Miami, the place that Blanco has come back to, that he goes to, again and again, the place from which he writes in the present, the place from which he emerged, as a Cuban American, a proud gay man, and as an author.

CONCLUSION

Your Hometown and Other Barriographies

A FEW years back I was in Mexico City researching Sandra Cisneros's gorgeous 2002 novel *Caramelo*. Between curbside snack stops for sweet fried plantains and pumpkin flower quesadillas (for research!), I traced the protagonist's steps, based on Cisneros's own frequent visits to the capital from her childhood: a long car ride from her hometown of Chicago with her six brothers, humorously recounted in the novel. As usual, the fictional account provided detailed and accurate descriptions of real-life streets and houses—one chapter is even titled, "Leandro Valle Street, Corner of Misericordia, Over by Santo Domingo" (111)—so I was able to walk Lala's walks from her grandmother's house on "Destiny Street" (Avenida la Fortuna, house "number 12") to Parque Alameda to the Zócalo to the Basílica de Guadalupe and back again. I learned a lot on that trip, about the making of Mexican shawls (the novel tells the intergenerational history of an inherited *rebozo de caramelo*) and the history of fringe work and various weaving traditions and how these crafts are strikingly gendered in their operation and geographically specific in their production. However, the most powerful revelation I had did not come from interviews or studying textiles or interpreting the text.

What one learns by visiting the streets and neighborhoods Cisneros describes is the importance of sound. Mexico City projects a maddening racket of sound. The streets are awash in noise and activity. The traffic of cars and trucks is part of this, and the sound of honking and screeching tires and car alarms, and the vibrations of heavy vehicles on uneven pavement, and the yelling of vendors or human windshield wipers snaking between cars at lights at rush hour; and, of course, the foot traffic of any major city is at work, with sidewalks thronged with pedestrians, or subways packed full at rush hour, with the Latin American tradition of subway-riding sellers: buskers singing from car to car while battling through the crowd, or hawkers of gum, flashlights, ChapStick, chanting about what they are selling and how much it costs; guitarists boarding buses and playing for several stops, only to be replaced by a new artist, or by the bus driver's radio. Mexican culture adds several more layers of sound: many sidewalks, even in the more suburban neighborhoods in the city, even in small towns, are lined with food vendors grilling and making fresh tacos, *tortas,* quesadillas, huaraches, *sopes,* selling fresh juices or sweets, churros, coffee, *elote, plátanos.* At any time of day from morning until late evening, there are men and women curbside yelling out their offerings, ringing bells or blowing whistles, and small clusters of men and women gathered standing or sitting to eat and drink. On the other side of the sidewalk are the storefronts, which quite often blast music from the inside of their establishments that floods out into the street. Add to this the propensity of Mexican men to comment audibly and directly to female passersby, and you have streets that become cacophonies. The noise is simply relentless. It is on a level that surpasses the sounds of an American city like Chicago, or even New York. It is overwhelming and exhausting, even for US city-dwellers like Cisneros and me.

In the novel, Lala seemed to find spaces to be alone: there are a few scenes where she walks the city on her own, including a climactic contemplative moment at the Basílica de Guadalupe. How profoundly I misunderstood these spaces was not clear until I went to them myself. The grandmother's house sits on a short street between two hectic thoroughfares in La Valle, itself a barrio near the heart of Mexico City. As I head from "Destiny Street" to the famous basilica, a walk our heroine takes to try to escape the claustrophobia and racket of her abuela's tight quarters, full of male family members, I am assailed by noise: The heavy traffic of cars and trucks, honking, engines revving, speeding past on the busy avenue; the soundtracks attempting to outdo each other emanating out of each storefront; the curbside food stalls full of people standing, yelling, conversing, eating, as you inch your way by on the sidewalk; finally, the sounds of men, "greeting" you from storefronts or benches, walking past you and whispering comments on your dress or your stature, whistling, exclaiming, and variously making themselves both menacing and irritating. When I arrive at the basilica, expecting a respite from the clamor, assuming Lala found a quiet spot, instead the noise intensifies: large groups of tourists and pilgrims mill about outside, while buskers, sidewalk vendors, and more food stalls await the caprices of the faithful. Even inside the church there is no peace. Pews are full and mass is delivered through a microphone and echoing surround sound.

By the time I enter the basilica, I get it. Cisneros's character-double Lala, who tries many times to find a sanctuary from her home of too many boys and no room of her own, is desperate for solitude. Before my trip I had pictured the moments in the book when she is on a park bench in *parque Alameda,* or on a balcony overlooking the Zócalo, or inside the Basílica, as scenes where she achieves calm, serenity, and her own space to think. It took being in these spaces to realize that for any pedestrian in Mexico City—*especially* a single female pedestrian—there is no quiet place.

Lala, like Cisneros in her own collection of autobiographical essays, *A House of My Own,* like Esperanza in *The House on Mango Street,* craves a place removed from the eyes and concerns of men, soundproofed from the messy racket of urban life, and set aside for listening only to the stories inside her own head. As Cisneros puts it in *Mango Street,* Lala needs "Not a man's house. Not a daddy's. . . . Only a house as quiet as snow, a space for myself to go, clean as paper before the poem" (*Caramelo* 108). The simile Cisneros chooses is perfect, as usual. A space as "clean as paper before the poem" is empty, silent, peaceful, and full of creative possibility. The page becomes the place where she can be alone, freed from her brothers, father, uncles, and boyfriends. Like Soledad at the end of Angie Cruz's *Soledad,* or even the F-troop of Helena María Viramontes's *Their Dogs Came with Them,* the space for female independence, creativity, and freedom from patriarchal pressures only exists on the page.

The sketch of *Caramelo*'s barriography reminds us of both what else is at stake in a local reading and just how far we might extend it. By homing in on place, we don't just get to point to real-life referents and make neat one-to-one equivalences between the text and the barrio. Since a culture is built by a place, inhabiting the place allows us to experience the culture, to understand the interplay of gender, sexuality, language, class, and race that emerge from any given locale. The noise and crowds of Mexico City are linked to the fear of the male gaze and the stifling machismo of Mexican life, all of which propel the stories of the distaff side that men seek to push to the margins of *Caramelo*'s tale.

I hope that *Walk the Barrio* has convinced you that when considering contemporary Latinx literature on and by immigrants, place matters. Cuba's fearsome antihomosexual laws, Miami's multiple diasporas (Cuban, Jewish, gay), and Little Havana's intense island nostalgia all contribute specific complications to Richard Blanco's coming-of-age and coming-out stories. Washington Heights' rough-and-tumble crack years created a neighborhood watchfulness Angie Cruz's Soledad cannot escape. Junot Díaz's performance of toxic masculinity doesn't make sense unless you see the gentrification of his housing projects and understand the instability of gender roles for the Dominican diaspora and its impact on a historically macho society. If William Archila hadn't landed in the cultural dead zone that is Van Nuys, he might never have needed to seek out the colonias of Lincoln Heights or Echo Park, or learned how to make his homeland in the poem. Without the intersection of Los Angeles's Central American barrios and police brutality against Blacks, Héctor Tobar's *The Tattooed Soldier* would literally not exist. If Helena María Viramontes hadn't witnessed the very real destruction of her childhood Eastside streets, she may not have invented the fictional quarantine to capture the atmosphere of hostility and alienation so many East Los Angeles Chicano/as experience. If Salvador Plascencia hadn't been a stranger to El Monte hailing from Guadalajara, he may not have noticed the rasquachismo of the barrio that both reminded him of home and suggested a new synthesis of Mexico and the US.

Earlier and Other Geographies

Walk the Barrio has dealt exclusively with Chicanx and Latinx writing from the last twenty-five years, but the barriography model can illuminate earlier works, given that they fulfill the criteria of this project: namely, writing that is place-detailed, concerns a transnational community or communities, and is written by an author who is inscribed in a binational social field. Numerous works of Latinx literature from the twentieth century can benefit from this methodology, including Américo Paredes' *George Washington Gómez*, Ernesto Galarza's *Barrio Boy*, Alfredo Vea's *Gods Go Begging*, and poetry by writers such as Julia Alvarez, Judith Ortiz Cofer, and Rafael Campo.[1]

A barriography of Red Hook, Brooklyn, in Francisco Goldman's *The Ordinary Seaman*, for instance, was initially in *Walk the Barrio*. The novel describes the neighborhood both on and off a ship that does not move in Brooklyn harbor, following a crew of Hondurans, Nicaraguans, and Salvadorans who are flown to the US to work as seamen, only to find their boat derelict and their employers absentee; Goldman narrates scenes from multiple vantages, introduces contradictory reckonings of time, and plays with grammatical tense to create literarily the disorienting sense of time that occurs on the boat, reflecting the consequences of globalization, transnational movement, and the exploitation of economic disparity. The Red Hook port, built for an anterior mode of commerce (shipping) and hence rendered anachronistic, serves as the economic dead space needed for two white, privately funded Americans to "own a secret slave ship" in its harbor (Goldman 304). In turn, the exclusion of the Central Americans from US capitalism mirrors the inequities at work in Red Hook's predominantly Black affordable housing projects just offshore.

I have pages and pages of more notes on Little Havana and on its sister Hialeah. Cristina García's novel *The Agüero Sisters* is another ideal barriography candidate: García's writing choices echo Little Havana's "fierce nostalgia" (45), as she employs a nonlinear narrative that toggles in time, place, and narrators to thematize the faultiness of memory, the impossibility of return, and the subsequent ferocity with which the neighborhood clings to its island memories. Ana Menéndez's short story collection *In Cuba I Was a German Shepherd* and Achy Obejas's *We Came All the Way from Cuba So You Could Dress Like This?*, while outside the time frame of my project, both dovetail nicely with Richard Blanco's work in their rich depictions of Little Havana's Golden Exile culture. Indeed, in *The Tower of the Antilles*, Obejas's latest collection, partially set in Miami, you can hear the echo of the Little Havana culture that haunts Blanco in the story "Exile": "We explained that where we come from the greatest achievement is to leave" (45).

As mentioned in the introduction, New York Puerto Ricans are glaringly absent from *Walk the Barrio*. Here at the end, please allow me to draw the contours of a nuyorican barriography. It begins with the electric Puerto Rican poetry movement of the 1960s and 1970s, fueled by the Young Lords. Poets like Pedro Pietri described the gritty realities of migration to El Barrio in New York City, using literature as an overt call for social change; such a mandate, combined with the nascent market for Latinx literature, necessitated a more conservative approach to form. In contrast, several contemporary Puerto Rican poets display a refreshing rejection of traditional narrative conventions. These innovative texts, such as performance artist Urayoán Noel's *Buzzing Hemisphere/Rumor Hemisférico*, continue rather than abandon the political project of the Young Lords by demonstrating how decolonizing literary form—through radically bilingual, nonlinear, fluid work—is its own social protest, while still anchoring their settings in the Puerto Rican barrio.

In the South Bronx, the other home of the Puerto Rican diaspora, New York Ricans enter a racial hierarchy far more rigid than that operating on the island, complicated by these neighborhoods' shared urban space with longstanding African American communities. Afro-Puerto Rican poets such as Maria "Mariposa" Fernandez and Carmen Bardeguez-Brown must thus navigate and nuance their self-presentation, caught between a US racial paradigm that flattens their identity to "Black" and their own community's attempts to define itself as distinct from African Americans. Barriographies of El Barrio and the South Bronx would include the El Museo de Barrio and the Nuyorican Poets Café, and a deep dive into NYC's graffiti and slam poetry traditions, ultimately locating the city streets underneath Noel's, Fernandez's, and Bardeguez-Brown's work, buttressing the linguistic and racial rootlessness they perform.

Walk the Barrio is also missing two important geographic areas: Houston and Chicago, which are among the top six cities for US Latinx immigration in the twenty-first century. Many scholars have elegantly contextualized The House on Mango Street in terms of its Chicago neighborhood,[2] and a barriography of Caramelo's Chicago scenes would be revelatory to scholarship about the role of the city's transnational Mexican community in its literary production. Achy Obejas's short stories of pan-Latinx coalition building ("The Sound Catalogue") and queer sexuality literally pushed to the shores of Lake Michigan ("Wrecks") could fill out the history of this city with both a dark, racially divided past but also proud, long-standing Puerto Rican and Mexican communities that have taken in newer Latinx diasporas. As for Houston, Bryan Washington's short story collection Lot would be a good place to start. NPR avers that "perhaps the most important character in Lot is Houston itself," which sounds a lot like the premise of my book. The main protagonist navigates gay, biracial, working-class, and ethnic identities against, or rather with, the backdrop of a Houston that is also evolving.

Mark McGurl closes The Program Era, his influential book on the consequences of institutional creative writing, with a critique of the "transnationalist turn" in literary criticism:

> Literary scholars have generally been on the side of excess . . . and this has found another expression in the recent rise to glory of the discourse of the "transnational." With its adjacent terminologies of transatlanticism, cosmopolitanism, diaspora, and the like, it offers itself as a critical response to the rhetoric (but also the facts) of capitalist globalization, and is founded on a recognition of the limits of the category that has always been the organizing force of the modern literature curriculum— the nation . . . It is characteristic of the cognitive expansionism of literary studies—a panic response, it may be, to anxieties about its irrelevance in the world at large—that most of its energy has been invested in extending outward from the nation rather than inward to the regions and localities, not to mention the institutions, that are equally corrective to the thoughtless assumptions of disciplinary nationalism. (401)

I share McGurl's suspicion of the meteoric "rise to glory" of transnationalism as a framework, despite its basis in the facts of capitalist globalization and the acknowledged limitations of thinking only within national boundaries. However, where McGurl sets up a dichotomy—to *either* expand outward from the nation *or* turn "inward to the regions and localities" in order to combat disciplinary nationalism—I propose a dialectic. My work operates from the premise that the global can be found and, even more important, can best be analyzed and understood at the local level. Transnationalism (and its attendant terminologies, to which I add to McGurl's list "hemispheric studies") requires grounding to be useful to the literary critic, to avoid the "excess" of expansiveness that ends up becoming mired in generalizations and abstractions.

In the case of US Latinx communities, the need to update our rubrics for comprehending contemporary transmigrancy has become particularly urgent. The US Census Bureau predicts that the Latinx population will triple in the coming decades. We are already the largest minority group in the Unites States. However, the appellation is misleading, as "Latinos" have never been a single group: the label includes indigenous groups who predate current US boundaries, Chilean descendants from the gold rush, Mexican braceros who helped build the railroads, Cuban exiles, Dominicans who escaped Trujillo, and Central Americans fleeing political upheaval. My work pushes back on the generalizing label of "Latino" by analyzing literary depictions of the immigrant experience in microcosm: each work reflects the identity of *one* community, in *one* neighborhood corner of the United States. I hope *Walk the Barrio* contributes a sorely lacking literary dimension to the social scientific discourses of transnationalism and human geography on the US Latinx immigrant experience, and conversely demonstrates how those same discourses can provide an innovative lens for interpreting Latinx literature. As a society, we need to nuance our understanding of Latinx identity, especially in the face of ever-increasing migration, immigration, and transmigration.

Where Are You Now?

Every few years I teach an upper-level course at Providence College called "The Neighborhood in Latinx Literature." Like most junior faculty at teaching institutions, I try to conserve my precious hours by teaching my research. I link each literary text to one of the many theorists I have relied on and find inspiring in my own work: Raúl Homero Villa and Mike Davis with Helena Maria Viramontes's *Their Dogs Came with Them;* Henri Lefebvre with Julia Alvarez's *The Other Side/El Otro Lado;* Dolores Hayden with Sandra Cisneros's *The House on Mango Street;* Gloria

Anzaldúa with Tomás Rivera's . . . *And the Earth Did Not Devour Him,* Jorge Duany and *Nations Unbound* with short stories by Junot Díaz and Ana Menéndez. However, the most generative part of the course does not come out of my close reading modeling or student application of theories of space to their interpretations of literature.

Without fail, the highlight of the class is when we use these theories to interrogate the spaces around us. Early in the spring 2020 semester, we took a "field trip" each week to a different location in Providence, Rhode Island, both on and off campus. The focus shifted slightly based on which theorist we were attempting to apply to the space, but a few of the guiding questions were always the same: Who is this space built for? Is it built for me? Why or why not? How do I feel in the space? Who uses this space, and how? How is movement in and out of the space controlled? Students were able to see Mike Davis's "class war at the level of the built environment" in their own college cafeteria, analyzing how the workers were separated and variously rendered invisible to the students and staff they serve; they saw how Raúl Homero Villa's concepts of both "barriology" and "barrioization" worked to make the Chad Brown low-income housing projects, mere steps from campus and its high-end student rentals, both a home for its residents and a geographic area cordoned off and isolated by roads, bus routes, foot traffic, and architecture; through Dolores Hayden's *The Power of Place,* they recognized how our campus touted its Catholic Dominican history in plaques and monuments but neglected to tell its past as a place of confinement for unwed pregnant women in the nineteenth century, commemorating some stories but not others; they realized, by walking the space, observing the flows of money and people, close reading the halls, layout, and geography, how our new "multicultural center" gave lip service to inclusivity without actually spending the money to back up the gesture.

In a normal, non-once-in-a-hundred-year pandemic semester, my students' final project entails choosing a site anywhere in Providence and conducting what I now call a barriography: they must interview at least two people, reference at least three sources, apply one of the space theorists we learned about, and include a first-person narrative of their own experience in the space. One former student, now a lawyer, studied the city courthouse, and laid out how the setup of the building encouraged a divide between the law and the defendant, architecturally presenting a presumption of guilt. Another went to his local dominicano barbershop, describing the feeling of being on the inside of belonging as an Afro-Latino, and pinpointing what made that space safe for him, if not for non-Spanish speakers.

This year, due to COVID-19, students unleashed close readings of space onto their own quarantine neighborhoods. Most students saw with new eyes how deliberate urban planning techniques and local policies have created an invisible wall around the wealth and racial privilege of their community. My students, from their homes in places like New Rochelle, New York; Georgetown; coastal New Jersey; and Chatham on Cape Cod, started to see the ways in which their neighborhood came to be; no longer innocent to the ways space is deployed as a weapon or as a shield, by some against others, and now trained in Lefebvre's mantra, "no space is neutral," they not only saw their own neighborhood as no accident but could actually, literally point to the tools of its construction.

I have (rightly) been asked if I want college students and my colleagues to descend upon the barrios of the US, flooding the streets with flimsy notepads, bothering residents, feeling awkward, and potentially causing gentrification, all in the service of place-based literary analysis. I do think barrios have been intentionally isolated and intentionally stigmatized by the mainstream, and one way to combat that is to educate oneself, to do the work to enter into the space and engage with a community on their terms. But, while there are many works of Latinx literature about place, the number of texts that explicitly ask for or require a barriography—through their level of place detail, their emphasis on real-life veracity, and the author's own documented connection to the place—is actually quite low. I don't think East L.A. or Quisqueya Heights is in any imminent danger of a scholarly invasion.

A more practical, less fraught (because less potentially appropriative or gentrifying or exoticizing), and more necessary application of the methodology is to turn it, as my students do, as I do, on ourselves. Where do *you* live? Why do you live there and not elsewhere? What are the attributes of your space? Who is it built for? How do people and money flow in or out? How did your space come to be? What is its history? Who is in charge of it? How do your neighbors feel in this space? What is it like for you to be in this space, walk through this space, inhabit this space? I guarantee there is always more to learn about where you live, more to analyze about how it has been constructed, managed, or transformed. A student (the future lawyer) told me at the end of my course that I had "ruined space" for him, that he couldn't unsee space and now constantly close read *where* he was. I confess this is my goal: to ruin space for you.

Whether that ruination takes the form of a more fine-combed attention to place setting in works of literature, or the new inability to experience a sidewalk, a playground, a housing complex, a supermarket, a prison, without questioning how it got there and how you got there and who made it and why, or, yes, when the novel or poem or short story or memoir warrants, going to the location you've been reading about and experiencing it for yourself, is up to you. I hope this book has provided a guide and a model for close reading space and for thinking deeply about neighborhoods, both your own and many others.

GEOGRAPHIES OF GRATITUDE

University of Virginia (Press): Thank you to Angie Hogan for letting me pitch my book at MLA, for being excited about the project, and for guiding me through. Thank you to Ellen Satrom for taking this book across the finish line. UVAP's book readers (especially Reader #2, whoever you are!) were incredibly generous and helpful, and I owe them big time. This team (literally, but also figuratively) made this book.

Providence College: I am indebted to PC for its unstinting support. Thank you to Provost Hugh Lena and President Brian Shanley for giving me the job, and the generous grants, that allowed me to complete my research, and thank you to Provost Sean Reid and President Kenneth Sicard for seeing fit to keep me around. The English department has taken such good care of me, providing feedback, freedom, and the conditions to produce *Walk the Barrio.* The commitment to letting us faculty teach what we do resulted in a few research breakthroughs for me; and teaching lit theory a few times also inspired me to write a better introduction (since don't we all just read theorists' book introductions?). Special thanks to Bruce Graver and Peggy Reid, department chairs who fiercely protect junior faculty and have endless patience with my questions. And extra special thanks to my students, who brought insights and curiosity, and pushed me to know my research better.

UC Irvine: Rodrigo Lazo, you are my guardian angel. You were the one who first told me that no one is patrolling the boundaries of our identities. You pushed this project in the right direction, with your suggestion to go to El Monte. Like a great teacher, you let me get there most of the way on my own, then agreed vigorously so I realized that you knew best all along. You introduced me to the cool folks in our field right at the moment in grad school when I wanted to give up. And you've coached me through every major step in academia. You even motivate me to go for a run from time to time. I cannot overstate what your mentorship, and friendship, has meant to me, and to this project.

Alejandro Morales, thank you for teaching Salvador Plascencia, Gloria Anzaldúa, and Bruce Novoa, and for getting us all thinking about *rasquachismo:* your stories about the Simons barrio first sparked my fascination with L.A. Arlene Keizer, thank you for your incisive feedback on early versions of several of these chapters, plus your emotional support during the crises of faith on the academic road. Your voice has carried me a couple times. I remember you telling me to figure out what I have to say that's different, sound advice for the rest of my days. John Smith, thank you for teaching me Hegel and Kant; you have saved me a lot of bluffing over the years.

Kathrine Ryan, Michael Andreasen, Nicole Kelly, Vinh-Paul Ha, Erin Sweeney, Anna Finn, Erin Pearson, Brian Fonken, Chris Dearner, Matt Mieskoski, Will Litton, Julian Smith-Newman: Thank you for the hot tub conversations (debates) (okay, arguments), potlucks, dance parties, and incredible insights about dwelling, authorship, space, time, Derrida, *Battlestar Gallactica,* ethnic identity, and dating.

JEFFREY CHESTER: Alison Espach, when you first proposed team teaching an autobiography class, I thought it sounded boring but went along. Now I know teaching with you changed the trajectory of my writing. Thank you for teaching me how to read from a craft perspective and giving me the courage—and training!—to bring the autobiographical into my work. The Jeffrey Chester fellowship gave me the time and focus I needed to finish huge chunks of the project. To Alison, and Mark Polanzak, and Michael Andreasen (again!): thank you for listening to portions of the project, making me not feel boring in a room of incredible fictioneers, and for encouraging me to push my thinking in the right direction.

CAMBERVILLE: Katherine Perry, light of my life, this book doesn't get done without your love and support. Lesley Ofrichter, thank you for the thought-provoking hikes and the readiness to talk out big issues. Tara Mulloy, you moved but are still at the beating heart of Boston for me. The Monkeys (Kari Kuelzer, Jackie Mercer, Josh Seiler, Dustin Frankus, Whitney Roberts, Emelia Peck): thank you for celebrating my academic victories but especially for keeping things in perspective, for the Skirt Days and Marathon Mondays and fun runs.

PACIFIC NORTHWEST: Hester Serebrin, thank you for showing me how to think about cities in more inclusive ways (and for being an incredible friend). Bill Ray, thank you for teaching me literary theory at Reed College. I have stolen everything from your class.

VAN NUYS/SILVER SPRING: Candi, thank you for enduring my job talk, for being interested in my research, and for moving to such a crazy city. I remember that even before I got into UCI, you had a good feeling about Irvine . . . and it brought us together. Mamu, I couldn't do any of this without you. Your wisdom is unerring, and your love buoys me in all things.

DUXBURY: Tracy and Susan Morrison, thank you for always making me feel welcome into your family and your home.

LAST BUT not least, Kyle, thank you for putting up with the stress of this book, for acknowledging the milestones and empathizing with the setbacks, and for always being sweet, thoughtful, and upbeat about the journey. Your work ethic and talent inspire me every day. No one else I'd rather walk this road with.

NOTES

Introduction

1. Imagine: a classroom of the sons and daughters of Chilean, Argentine, and Uruguayan diplomats and ambassadors, here in the US for brief stints before returning to their native countries, for whom South American history, language, culture, and schooling was the air they breathed; then, me, a little kid with heritage Spanish (despite my mom's verb drills), for whom ordering lunch in the Spanish-only cafeteria was a humbling ordeal requiring rehearsal, who could barely eke out a passing-grade *dictado,* let alone participate in class discussion. For a nascent insufferable know-it-all like me, Argentine School provided the important experience of being very, very bad at school.
2. I didn't know yet this was the single best thing to ever happen to my career, or frankly, to me. "God bless Rodrigo" goes my mom's refrain.
3. I suspect this anxiety over recognition is what led my mom to keep "Rodríguez" as her last name, long after the divorce, to signpost to Americans she was *una hispano hablante.* Even other Spanish speakers in the US generally have no referent for her (unless they've known an Argentine), so much so she has made it into a game: when strangers ask, "where are you from?" she offers them five chances to guess the correct answer. She's way ahead in the score: people will guess Israel or Denmark before thinking of the Southern Cone.
4. "Latinx" refers to people in the US of Latin American descent; their position within the US is implied. As Richard Rodriguez jokes in his ludic essay "Hispanic," Latin Americans don't become Hispanic, or Latinx, until they are incorporated into the United States. When I say "Latinx immigration," I am referring to immigration to the United States from various countries in Latin America.
5. Although Guarnizo coins the term to refer to how Dominicans in the diaspora adjust their identities to navigate the cultures of both the island and the US (40), the phrase can be used to describe individuals living in any transnational community or who themselves form part of transnational networks.
6. Please see the section "Where are the Puerto Ricans?" at the end of this introduction, and the conclusion.
7. I know because I checked.

8. I'm aware that for other communities or members of other economic brackets the desire to brag may go the other way, i.e., a wish to assure others that one's neighborhood used to be much better than it appears now. For instance, this is my mom's impulse when describing her childhood homes in Buenos Aires and Ramos Mejía.

9. Before Latin Americans begin their angry tweets at me for centering the Iberian Peninsula, the Larousse also defines *colonia* this way, even adding an entry defining it explicitly as a "*barrio urbano.*"

10. Mary Pat Brady gestures to the underutilization of this discourse in contemporary postmodern geography: "Yet the work of critical geography has largely emerged without reference to the spatial epistemologies of Chicana literature. That is indeed unfortunate, since so many of its spatial claims and discoveries had been anticipated, theorized, and illustrated by Chicanas" (204).

11. I've written elsewhere about the benefits of using Lefebvre as a theoretical model, despite the very real pitfalls and lacunae in his theory, as delineated by David Harvey, Neil Smith, and Manuel Castells, et al. See my "'Relentless Geography'"; for further reading, see also Smith; Curry; Harvey, *Social Justice in the City* (which offers a very qualified approval of Lefebvre); and Castells.

12. Not quite Marxists, and not direct influences upon my project, but certainly important to mention as intellectual forebears, are Michel de Certeau, whose *The Practice of Everyday Life* is endlessly referenced, and Gaston Bachelard's *The Poetics of Space.*

13. In their foundational book *The Elements of Journalism,* Bill Kovach and Tom Rosenstiel identified the essential journalistic principles and practices from which this is a partial list.

14. Under the instruction of Neiman Fellow Cathy Grimes at the Harvard Extension School and for the following newspapers from 2006 to 2008: The *Boston Phoenix,* the *Weekly Dig,* and *Boston NOW.*

15. Each conducted over a series of days, from 2013 to 2019. I'm indebted to UC Irvine and Providence College for their support. From 2013 to 2015, UC Irvine funded two research trips to El Monte and East L.A., as well as a visit to the Viramontes archives in Santa Barbara, and a trip to Red Hook Brooklyn (for a now defunct chapter on Francisco Goldman's *The Ordinary Seaman*); From 2015 to 2019, Providence College funded barriographies of Chicago, Mexico City, Washington Heights, and Miami. Trips to New Jersey, downtown L.A., and Van Nuys were self-funded.

16. It is impossible to broach this topic without reference to the spectacular work of Juan Flores; *From Bomba to Hip Hop: Puerto Rican Culture and Latino Identity* has already analyzed the formative role of Puerto Ricans in New York City street culture as well as the relationship between Puerto Ricans and place identity in the South Bronx and Spanish Harlem.

PART I. MEXICAN AMERICAN EAST LOS ANGELES

1. I largely use "Mexican American" in this introduction to indicate the dual populations of the region: Chicano/as whose ancestors conceivably never left the area, and the ongoing migrations of native Mexicans to the metropolis. The term spans first-generation Mexicans to Chicano/as with deep Southwestern US roots.

2. One of the earliest barrios and a result of this need for exploitable labor was Simons, in what is now Montebello in Los Angeles County. Founded in 1905, Simons Brick Company imported workers by train, mostly from the Mexican states of Michoacán, Jalisco, and Guanajuato, to form their workforce (Uyeda). Workers were settled in a segregated "company town," with their own school, church, stores (where company credit or tokens were taken rather than cash), sports teams, and their own regulations such as company curfew (Interview with Alejandro Morales; "Restoring History"). Variously called Simons barrio, el pueblo de Simons, or just plain Simons by its residents, the town population peaked at three thousand in the 1920s (López López). The brickyard shut down in 1952 (though it was reopened in 1989) (López López). Writer and scholar Alejandro Morales, a mentor of mine at UCI, grew up in Simons and captured its world in his novel *The Brick People*. Simons bricks are a commonplace of Los Angeles Chicanx literature, and citizens of LA are still walking over them. My sister's patio in Van Nuys has Simons bricks.

1. "A WORLD BUILT ON CEMENT"

1. I visited the El Monte Historical Museum in May of 2013.

2. Immediately following Liz's request is a page that simply reads, "*cunt,*" before the new title page and dedication—this time without her name—appear.

3. I am indebted to Professor Alejandro Morales for introducing me to this work by Ybarra-Frausto and for pairing it with *The People of Paper* in his course.

4. Even philologically, the word *rasquache* (or *rascuache*) expresses a relationship between the international and the national or, more specifically, the colonized and the indigenous. The "qua" letter group immediately marks the word off as a loan word into Spanish. Its limited use in Honduras, El Salvador, and Mexico to mean "[a person or thing] of low quality or value" (according to the *Diccionario de la Lengua Española* of the Real Academia Española, 22nd edition) implies that it derives from an indigenous language native to those regions; the Spanish philologist Víctor M. Suárez affirms the word is Mayan in origin, and as one commentator asserts, "[la palabra] es, sin duda, un mexicanismo" (Campos 177). *Rascuache*'s more contemporary variant, *rasquachismo,* appears to be unique to

Caló or Chicanx Spanish (as is the orthographic choice of a "q" instead of a "c"). The shift in the word's connotation, from negative to positive, is also specifically Chicanx. *Rascuache/rasquache* thus originates from the encounter of colonial Spanish and indigenous Mayan and Nahuatl languages, and the geographic limits of its usage and the peculiarities of its etymology demonstrate that it could only come out of this region.

2. "Earthquakes or Earthmovers"

1. Throughout the *Their Dogs Came with Them* manuscript, Viramontes writes marginalia explaining aspects of Chicanx culture to her editor, who seems unaware of the meaning of phrases like "*con safos.*" Elsewhere Viramontes elucidates phrases for her non-Chicanx reader(s): in the margins of one passage she writes, "La Bootie is a person," with checkmarks to make sure the copyeditor does not substitute the "she" pronoun: "La Bootie had an adding machine that she punched and cranked with amazing precision" (Manuscript 76). To a Spanish speaker, "La Bootie" is clearly a female name (if an unusual one), but apparently the copyeditor conflated the store name and the store owner's name in earlier drafts.
2. These are only a few of Viramontes's literary devices. Alicia Muñoz delineates the novel's use of metaphor to convey the effects of displacement and dislocation; Hsuan Hsu focuses on how Viramontes utilizes metonymy to capture the contiguity of spatial transformation impacting the Eastside.
3. Sarah Wald argues that the novel critiques the injustice of differential access to transportation through consistent reference to the characters' frustrations moving around the barrio. Yet the descriptions of waiting at bus stops, transferring, walking, and variously attempting to navigate streets without a car also pervade the reader with the atmosphere of claustrophobia and entrapment that plague the characters.
4. Hadley Meares, in a piece for KCET, reports that beginning in the 1950s the Christian Serbian community relocated to the San Gabriel Valley but still use this cemetery for its faithful dead. According to the article, the last Serbian parishioner to live in the Eastside died in 2005.
5. Wald aptly connects the social and, more important, spatial displacement of the characters by urban planning schemata to the street violence that closes the novel (77).

Part II. Central American Downtown Los Angeles

1. Nicaraguan and Honduran immigration is outside the scope of this book, but rest assured that the US backed dictatorial rule in Nicaragua throughout the 1970s, tried to topple a democratically elected government throughout the 1980s, and maintained an armed military presence

in Honduras throughout the twentieth century to protect the agricultural business monopolies it had established in the late nineteenth century (J. Gonzalez 132).

2. I talk more extensively about the political economy of L.A. and its relationship to inner-city space in my article, "'Relentless Geography: Los Angeles' Imagined Cartographies in Karen Tei Yamashita's *The Tropic of Orange.*"

3. "Center" is a tough word when referring to Los Angeles, which, as Jorge Luis Borges might put it, is a circle whose center is everywhere and whose circumference is nowhere. Here I mean what is labeled "Downtown Los Angeles" on maps, next to both Skid Row and the Fashion District (a classic L.A. juxtaposition).

3. "Los Angeles Was the Problem"

1. By being set in both Guatemala and the US, the novel creates a comparison between the two nations' struggles for national unity and the revolts of oppressed populations against silencing, which has been expertly handled by several critics. See Vargas; A. Rodríguez, *Dividing the Isthmus;* Pattinson.

2. Please see the introduction.

3. "Inhabitants and users" are Lefebvre's terms for those operating in what he calls "lived space." Please see the introduction.

4. As a reporter for the *Los Angeles Times* in the late 1980s, Tobar went to the *rescate,* or refugee office, on South Bonnie Brae Avenue to interview immigration officers. The woman working told him that what differed in Central American immigration today was "now we've got a lot of soldiers coming. Before we had refugees, leftists, and all of a sudden now we've got people from the squads and armies" (Tobar, personal interview). One of her clients related that he had seen a former soldier, a person who participated in a massacre in his village, in MacArthur Park, and that he was planning to kill him. The refugee worker talked him out of it, telling him if he killed someone, he would ruin his asylum application (surely an understatement). Tobar turned it into a Column 1 story for the *Times.* Later, when he went to get his MFA, he resurrected the story, transforming it into a revenge tale.

5. The Rodney King riots will of course provide another site of "crossing" in the novel.

6. Julie Avril Minich offers a trenchant interpretation of the function of the Quiché language in *The Tattooed Soldier* as demonstrating the complicit role of the Guatemalan left in perpetrating a racialized hierarchy even as it reclaims "indigenous languages as a progressive political act" (217).

7. In this aspect, his neighborhood echoes my Silver Spring; see the introduction.

4. "The Blackouts of a Tiny Country"

1. While the author himself asserts the poems are not strictly autobiographical (Archila, Electronic correspondence), I am not alone in reading *The Art of Exile* as displaying autobiographical elements. Karina Alvarado writes: "While Archila's work cannot be defined as purely testimonial poetics, the poems show a collapse between the author and narrator, a male-gendered youth experience of the Salvadoran Civil War. Archila's poems become part of the cultural memory of U.S. Salvadorans considering the embodied experience of civil war in El Salvador but engaged through the imagistic and emotive language of poetry by a 1.5 writer" (481).

2. Interestingly, this is despite the fact that he writes in English and has said that he has lost some of his native Spanish (Archila, Interview by Mariano Zaro). This makes Czeslaw Milosz's epigram to the collection, "Language is the only homeland," slightly ironic in addition to poignant.

3. Of course, some of the abstraction is because of the shift in genre from fiction to poetry; however, we will see with Richard Blanco's poetry in chapter 7 that such attention to place detail is still possible.

4. Karina Oliva Alvarado picks up on this aspect of Archila's work when she claims that his poetry can "signify directly onto Central America through a lens of the imagined from within the United States" (476).

5. Archila says in a *Poetry L.A.* interview with Mariano Zaro that he naturally writes verse in English.

6. Translations are mine.

7. The major bus line actually stops at Broadway and Daly, a main street in Lincoln Heights.

8. *The State of Van Nuys* is a 2013 report created by UCLA Urban Planning students in concert with the Van Nuys Neighborhood Council. The authors, Daisy Miguel and Jenny Chhea, chiefly pull from Decennial census reports from 1970–2010, the 2007–2011 American Community Survey, and the Longitudinal Employer-Household Dynamics reports of 2002–2010.

9. Despite the affordable buying market, almost three-fourths of Van Nuys residents are renters, about 10 percent more than L.A. proper, and single-family homes are handily outnumbered by apartment complexes and multi-family homes. With depressed incomes in the neighborhood, the housing stock remains abundant, for the few who can afford to buy rather than rent.

10. At the time of writing (summer 2020), my mom tells me this encampment was recently cleaned out; a new one has cropped up in a fenced-off parking lot at the corner of Sepulveda and Sherman Way.

11. The name for downtown L.A. in the nineteenth century; please see the introduction to part 1.

12. It seems unnecessary, not to mention rude, to call immigrants *both* "undocumented" and "illegal"; Colvin is a bit sour on the neighborhood.

Part III. Dominican New York City

1. According to CUNY's Center for Latin American, Caribbean and Latino Studies (Hernández, and Rivera-Batíz).
2. When referring to demographics, I follow Duany in using the terms "diasporic" and "transnational" interchangeably. However, when discussing culture and identification, I follow Peggy Levitt in viewing the two terms as often overlapping but not necessarily coincidental: "Transnational communities are the building blocks of diasporas that may or may not take shape. Diasporas form out of transnational communities spanning sending and receiving countries and out of the real or imagined connections among migrants from a particular homeland" (Levitt 15). My contention is that not all transnational communities result in diasporic identity formation, and such identities, when formed, will be unique to the experiences of that transnational community.
3. Jesse Hoffnung-Garskof cautions that US history often overemphasizes the role of 1965 immigration reform in increased international migrations: "The categorization 'post-65' erroneously attributes the rise in Latin American immigration (by far the greatest proportion of arrivals since 1965) to the liberalization of national-origins restrictions in the US that year. In fact, after a brief lull in the 1930s, millions of Latin Americans came to the United States beginning in the mid 1940s . . . indeed the authors of the 1965 legislation aimed to reduce the number of Latin Americans coming to the United States" (xiv). Still, immigration reforms did contribute to shifts in transmigratory patterns.
4. Further evidence of this is the US census: "most Dominicans, like many Mexican Americans, Puerto Ricans, and Cubans, remained profoundly ambivalent toward the prospect that their national or ethnic identities marked a racial difference in the United States. For each of these groups the category Hispanic has sometimes seemed to offer an escape, an ethnicity rather than a race, and a clear alternative to being black. Indeed, although Dominicans generally recognized that many in the United States perceived them as black, on both the 1990 and 200 censuses, nine out of ten Dominicans in the United States reported themselves as either 'white' or 'some other race,' most frequently Dominican or Hispanic" (Hoffnung-Garskof 114).
5. See Guarnizo, Pessar and Grasmuck 1991, Ricourt, Hoffnung-Garskof, Duany.

5. "No Promises Can Survive That Sea"

1. The controversy surrounding Díaz and his behavior sadly lies outside the scope of this chapter. However, it is important to address one aspect

of the media fallout as it pertains to literary criticism. In the wake of the accusations, many readers expressed sadness that Díaz's fiction *apparently* was celebrating rather than critiquing misogyny and machismo; there were also righteous proclamations that suspicions about Díaz's fiction as glorification of bad conduct were now confirmed (see for instance the myriad responses to Zinzi Clemens's initial Twitter accusation). I strongly disagree that these accusations should change our interpretations, which are based in the various narrative techniques Díaz uses to complicate and criticize his characters' positions. While my own reading pulls from the author's autobiography, it still sees affirmed in the text a narrative distance between the actions of the protagonist and the beliefs of the writer.

2. I agree with Maia Gil-Adí that the apology is highly qualified and that Díaz's approach to depicting women, in this piece as well as in his fiction, often denies female agency and has a long way to go before we can call it "decolonizing"; see her excellent essay in *Latino Studies*, "'I think about you, X—': Teaching Junot Díaz after 'The Silence.'"

3. Gil-Adí is again instructive here: it's worth noting that therapy, like Díaz's fiction, is self-directed in its rehabilitation and doesn't necessarily center female subjectivity.

4. Julie Avril Minich argues that "the realist aspects of Díaz's fiction" aid her disability critique (51), and asserts that Rafa's stories in *This Is How You Lose Her* draw "directly from Díaz's life" (57); Silvio Torres-Saillant treat's Díaz's own "layered" identity as a Dominican American and public intellectual as crucial contextual elements to consider for literary analysis (115).

5. When asked why he uses the name "Yunior," his own nickname, for his chief narrator, since using that name encourages people to read his stories autobiographically, Díaz retorts: "But they will anyway. So the approach is never to distance. . . . If you distance yourself from the reader, it ends up backfiring. But to try to play with people's expectations—. . . to productively engage in someone's expectations about this as biography" (Scarano).

6. Harford Vargas ("Dictating a Zafa") and several others, most notably Monica Hanna ("'Reassembling the Fragments'"), Ramón Saldívar ("Historical Fantasy"), and Elena Machado Sáez ("Dictating Desire, Dictating Diaspora"), present incisive close readings of the form of *Oscar Wao* and make the case that Díaz's stylistic choices work to decolonize the text. Other critics such as Lourdes Torres ("In the Contact Zone") more generally analyze Díaz's use of formal elements to represent a diasporic identity. Yet there are no essays on the role of neighborhood geography in Díaz's work, and to date there are very few focused literary analyses of the more recent *This Is How You Lose Her*, with the happy exception of *Reading Junot Díaz* by Christopher González.

7. Although it is a collection of short stories, the thematic unity of *This Is How You Lose Her* allows us to interpret it as a whole. Indeed, Díaz claims this was his intent: "I wanted, to be precise, a story collection with a novelistic arc" (Barrios). Yunior's consistent narration gives the collection a cohesive storyline, and although the work is nonlinear, Yunior undergoes chronological change.

8. See the introduction.

9. Christopher González, translating "otravez" more literally, comes up with "Another Life, Once Again" (91).

10. On a single block I see Irish-themed door decor on several different houses, including Celtic crosses, proclamations such as "Failte! Welcome!" and "Irish blessings!" and a sign that reads "O'Hara."

11. "Papi" remains unnamed, but he can function as a double for Ramón in "Otravida, Otravez." Where that story follows the new life the male immigrant creates in the US, this story tracks the family that was left behind on the island. Rereading this story into that one underlines the impossibility of Yasmin truly starting a new life, since Papi eventually brings his family over, though he clearly maintains a relationship with a mistress in the US.

12. *Soledad*'s closing chapter in the Dominican Republic reflects a similar shift from the ultradetailed and architecturally focused setting descriptions of the US neighborhood to more sweeping, less specific landscape descriptions of the Dominican countryside.

13. Please see the introduction to part 3.

14. Díaz has said, "I definitely would never try to pass for an island person. But I know that I'm Dominican. In this country that's what you're called if you are not called other things first" (Céspedes and Torres-Saillant 896).

15. Díaz consistently uses the characteristics of a neighborhood, region, or nationality to stand in for a description of a woman: Magda was "a Bergenline original" from the Latinx part of New Jersey (5); Alma "grew up in Hoboken" and has a "big Dominican ass" (45); Flaca was "whitetrash from outside of Paterson" (82); Pura was "Dominican," "fresh-off-the-boat-didn't-have-no-papers-Dominican" (100); Paloma was "the only Puerto Rican girl on the earth who wouldn't give up ass for any reason" (151); Miss Lora is from La Vega (154); and the fiancée in the final story is a "bad-ass salcedeña" (175).

16. The most noteworthy examples: In "The Sun, The Moon, and the Stars" Magda receives a letter from the other woman; "Otravida, Otravez" has Yasmin reading of Ramón's unfaithfulness to his wife; "The Cheater's Guide to Love" recounts Yunior's fiancée's discovery of dozens of sexual exploits via email.

17. Indeed, while the collection's title refers to a story in which Yunior loses a girl, the "Her" could figuratively refer to losing the island (the Dominican Republic) itself.

18. While I personally find my own Cambridge sightings of Díaz in the early 2000s to be interesting, I doubt they are germane to the chapter. But for my Cantabrigian readers: he lived on Dana Street.

19. A phrase, it's worth noting, that would only be said in English.

6. "Washington Heights Is Like a Prison Sentence"

1. In a study from January 2018, Ramona Hernández et al. found that "the demographic changes that New York City has experienced since 1990 put into serious question whether neighborhoods such as Washington Heights/Inwood, which have been the home to generations of Dominicans, will continue to be spaces for low-income, immigrant, and working-class people" (2).

2. It is telling that the only character who is able to change within the space is Victor, our only male protagonist and the only male recipient of third-person-limited narration, who learns to stop cheating on his girlfriend. For Cruz (if not Díaz), the neighborhood provides space for men to grow but not women.

3. The spot they go to, Lily Brown playground on 163rd and Riverside, is tiny: they would be in the midst of the scene and quite visible.

4. Her paranoia is warranted: this "private" sex act is witnessed by Flaca and Cady.

5. Victor is instructive regarding this point: a womanizer unfaithful to his longtime girlfriend, he is abetted by his family, who cover for him, and never castigated for his behavior.

6. Dominicans in Washington Heights were far more insulated than Dominicans in the Bronx, for instance, who only reported that 69 percent of those they lived with were fellow Dominicans and had higher rates of friendship and coworkers with non-Dominicans (Hernández and Ortega 9–10).

7. Mujcinovic argues that some protagonists are shown "embracing exile" as a "comforting distance" from the source of pain, but "their life in exile does not succeed as a process of rebirth because they fail to negotiate their past traumas" (169).

8. Francis astutely points out how Olivia's past haunting her daughter points to the multigenerational inheritance of sex work and the uneven effects of migration: "This attention to how the children fare in the aftermath of their mother's labor shows that bodies bear archival memories that cannot be simply erased with geographical relocation" (133).

9. Cruz's comfort fictionalizing Dominican locations but not fictionalizing details from her own neighborhood is further evidence of her identification with Manhattan rather than the DR.

10. I agree with Herrera that Olivia speaks without literally speaking in the text. However, Herrera argues that motherhood is what finally allows

Olivia to speak *aloud,* whereas the focus on the Dominican Republic as home versus the stifling descriptions of Washington Heights leads me to attribute Olivia's newfound agency to *place:* both the recuperative space of the island for the first generation and, more profoundly, the space in writing for Dominican and Dominican American women's voices.

PART IV. CUBAN MIAMI

1. Less than 2 percent were common criminals, but the stereotypical perception, especially in Miami, was that Castro was offloading unwanted social elements onto the US (Duany 45).

7. "WHY DON'T I GOT A STREET?"

1. Crenshaw literally invents the word "intersectionality" in the context of legal discrimination ("Demarginalizing the Intersection of Race and Sex"); Audre Lorde as a poet and activist calls for intersectionality as a tool for social change ("Age, Race, Class"); bell hooks insists on applying an intersectional lens in the academy ("Postmodern Blackness").
2. For example, to be a black woman is not the same as to be black, and to be a woman, as two separate identities: the intersection of race and sex results in a different social position than either a black man or a white woman would occupy.
3. By "queer" here, I'm thinking of Eve Sedgwick, and her claim in *Epistemology of the Closet* that Western cultural productions, including narrative form, operate according to an onerous homo/hetero "master term." To queer that binary is to read against and undo dichotomous constructions of thought.
4. Sightings of the Virgin Mary in different parts of the world inspire particular forms of devotion based on various aspects: "Our Lady of Guadalupe," for example, has become synonymous with Mexico. "Our Lady of Charity" is the patroness of Cuba.
5. Many depictions have Mary and the baby Jesus as Black, though not this one.
6. Possibly the inspiration for Máximo's Cuban restaurant in Menéndez's collection *In Cuba I Was a German Shepherd,* which links several of the short stories.
7. Or, ahem, US interventionism.
8. See the introduction to part 4.
9. Gustavo Pérez Firmat picks up on this in his analysis of "Havanasis": "Then and now, travel writing about Cuba is full of paradisal imagery"; however, "what is surprising is that a Cuban-American writer would resurrect these clichés and stereotypes" (26). I follow Firmat in linking this language to Blanco's tenuous connection to the island ("Spell of the Hyphen").

10. To avoid confusion, I will refer to the young Blanco as "Richard" in my discussion of the memoir, to distinguish him from Blanco, the adult author.

11. I note the language of the patrons and workers because whiteness is not an indicator of nationality in these neighborhoods. The Cubans I encounter, especially from that first exile generation, are overwhelmingly white. Miami is also now home to many Central Americans and South Americans, so that I come perilously close to racial or ethnic profiling to try to determine at a glance the population of a given area. I've learned that newer immigrants do not respond well to questions of "where are you from?" from strangers, and so I try to suss out the accent and listen for tells (Central Americans tend to use "*usted*" more, or the occasional "*vos*"; Cubans have a Caribbean accent, which to my ears means it is harder to understand). However, I'm not a linguist or Spanish expert.

12. And not downtown Miami, as evidenced in the political history of the two neighborhoods: Miami has only had one Jewish mayor in its history; Miami Beach has had fifteen.

13. I don't mean to suggest here, against Judith Butler, that identities are not performative; yet while identities are not wholly fixed, they do have a grounding, however tenuous, in the psyche, and no part of Richard's performance of heterosexuality stems from his own internal drives.

CONCLUSION

1. Transnational flows are, of course, not exclusive to Chicanx and Latinx communities, and a number of works in multiethnic US literature, by authors such as Karen Tei Yamashita, E. C. Osundo, Theresa Hak-Kyung Cha, Chang-Rae Lee, and Gayl Jones, would produce enlightening barriographies. *Building Stories*, Chris Ware's wildly imaginative graphic novel, is neither transnational nor Latinx, but it does use place identity (Hyde Park in Chicago) to anchor its narrative of disability, loneliness, and female strength in the city. My intervention is in Latinx literary criticism, but the methodology is portable, and adaptable to literature from various traditions.

2. Julián Olivares, Monica Kaup, John Alba Cutler (who has an excellent retort to Mark McGurl's reading of Cisneros), et al.

BIBLIOGRAPHY

Alvarado, Karina Oliva. "Cultural memory and making by US Central Americans." *Latino Studies,* vol. 15, 2017, pp. 476–97.

Anderson, Jon Lee. "Donald Trump Reverses Barack Obama's Cuba Policy." *New Yorker,* 16 June 2017, www.newyorker.com/news/daily-comment /donald-trump-reverses-barack-obamas-cuba-policy.

Anzaldúa, Gloria. *Borderlands/La Frontera.* Aunt Lute Books, 1987.

Archila, William. *The Art of Exile.* Bilingual Review Press, 2009.

———. Electronic correspondence with author. 19 Sept. 2019.

———. Interview by Mariano Zaro. *Poetry.LA,* 13 Apr. 2013, www.poetry.la /Archila,%20William.html.

Atkins, G. Pope, and Larman C. Wilson. *The Dominican Republic and the United States: From Imperialism to Transnationalism.* U of Georgia P, 1998.

Baca, Mandy. "From Pride to the Palace: Miami's LGBT Community through the Years." *The New Tropic,* 6 Aug. 2015, thenewtropic.com/miami-lgbt-history/.

Baeder, Ben. "El Monte street gang is one of the area's largest, oldest." *San Gabriel Valley Tribune,* 14 May 2009.

Barrios, Greg. "'He is a writer of fiction. He puts on masks for a living': An Interview with Junot Díaz." *LA Review of Books,* 7 Oct. 2012.

Barton, Jack. "A Brief History of El Monte." El Monte Union High School District, 1988.

Basch, Linda, et al. *Nations Unbound.* Routledge, 1994.

Benavidez, Max. "Salvador Plascencia." *BOMB,* 98, Winter 2007, p. 26.

Bernstein, Emily M. "Neighborhood Report: Washington Heights; Homicide Rate Falls by 27 Percent." *New York Times,* 31 Oct. 1993, www.nytimes.com /1993/10/31/nyregion/neighborhood-report-washington-heights-homicide -rate-falls-by-27-percent.html.

Blanco, Richard. *City of a Hundred Fires.* U of Pittsburgh P, 1998.

———. *The Prince of Los Cucuyos: A Miami Childhood.* Harper Collins, 2014.

Brady, Mary Pat. *Extinct Lands, Temporal Geographies.* Duke UP, 2002.

Brick, Kate, et al. *Mexican and Central American Immigrants in the United States.* Migration Policy Institute, June 2011.

"Broadway Malls." NYC Parks, www.nycgovparks.org/parks/broadway-malls /history.

Bruce-Novoa, Juan. *Retrospace.* Arte Público, 1990.

Campos, Jorge Hernández. Review of *El español que se habla en Yucatán, apuntamientos filológicos* by Victor M. Suárez, Mérida, Yucatán, México, 1945. *Nueva Revista de Filología Hispánica,* año 3, no. 2, 1949, pp. 175–79.

Castells, Manuel. *The Urban Question.* MIT Press, 1979.

Céspedes, Diogenes, and Silvio Torres-Saillant. "Fiction Is the Poor Man's Cinema: An Interview with Junot Díaz." *Callaloo: A Journal of African-American and African Arts and Letters* vol. 23, no. 3, 2000, pp. 892–907.

Cheung, Michael, and Joe Chiu. "The Renovation of the Eastern Avenue Chinese Cemetery." Informational Plaque, Chinese Cemetery, 102 S. Eastern Avenue, Los Angeles, 2007.

Cisneros, Sandra. *Caramelo.* Knopf, 2002.

———. *A House of My Own.* Vintage, 2016.

———. *The House on Mango Street.* Vintage, 1984.

Colvin, Richard Lee. "Anglos Predominate but Majority Status Slipping." *Los Angeles Times,* 31 Mar. 1991.

Cooney, Kevin. "Metafictional Geographies: Los Angeles in Karen Tei Yamashita's *Tropic of Orange* and Salvador Plascencia's *People of Paper.*" *On and Off the Page: Mapping Place in Text and Culture,* edited by M.B. Hackler, Cambridge Scholars Publishing, 2009, pp. 189–218.

Cortez, David Pierre. Personal interview with author. 1 Nov. 2019.

"Country of Immigrants." Moderated by Simon Ríos. WBUR panel at Boston Book Fair, Copley Square, Boston, MA, 19 Oct. 2019.

Coutin, Susan Bibler. "Re/membering the Nation: Gaps and Reckoning within Biographical Accounts of Salvadoran Émigrés." *Anthropological Quarterly,* vol. 84, no. 4, Fall 2011, pp. 809–34.

Crenshaw, Kimberlé. "Demarginalizing the Intersection of Race and Sex: A Black Feminist Critique of Antidiscrimination Doctrine, Feminist Theory, and Antiracist Politics." *University of Chicago Legal Forum,* issue 1, 1989, pp. 139–67.

Crippen, Donna. Personal interview with the author. 9 May 2013.

Crucet, Jennine Capó. *How to Leave Hialeah.* U of Iowa P, 2009.

Cruz, Angie. *Soledad.* New York: Simon and Schuster, 2001.

———. "A Sublet in Washington Heights." *New York Times,* 3 Sept. 2006, www.nytimes.com/2006/09/03/nyregion/thecity/03angi.html.

Curry, Michael R. *The Work in the World.* U of Minnesota P, 1996.

Cutler, John Alba. *Ends of Assimilation.* Oxford University Press, 2015.

Davis, Mike. *City of Quartz.* Verso, 1990.

———. *Magical Urbanism: Latinos Reinvent the U.S. City.* Verso, 2000.

"Diamond Street Gang Member Takes Murder Rap 'for the Gang.'" *The Daily Mirror,* 28 Aug. 2018, https://ladailymirror.com/2018/08/28/aug-28-1947-diamond-street-gang-member-takes-murder-rap-for-the-gang/.

Díaz, Junot. *The Brief Wondrous Life of Oscar Wao.* Riverhead, 2007.

———. *This Is How You Lose Her.* Riverhead, 2012.

Dr Jedly. "Van Nuys Tourism Video." *YouTube,* 12 Oct. 2010, www.youtube.com/watch?v=uMiEAr6oyMY.

Duany, Jorge. *Blurred Borders.* University of North Carolina Press, 2011.

Firmat, Gustavo Pérez. "The Spell of the Hyphen." *Cuban-American Literature and Art: Negotiating Identities,* edited by Isabel Alvarez Borland and Lynette M. F. Bosch, SUNY Press, 2009, pp. 15–30.

Flores, Arturo. "Con Safos Glossary." *Con Safos,* vol. 7, Winter 1971, p. 65.

Flores, Juan. *The Diaspora Strikes Back.* Routledge, 2009.

Foster, Sesshu. "Los Angeles, City of Poets." *Los Angeles Review of Books,* 24 Oct. 2018, https://lareviewofbooks.org/article/los-angeles-city-of-poets/.

Francis, Donette. "Love in the Age of Globalized Sex Work, Secrets, and Depression." *Fictions of Feminine Citizenship: Sexuality and the Nation in Contemporary Caribbean Literature.* Palgrave, 2010, pp. 115–39.

Galarza, Ernesto. *Barrio Boy.* U of Notre Dame P, 1971.

Garces, Bibi. Personal interview with author. 1 Nov. 2019.

García, Cristina. *The Agüero Sisters.* Random House, 1997.

Gil'Adí, Maia. "'I think about you, X—': Teaching Junot Díaz after 'The Silence.'" *Latino Studies,* vol. 18, no. 4, 2020.

"Global Landfill." Site Remediation Program, New Jersey Department of Environmental Protection, 1 June 2014.

"Global Sanitary Landfill." Region 2 Superfund. U.S. Environmental Protection Agency, 1 June 2014.

Goldman, Francisco. *The Ordinary Seaman.* Grove Press, 1997.

González, Christopher. *Reading Junot Díaz.* U of Pittsburgh P, 2015.

Gonzalez, Juan. *Harvest of Empire: A History of Latinos in America.* Penguin, 2000.

Grasmuck, Sherri, and Pessar, Patricia. *Between Two Islands: Dominican International Migration.* University of California Press, 1991.

Grider, Sylvia Ann. "Con Safos: Mexican-Americans, Names and Graffiti." *The Journal of American Folklore,* vol. 88, no. 348, 1975, pp. 132–42.

Guarnizo, Luis Eduardo. "Going Home: Class, Gender, and Household Transformation among Dominican Return Migrants." *Caribbean Circuits: New Directions in the Study of Caribbean Migration,* edited by Patricia R. Pessar, Center for Migration Studies, 1997, pp. 13–60.

Gutierrez, José. Personal interview with author. 1 Nov. 2019.

Hanna, Monica. "'Reassembling the Fragments': Battling Historiographies, Caribbean Discourse, and Nerd Genres in Junot Díaz's *The Brief Wondrous Life of Oscar Wao.*" *Callaloo,* vol. 33, no. 2, 2010, pp. 498–520.

Hanna, Monica, et al., editors. *Junot Díaz and the Decolonial Imagination.* Duke UP, 2016.

Harford Vargas, Jennifer. "Dictating a Zafa." *Junot Díaz and the Decolonial Imagination,* edited by Monica Hanna et al., Duke UP, 2016, pp. 201–30.

Harvey, David. *The Condition of Postmodernity.* Blackwell, 1989.

———. *Social Justice in the City.* U of Georgia P, 2009.

Hayden, Dolores. *The Power of Place.* MIT Press, 1995.

Hernandez, Daniel. "North of Tijuana." *Los Angeles Times,* 3 July 2006.

Hernández, Ramona, et al. *Restoring Housing Security and Stability in New York City Neighborhoods: Recommendations to Stop the Displacement of Dominicans and Other Working-Class Groups in Washington Heights and Inwood.* CUNY Dominican Studies Institute, July 2018, www.ccny.cuny.edu/dsi/publications.

Hernández, Ramona, and Pedro Ortega. *Estudio comparativo sobre la vida cotidiana de la población de descendencia dominicana residente en los condados del Bronx y Manhattan en la ciudad de New York.* CUNY Dominican Studies Institute, 2010, www.ccny.cuny.edu/dsi/publications.

Hernández, Ramona, and Francisco Rivera-Batíz. *Dominican New Yorkers: A Socioeconomic Profile.* CUNY Dominican Studies Institute, 1997, https://academicworks.cuny.edu/cgi/viewcontent.cgi?article=1019&context=dsi_pubs.

Herrera, Cristina. "The Madwoman Speaks: Madness and Motherhood in Angie Cruz's *Soledad.*" *Journal of Caribbean Letters,* vol. 7, no. 1, Spring 2011, pp. 51–67.

Hinton, James, and Herbert Kohl. "Names, Graffiti, and Culture." *Rappin' and Stylin' Out: Communication in Urban Black America,* edited by Thomas Kochman, U of Illinois P, 1972, pp. 109–33.

Hoffnung-Garskof, Jesse. *A Tale of Two Cities: Santo Domingo and New York after 1950.* Princeton UP, 2008.

hooks, bell. "Postmodern Blackness." *Postmodern Culture,* vol. 1, no. 1, Fall 1999.

Hornblower, Simon, and Antony Spawforth, editors. *The Oxford Classical Dictionary.* Oxford UP, 2003.

Hsu, Hsuan L. "Fatal Contiguities: Metonymy and Environmental Justice." *New Literary History,* vol. 42, no. 1, Winter 2011, pp. 147–68.

Hutchinson, Sikivu. *Imagining Transit: Race, Gender, and Transportation in Los Angeles.* Peter Lang Publishing, 2003.

Irizarry, Ylce. *Chicana/o and Latina/o Fiction: The New Memory of Latinidad.* U of Illinois P, 2016.

Jacobs, Jane. *The Death and Life of Great American Cities.* Vintage, 1992.

Jones, Gayl. *Mosquito.* Beacon Press, 1999.

Juan and Anita. Personal interview with author. 1–2 Nov. 2019.

Kaup, Monica. "The Architecture of Ethnicity in Chicano Literature." *American Literature,* vol. 69, no. 2, June 1997.

Kripke, Saul. *Naming and Necessity.* Harvard UP, 1980.

Labott, Elise, et al. "U.S. ending 'wet foot, dry foot' policy for Cubans." *CNN.com,* 13 Jan. 2017, www.cnn.com/2017/01/12/politics/us-to-end-wet-foot-dry-foot-policy-for-cubans/index.html.

Lee, Chang-Rae. *Native Speaker.* Riverhead, 1995.

Lefebvre, Henri. *The Production of Space.* Blackwell, 1974.

Lesser, Gabriel, and Jeanne Batalova. *Central American Immigrants in the United States.* Migration Policy Institute, 5 Apr. 2017.

Levi, Yashohua. Personal interview with the author. 18 July 2018.

Levitt, Peggy. *The Transnational Villagers.* U of California P, 2001.

Lissardy, Gerardo. "La fascinante historia de Juan Rodríguez, el 'proto-dominicano' que fue el primer inmigrante de Nueva York." *BBC News Mundo*, 5 June 2021.

López, Gustavo. *Hispanics of Dominican Origin in the United States*. Pew Research Center's Hispanic Trends Project, 15 Sept. 2015.

López, Margarita. "Restoring History, Brick by Brick." *Latinx Talk*. 24 March 2020. latinxtalk.org/2020/03/24/restoring-history-brick-by-brick/

Lorde, Audre. "Age, Race, Class, and Sex: Women Redefining Difference." *Sister Outsider: Essays and Speeches*. Crossing Press, 1984, pp. 114–23.

"The Mariel Boatlift of 1980." *Florida Memory*, State Library and Archives of Florida, 10 May 2017, www.floridamemory.com/items/show/332816.

Massey, Douglas S., et al. "International Migration and Gender in Latin America: A Comparative Analysis." *International Migration*, vol. 44, no. 5, 2006, pp. 63–91.

McGurl, Mark. *The Program Era*. Harvard UP, 2009.

Meares, Hadley. "The Faces of a People: The Serbian Cemetery of East L.A." *KCET.org*, 16 Sept. 2015.

Menéndez, Ana. *In Cuba I Was a German Shepherd*. Grove Press, 2001.

Mesa-Bains, Amalia. "Domesticana: the sensibility of Chicana rasquache." *Aztlan: A Journal of Chicano Studies*, vol. 24, no. 2, 1999, pp. 157–67.

Miguel, Daisy, and Jenny Chhea. *The State of Van Nuys*. School of Public Affairs, University of California, Los Angeles, 2013.

"Migrant caravan: What is it and why does it matter?" *BBC News*, 26 Nov. 2018, www.bbc.com/news/world-latin-america-45951782.

Minich, Julie Avril. "Mestizaje as National Prosthesis: Corporeal Metaphors in Héctor Tobar's *The Tattooed Soldier*." *Arizona Journal of Hispanic Cultural Studies*, vol. 17, 2013, pp. 211–25.

Morales, Alejandro. Personal Interview with the author, 20 October 2011.

Morales, Daniel. "El Monte's Hicks Camp: A Mexican Barrio." *KCET.org*, 18 July 2014.

Mujcinovic, Fatima. "Multiple Articulations of Exile in US Latina Literature: Confronting Exilic Absence and Trauma." *MELUS*, vol. 28, no. 4, Winter 2003, pp. 167–86.

Muñoz, Alicia. "Articulating a Geography of Pain: Metaphor, Memory, and Movement in Helena María Viramontes's *Their Dogs Came with Them*." *MELUS*, vol. 38, no. 2, Summer 2013, pp. 24–38.

"New Brunswick, New Jersey Population: Census 2010 and 2000 Interactive Map, Demographics, Statistics, Quick Facts." CensusViewer.com, 1 June 2014.

"New Jersey Landfill Database." New Jersey Department of Environmental Protection, Division of Solid and Hazardous Waste, www.nj.gov/dep/dshw/lrm/landfill.htm. 1 June 2014.

Noe-Bustamante, Luis, et al. *Facts on Hispanics of Dominican Origin in the United States, 2017*. Pew Research Center's Hispanic Trends Project, 16 Sept. 2019.

Olivares, Julián. "Sandra Cisneros' *The House on Mango Street*, and the Poetics of Space." *The Americas Review*, vol. 15, Fall–Winter 1987, pp. 160–70.

Paredes, Américo. *George Washington Gómez*. Arte Público Press, 1990.

Pattinson, Dale. "Born in the U.S.A.: Breeding Political Violence in Héctor Tobar's *The Tattooed Soldier.*" *Studies in American Fiction,*" vol. 44, no. 1, Spring 2017, pp. 113–37.

Pérez, Louis Jr. *Cuba and the United States: Ties of Singular Intimacy*. U of Georgia P, 2003.

Pessar, Patricia R. "New Approaches to Caribbean Emigration and Return." *Caribbean Circuits: New Directions in the Study of Caribbean Migration*, edited by Patricia R. Pessar, Center for Migration Studies, 1997, pp. 1–11.

Piedra, Lilian. Personal interview with the author. 18 July 2018.

Plascencia, Salvador. *The People of Paper*. New York: Harcourt, 2005.

Poole, Steven. "The War on Saturn." *The Guardian*, 17 Nov. 2006.

Raju, Mohammed. Personal interview with author. 18 July 2018.

Rasmussen, Cecilia. "The Heyday and Decline of a Lively Barrio." *Los Angeles Times*, 27 Nov. 1995.

Review of *The People of Paper* by Salvador Plascencia. *Publishers Weekly*, 16 May 2005.

Rich, Nathaniel. "'Music of the Mill' and 'The People of Paper': Cal-Mex." *New York Times*, 10 July 2005.

Ricourt, Milagros. *Dominicans in New York City: Power from the Margins*. Routledge, 2002.

Rivero, Daniel. "Cuban Immigrants Were Given a Haven in the U.S.; Now They're Being Deported." *NPR*, 11 May 2019, www.npr.org/2019/05/11 /722201692/cuban-immigrants-were-given-a-haven-in-the-u-s-now-theyre -being-deported.

Rodríguez, Ana Patricia. "Diasporic Reparations: Repairing the Social Imaginaries of Central America in the Twenty-First Century." *Studies in 20th & 21st Century Literature*, vol. 37, no. 2, 2013, article 3; pp 27–43.

———. *Dividing the Isthmus*. U of Texas P, 2009.

Rodriguez, Cristina M. "'Relentless Geography: Los Angeles' Imagined Cartographies in Karen Tei Yamashita's *The Tropic of Orange.*" *Asian American Literature: Discourses and Pedagogies*, vol. 8, 2017, pp. 104–30.

Romo, Ricardo. *East Los Angeles: History of a Barrio*. U of Texas P, 1983.

Sáez, Elena Machado. "Dictating Desire, Dictating Diaspora: Junot Díaz's *The Brief Wondrous Life of Oscar Wao* as Foundational Romance." *Contemporary Literature* vol. 52, no. 3, Fall 2011, pp. 522–55.

Saldaña, Humberto Lopez. Personal interview with author. 1 Nov. 2019.

Saldívar, Ramón. *The Borderlands of Culture*. Duke UP, 2006.

———. "Historical Fantasy, Speculative Realism, and Postrace Aesthetics in Contemporary American Fiction." *American Literary History*, vol. 23, no. 3, 2011, pp. 574–99.

———. "The Second Elevation of the Novel: Race, Form, and the Postrace Aesthetic in Contemporary Narrative." *Narrative,* vol. 21, no. 1, 2013, pp. 1–18.

Sánchez, George J. *Becoming Mexican American: Ethnicity, Culture, and Identity in Chicano Los Angeles, 1900–1945.* Oxford UP, 1993.

Saussure, Ferdinand de. *Course in General Linguistics.* Edited by Charles Bally and Albert Sechehage. Translated by Wade Baskin. Philosophical Library, 1959.

Scarano, Ross. "Junot Díaz Talks Dying Art, the Line between Fact and Fiction, and What Scares Him Most." www.complex.com, Dec. 2012/Jan. 2013.

Schaub, Michael. "'Lot' Paints an Unforgettable Portrait of Houston and Its People." *NPR,* March 19, 2019.

Sedano, Matilde and Juan. Personal interview with author. 18 July 2018.

Sedgwick, Eve Kosofsky. *Epistemology of the Closet.* U of California P, 2008.

Seliger, Mary A. "Racial Violence, Embodied Practices, and Ethnic Transformation in Helena María Viramontes's 'Neighbors' and *Their Dogs Came with Them.*" *Bilingual Review / La Revista Bilingüe,* vol. 31, no. 3, Sept.–Dec. 2012–2013, pp. 262–78.

Shaw, Douglas V. *Immigration and Ethnicity in New Jersey History.* New Jersey Historical Commission, 1994.

Siu, Oriel María. "Central American Enunciations from US Zones of Indifference, or the Sentences of Coloniality." *Studies in 20th & 21st Century Literature,* vol. 37, no. 2, 2013, article 7, pp. 94–110.

Smith, Neil. "Antinomies of space and nature in Henri Lefebvre's *The Production of Space.*" *Philosophy and Geography II: The Production of Public Space,* edited by Andrew Light and Jonathan Smith. Rowman and Littlefield, 1998, pp. 49–68

Snyder, Robert W. *Crossing Broadway: Washington Heights and the Promise of New York City.* Cornell UP, 2015.

Soja, Edward, et al. "Urban Restructuring: An Analysis of Social and Spatial Change in Los Angeles." *Economic Geography,* vol. 59, no. 2, 1983, pp. 195–230.

Soy, Rosie M., and Stefan Bosworth. *Dominican Women across Three Generations: Educational Dreams, Goals and Hopes.* CUNY Dominican Studies Institute, Dominican Studies Research Monograph Series, 2008.

Statistical Atlas. www.statisticalatlas.com.

Tobar, Héctor. "Homeless Camps Thrive on L.A.'s Most Expensive Land: Survival: Weak economy has stalled redevelopment of Crown Hill and pushed more people onto the streets." *Los Angeles Times,* 23 Feb. 1992.

———. Personal interview with author. Los Angeles, 15 July 2017.

———. *The Tattooed Soldier.* Penguin, 1998.

Torres, Lourdes. "In the Contact Zone: Code-Switching Strategies by Latino/a Writers." *MELUS,* vol. 32, no. 1, Spring 2007, pp. 75–96.

Torres-Saillant, Silvio. "Writing has to be Generous: An Interview with Angie Cruz." *Calabash,* vol. 2, no. 3, Summer/Fall 2003, pp. 108–27.

Tropical Dreams: A People's History of South Florida. Permanent Exhibit, History Miami Museum, Miami, Florida.

Ulin, David, editor. *Another City: Writing from Los Angeles.* City Lights, 2001.

Uyeda, Elizabeth. "Simons Brick Company." *Los Angeles Revisited,* accessed 30 August 2021, https://losangelesrevisited.blogspot.com/p/simons-brick-co-album.html.

Van Nuys Neighborhood Council. "History," https://vnnc.org/about/history/.

Vargas, Jennifer Harford. *Forms of Dictatorship: Power, narrative, and Authoritarianism in the Latina/o Novel.* Oxford UP, 2017.

Véa, Alfredo. *Gods Go Begging.* Plume, 1999.

Villa, Raúl Homero. *Barrio-Logos: Space and Place in Urban Chicano Literature and Culture.* U of Texas P, 2000.

Viramontes, Helena María. *Their Dogs Came with Them.* Washington Square Press, 2007.

———. "Their Dogs Came with Them." California Ethnic and Multicultural Archives, University of California Santa Barbara, Santa Barbara, CA. Manuscript.

Wald, Sarah D. "'Refusing to Halt': Mobility and the Quest for Spatial Justice in Helena María Viramontes's *Their Dogs Came with Them* and Karen Tei Yamashita's *Tropic of Orange.*" *Western American Literature,* vol. 48, no. 1/2, Spring 2013, pp. 70–89.

Ware, Chris. *Building Stories.* Pantheon, 2012.

Waugh, Patricia. *Metafiction: The Theory and Practice of Self-Conscious Fiction.* Methuen, 1984.

Wile, Rob. "Miami Immigration Evolves; Cuban Dominate." *Miami Herald.* 5 August 2019.

Yamashita, Karen Tei. *Tropic of Orange.* Coffee House Press, 1997.

Ybarra-Frausto, Tomas. "Rasquachismo: A Chicano Sensibility." *Chicano Art: Resistance and Affirmation, 1965–1985,* edited by Richard Griswold del Castillo, et al. Wight Art Gallery, 1991, pp. 155–62.

Yúdice, George. *The Expediency of Culture.* Duke UP, 2003.

Zerivitz, Marcia Jo. "Miami's Jewish History." Greater Miami Jewish Federation, https://jewishmiami.org/about/federation/miami_jewish_history/.

INDEX

Cultural Frames, Framing Culture

Fashioning Character: Style, Performance, and Identity in Contemporary American Literature
Lauren S. Cardon

Neoliberal Nonfictions: The Documentary Aesthetic from Joan Didion to Jay-Z
Daniel Worden

Dandyism: Forming Fiction from Modernism to the Present
Len Gutkin

Terrible Beauty: The Violent Aesthetic and Twentieth-Century Literature
Marian Eide

Women Writers of the Beat Era: Autobiography and Intertextuality
Mary Paniccia Carden

Stranger America: A Narrative Ethics of Exclusion
Josh Toth

Fashion and Fiction: Self-Transformation in Twentieth-Century American Literature
Lauren S. Cardon

American Road Narratives: Reimagining Mobility in Literature and Film
Ann Brigham

The Arresting Eye: Race and the Anxiety of Detection
Jinny Huh

Failed Frontiersmen: White Men and Myth in the Post-Sixties American Historical Romance
James J. Donahue

Composing Cultures: Modernism, American Literary Studies, " and the Problem of Culture
Eric Aronoff

Quirks of the Quantum: Postmodernism and Contemporary American Fiction
Samuel Chase Coale

Chick Lit and Postfeminism
Stephanie Harzewski

American Iconographic: "National Geographic," Global Culture, and the Visual Imagination
Stephanie L. Hawkins

CPSIA information can be obtained
at www.ICGtesting.com
Printed in the USA
LVHW040005080622
720747LV00002B/235

9 780813 948065